AMERICAN PROSODY

AMERICAN PROSODY

BY

Gay Wilson Allen

Professor of English
New York University

1966
OCTAGON BOOKS, INC.
New York

Reprinted 1966
by special arrangement with American Book Company

OCTAGON BOOKS, INC.
175 FIFTH AVENUE
NEW YORK, N. Y. 10010

LIBRARY OF CONGRESS CATALOG CARD NUMBER: 66-17498

Printed in U.S.A. by
NOBLE OFFSET PRINTERS, INC.
NEW YORK 3, N. Y.

TO
ROBERT AND ETHEL
ALLEN

PREFACE

AMERICAN literature now occupies an important and respected position in the curriculum of nearly every college and university in the United States, and even in some leading universities abroad. Yet this book is the first attempt to trace the historical development of the prosodic theory and practice of the chief American poets. The versification of a few of the major poets (especially Poe and Whitman) has been discussed in the philological and linguistic journals, and most of the histories of American literature contain a few general statements on the versification of particular poets. But the scholarly articles are often inaccessible or inconvenient for the general use of students, and in the histories of literature the subject of verse-technique is almost always crowded out by the many other aspects of a poet's life and works.

No doubt the comparative infancy of genuinely scholarly research in American literature has something to do with the almost total neglect of so important a subject as prosody; but if American poetry deserves to be studied as *poetry*, then we can no longer afford to ignore this fundamental subject.

For the most part I have held to the plain historical and descriptive method in this book. My purpose has been to provide the facts and general outlines of the prosodic developments found in the works of the chief American poets. I have made no attempt, therefore, to indicate an ideal prosody or to advance any original theories. In fact I have even attempted, so far as possible, to suppress critical estimates, though I have tried in several places to trace out a poet's inconsistent practice of his own theories, since the student may frequently need such guidance.

I am particularly indebted to Professor Harry Hayden Clark, of the University of Wisconsin, who first suggested that I write this book. He has also graciously given me the benefit of his scholarly advice and his friendly help during the preparation of the manuscript. I am doubly grateful to Professor J. F. A. Pyre, first, for his helpful little book, *A Short Introduction to English Versification*, and, second, for reading several of my chapters and giving me many valuable criticisms and suggestions. To Professor William Ellery Leonard, I am indebted for general guidance in my prosodic thinking and in particular for examining and criticizing my interpretations of Walt Whitman's versification. Professors R. E. N. Dodge and H. B. Lathrop have given me many criticisms from which I have profited in the revision of the manuscript. I wish also to thank Professor Jay B. Hubbell, editor of *American Literature*, for permitting me to quote from his magazine and for his many other kindnesses; Professor Killis Campbell, of the University of Texas, for kindly allowing me to quote from his excellent edition of *The Poems of Edgar Allan Poe;* Professor W. Freeman Twaddell, a Germanic philologist of the University of Wisconsin, for his valuable philological suggestions; my wife, for her expert bibliographical services; the library staff of the University of Wisconsin for its generous assistance; and the various publishers (acknowledged in detail on the next page) who have permitted me to quote illustrative material from their publications.

G. W. A.

PREFACE FOR SECOND EDITION

This second edition is unrevised except for one misleading footnote (p. 157) to a book never published. Since Chapter XI was written, Thomas H. Johnson has edited a definitive text of Emily Dickinson's poems, thus outdating the comments in sections 1 and 2; however, the analyses of the versification have not been invalidated.

G.W.A.
January 1966

ACKNOWLEDGMENTS

The appreciative thanks of the author are hereby offered to the following publishers who have courteously granted permission for the reprinting of extracts from their publications:

D. APPLETON & COMPANY, New York. For extracts from *The Poetical Works of William Cullen Bryant*, Parke Godwin, ed.; *Prose of William Cullen Bryant*, Parke Godwin, ed.; and *Life of William Cullen Bryant*, by Parke Godwin.

COWARD-MCCANN, New York. For extracts from *Our Singing Strength*, by Alfred Kreymborg.

DOUBLEDAY, DORAN & COMPANY, Garden City, N. Y. For extracts from Walt Whitman's *Leaves of Grass*, Emory Holloway, ed.; and *Uncollected Poetry and Prose of Walt Whitman*, Emory Holloway, ed.

HARCOURT, BRACE AND COMPANY, New York. For extracts from *Poems of Freneau*, Harry Hayden Clark, ed.

HARPER & BROTHERS, New York. For extracts from *The Letters of James Russell Lowell*, Charles Eliot Norton, ed.

HOUGHTON, MIFFLIN COMPANY, Boston. For extracts from the following books: the *Poems, Essays*, and *Journals* of Ralph Waldo Emerson; *The Poems of Oliver Wendell Holmes* (Cambridge Edition), *Pages from an Old Volume of Life*, and *Life and Letters of Oliver Wendell Holmes*, J. T. Morse, ed.; the *Poems* (Cambridge Edition) and *Journals* of Henry Wadsworth Longfellow; *The Complete Poetical Works of James Russell Lowell* (Cambridge Edition); *The Complete Poetical Works of John Greenleaf Whittier* (Cambridge Edition); *American Criticism*, by Norman Foerster; *Whittier, a Sketch of His Life*, by Bliss Perry; *The Genius and Character of Emerson*, by B. F. Sanborn; *Tendencies in Modern American Poetry* and *Poetry and Poets*, by Amy Lowell;

The Poets of Transcendentalism, George Willis Cooke, ed. Used by permission of and by arrangement with, Houghton Mifflin Company.

LITTLE, BROWN & COMPANY, Boston. For extracts from *The Poems of Emily Dickinson*, and the prefaces of the "First" and "Second Series."

HORACE LIVERIGHT, New York. For extracts from *American Writers on American Literature*, John Macy, ed.

THE MACMILLAN COMPANY, New York. For extracts from *The Cambridge History of American Literature* (formerly published by Putnam).

DAVID MCKAY COMPANY, Philadelphia. For extract from *In Re Walt Whitman*, by Traubel, Bush, and Harned.

MITCHELL KENNERLEY, New York. For extracts from *With Walt Whitman in Camden*, by Horace Traubel; and *Walt Whitman*, by Basil de Selincourt.

CHARLES SCRIBNER'S SONS, New York. For extracts from Poe's *Works*, Stedman and Woodberry, editors; and *Poems of Sidney Lanier, The Science of English Verse*, and *Music and Poetry*.

CONTENTS

GENERAL INTRODUCTION

CHAPTER I
PHILIP FRENEAU

CHAPTER II
WILLIAM CULLEN BRYANT

CONTENTS

CHAPTER VI
HENRY WADSWORTH LONGFELLOW

CHAPTER VII
OLIVER WENDELL HOLMES

CONTENTS

CHAPTER VIII
WALT WHITMAN

CHAPTER IX
JAMES RUSSELL LOWELL

CHAPTER X
SIDNEY LANIER

CHAPTER XI
EMILY DICKINSON

General Introduction

I. DEFINITION OF TITLE

For convenience, this book is called simply *American Prosody*. The word *prosody*, however, must be defined, because it is often used ambiguously to mean either the technique of versification or the theory of versification. And even *versification* is used sometimes to mean the art or processes of poetic composition and at other times to signify the principles and history of metrical practice.

Since it is the double purpose of this book to trace the theories of the American poets in regard to the technique of their craft and to analyze in chronological order their practices in technique, we need separate words to indicate the two functions. Coining new words would be confusing; so we will specialize *prosody* to mean the *theory*, and *versification* to mean the *practice*. When we speak of Poe's prosody, therefore, we mean his theories of technique, especially those contained in *The Rationale of Verse*. We will also use the term "prosody" for the underlying principles of Walt Whitman's poetic technique; for despite the fact that Whitman did not write anything specifically on "prosody," his practice rests upon and presupposes a "system" which he either consciously or intuitively worked out before he wrote *Leaves of Grass*. It is sometimes difficult to decide whether a poet was consciously following a theory (either an established or an original one) or whether he simply accepted uncritically the practices which he had learned by daily contact, just as he learned to write sentences before he knew how to analyze their grammatical parts. Yet in most cases the distinction is possible. Thus we can speak of Bryant's special prosodic theory regarding the use of the trisyllabic foot, and of Walt Whitman's novel prosodic system; but Freneau and Whittier, for example, merely followed long-established, conventional ways of verse-technique — thus, we shall refer to their "versification" rather than their "prosody."

The act of writing poetry is, to be sure, psychological and æsthetic as well as mechanical and objective, but in this book we must limit our analyses to principles of *technique* (there seems to be no better word). That is to say, we intend to concern ourselves not with how the poet wrote what he did (which would involve psychology as well as literary sources), but with those elements of words and sounds which compose the final printed or recited poem. We are interested, furthermore, not in the thought of the poem but in the *spoken* words and sounds.

This study of the prosody and versification of the American poets is still further limited by its scientific scope; the purpose is to analyze objectively, suppressing, as much as possible, general estimates, criticism, and personal opinions (though it would be fatuous to believe that such an ideal can always be realized). Since the chapters are devoted chiefly to the major American poets, it is assumed that the poems analyzed in detail have some literary merit.

We may urge further, in justification of the objective method, that whereas mere literary criticism is liable to influence the student to rely on borrowed opinions, a descriptive and historical account of American prosody and versification should teach him critical self-reliance.

2. THE DIFFICULTIES OF REDUCING VERSIFICATION TO A SCIENCE

Though it is possible to treat the phenomena of verse-structure as a linguistic science, there are a number of difficulties. First of all, there is the unfortunate obstacle of conflicting "systems," *i.e.*, different methods and terminology for explaining the same objective facts. The scholars of this subject are sometimes referred to as "a fair field of fighting folk." Often their fights are over minor points or different ways of saying the same things, but the controversies and the lack of a uniform set of terms are exceedingly confusing to the student who is just beginning to study the subject. And only too often the author of a book on versification seems to take the attitude that no other author of a similar book is quite sane. The student is all the more bewildered if the author asserts, as he frequently does, that any one who has "a good ear" will read verse as he does.

Herein lies a major difficulty: every one does not read poetry in the same way, *i.e.*, stress the syllables in the same manner. Frequently there is no excuse for dogmatism; some lines of poetry can be read in many different ways, all of which are natural and correct. Some people read verse as if they were scanning it. Others try to read it as nearly like prose as possible. And there are many stages between these two methods. Which is right? Miss Amy Lowell said that between the two extremes she preferred the scanning, singsong manner, if she had to choose one or the other.[1] But of course a compromise is preferable — sufficient allowances being made for the type and mood of the poem and the metrical context of individual passages.

A further difficulty is the fact that *feeling* rhythm, either in the writing or reading of a poem, is subjective to a considerable extent. Different habits in the reading of verse are easier to deal with than the subjective feeling that a given line ought to be read in a certain manner; for habits repeat the same performances, whereas the imagination often follows an uncharted course. A practical example of subjective rhythm is our interpretation of the ticking of the clock. Does it actually say *tick, tock, tick,*

[1] Amy Lowell, *Poetry and Poets* (Boston, 1930), p. 21.

tock, as we think it does, or does it really say *tick, tick, tick, tick?* The chances are that the former is merely our subjective feeling. For an actual instance of subjectivity in the reading of poetry, let us consider Tennyson's *Break, Break, Break:*

> Break, break, break,
> On thy cold grey stones, O sea!
> And I would that my tongue could utter
> The thoughts that arise in me.

The first line, with its three accented syllables, is usually scanned with "metrical pauses"; that is, the pauses that we make in reading the first line are counted as if they were unaccented syllables. Where do those pauses occur? The inexperienced reader would immediately say *after* each "break." But since the unaccented syllables come *before* the accented ones in the following lines, the person who is familiar with the poem may say that he *feels* a pause before the first "break." In other words, he pauses before he actually begins reading! One professor insists that the first line is anapestic, like the first foot of the second line. Yet this opinion is entirely subjective, as we can prove from Arthur C. Coxe's poem:

> March! March! March!
> Making sounds as they tread, —
> Ho! ho! how they step,
> Going down to the dead!

Here the unaccented syllables follow the accented ones in the last three lines, and after we have read the poem we would not hesitate to say that the first line does not sound anapestic, or even iambic, though we stress it exactly the same as "Break, break, break."

But the greatest of all confusions in the field of prosody results from the fact that the principles of English versification, including the terminology, have French and classical origins, whereas English is a Germanic language. As a result, the long-established conventional system does not fit perfectly the versification practiced by the English poets. The "classical" system is "quantitative," which is to say, it measures the *length* of syllables, and is based on the number of "long" and "short" syllables in a line or verse. But "long" and "short" do not mean the same thing in the pronunciation of French, Provençal, Latin, or Greek that they do in English.

The consequence is a twofold difficulty. First, English versification in practice is irregular. Students often complain that they have trouble in scanning English poetry because the accentuation does not follow the "rules." Second, many people who talk about versification do not understand the nature of the English language. (This is especially true of the prosodists of two or three generations ago, particularly of Poe and Lanier.)

English, unlike the classical and Romance languages, has strong expiratory stress, *i.e.*, certain syllables are pronounced very vigorously while the stream of breath is being exhaled. These heavily accented syllables are usually of greater duration than the syllables pronounced with less expiratory stress, but it is very difficult to work out rules for their length. Hence, it is much safer to speak of the "stress" or "accent" in English verse without trying to define length, since actual *length* in English pronunciation can only be determined by laboratory apparatus, in complicated experiments.[2]

The main principle in any system of versification in any language is rhythm, consisting usually of recurrent patterns of sounds.[3] Most grammar-school children associate rime with poetry. Rime is a certain kind of rhythm, because it recurs at certain intervals. But rime was borrowed from the Provençal through the French; the oldest English versification did not have it.[4] Even the principle

---

[2] *Cf.* Paull F. Baum, *The Principles of English Versification* (Harvard University Press, 1923), pp. 56–65.

[3] "Thought rhythm" is discussed in Chapter VIII.

[4] That is, rime was not a recognized principle in Anglo-Saxon and

of the alternation of combinations of stressed and unstressed syllables was borrowed from the classical system
of "longs" and "shorts." Old English, or Anglo-Saxon,
versification, however, did have a rhythm, and it is analogous to rime. We call it alliteration. In every line there
were four heavily stressed syllables, two, three, or all four
of which began with the same letter (all vowels were
counted as alliterative whether or not they had the same
sound).[5] There was no definite rule for the number of unaccented syllables that could occur between these strongly
accented, alliterative syllables. The recurrence, however,
of similar sounds produced a rhythm, as in these lines from
Beowulf:

> Ge*w*at tha ofer *w*aegholm, *w*inde gefysed
> *F*lota *f*amiheals *f*ugle gelicost,

which we may translate literally:

> *W*ent then over the *w*aves, by the *w*ind guided
> The *f*loater *f*oamy-necked, to a *f*owl likest

The use of alliteration did not die out with the adoption
of a "classical" prosody for English verse, but survived
even in American versification, in Bryant and Longfellow
and Poe, for instance. This is not because these poets
necessarily cherished the old Anglo-Saxon tradition (Poe
knew little or no Anglo-Saxon) but because this old
Germanic tradition never died out; it was too much a
part of the English language itself to be killed even by the
Norman Conquest. Yet this survival of alliteration as a
poetic technique is most important as an illustration of the

---

early Germanic versification, though there are some rimes, for example,
in the Christian epic, *The Phoenix*. And then there is the curious
Rhyming Poem.

[5] By marking secondary stresses and "rest beats" Professor
William Ellery Leonard scans the Old English epic line as eight-beat
(four beats to the half-line). See his "*Beowulf* and the Nibelungen
couplet," *University of Wisconsin Studies in Language and Literature*
(September, 1918), No. 2, 99–152.

fact that when classical prosody was grafted on the Anglo-Saxon stock, the stock lived and grew along with the scion. Continuing the same metaphor, modern English versification may be likened to the fruit of the tree, still nourished by Germanic sap. These fundamental facts not only account for the many difficulties and misunderstandings in English versification, but also indicate why there have been so many prosodic revolutions in English and American poetry. And incidentally, they may help us to be more tolerant of changing prosodic ideals.

Bearing all these things in mind, we must now return to one of the difficulties already touched upon. We must agree upon a set of terms, definitions, and principles which will enable us to analyze intelligibly the prosody and versification of the American poets. Since this book is intended to be historical and descriptive, our terms and principles must be as widely accepted as possible. We do not intend deliberately to avoid novel explanations or methods of analysis where they are needed, yet this is not the place for new prosodic theories. In the following section, an attempt is made to define and explain the principles and terminology on which this book is based. But for a complete list of definitions see the Glossarial Index.

3. DEFINITION OF TERMS AND PRINCIPLES

The rhythms of poetry may be analyzed by units, one of which is the verse, *i.e.*, the single line. A larger unit is the strophe or stanza, ranging anywhere from the couplet to long, complicated arrangements like the sonnet or the sestina. But a shorter unit, and the one with which our discussion should logically begin is the *foot*, or the unit which names the *meter*.

Metrical Rhythms. The very word *meter* itself indicates a measurement, and when we speak of "metrical rhythms" we mean a group of recurrences (repetition being the main characteristic of rhythms of any kind) which are short yet definite enough to be used as measuring units. But before naming and discussing these units, we need to go still farther back and find out what composes a foot. That, of course, brings us to the pronunciation of syllables. Occasionally we may be concerned with isolated spoken sounds, represented by *letters,* or single phonetic units, but the *syllable* is the smallest unit that need concern us at present. Counting the number of syllables in a verse is one way of measuring it, yet we do not know a great deal about the rhythm of the line until we have taken into account both *the number* and *the order of occurrence* of *accented* and *unaccented* syllables; and since there are various degrees of accent or expiratory stress, we must agree upon a scale of stress-measurements.

Stress (or *Accent*) *Marks.* The older books on English prosody diagram or "scan" the rhythm of a verse or line of poetry by using marks to indicate "long" (⁻) and "short" (˘) syllables. This terminology is confusing for two reasons. First, what our dictionaries call "long" syllables are not necessarily long in duration of pronunciation. And second, there are two main schools of prosodists: those who regard time as the most important element in English versification,[6] and those who regard accent as the most important.[7] Professor Saintsbury recognizes the accentual nature of the English language, without minimizing the time element in verse, but for convenience he uses the "long-short" terminology.[8] It seems better, however, to use "accent" marks. In this book we use four: Primary (ʹ), secondary (ˋ), weak secondary (ˮ), "metrical accent" (ˀ), and unaccented or unstressed (×). (The terms "stress" and "accent" may be used interchangeably.) All of these grades of accent or stress are found in normal speech. The American pronunciations

---

[6] *Cf.* Lanier's *Science of English Verse,* discussed in Chapter X.

[7] Notably Professor W. W. Skeat.

[8] George Saintsbury, *A History of English Prosody* (New York and London, 1906), I, 5.

of the words "primary" and "secondary" illustrate three of our symbols:

(prí-mà-ry) (séc-on-dà-ry)

Thus we scan a normal line of poetry:

I néver thought to ásk, I néver knéw:

The secondary accent is found most often in words with natural secondary speech stress, or in compounds:

Amóng the pálms of México and vínes . . .

The spéechless bábe, and the gráy-héaded mán . . .

while the primary accent is used only for syllables which receive primary accent in natural speech, the dictionary usually being a safe guide. The secondary accent, however, is less definite, for most poetry is not read precisely like prose, though normal pronunciation is a fairly sure indication of the use of the secondary accent in verse. But the scansions in this book should be regarded as only approximate, particularly with respect to secondary accents and "metrical accents" (*cf.* p. xxvii), since individual habits of reading, and the impression the poet is trying to convey, make it impossible to lay down ironclad rules. Most people, for instance, will probably read the following line as it is marked here:

The lóose whìte clóuds are bórne awáy.

Yet there might be some special reason for wishing to give "white" stronger stress. Ordinarily, when three accented syllables occur consecutively, normal pronunciation does give the second syllable secondary stress (as in "loose white clouds"), but sometimes the thought of the line may demand equal stress for three consecutive syllables, as in:

Séven lóng yéars of sórrow and páin [9]

---

[9] In natural pronunciation, *seven* is practically a monosyllable, though of course the *en* can be given weak syllabification.

Primary-secondary-primary accentuation might actually make this line sound flippant. "Seven" and "years," by the way, are not only heavily stressed here, but the sense of the line requires that they be pronounced slowly; therefore, they are long in time quality.

Feet. It would probably be better to speak of the number of accents or stresses in a verse of English poetry rather than its number of "feet," for the foot-division is often arbitrary. Still, it is a well-established convention and we may use it for convenience, since it enables us to label the different kinds of rhythms.[10] Thus if the line has an alternation of unaccented plus accented syllables, we use the ($^{×}$ $^{′}$) divisions as our rhythmical units. The main rhythms in English verse may be tabulated with illustrative words in this fashion:

Iamb	× /	I-am-
Trochee	/ ×	Trochee
Anapest	× × /	Uninten | tional
Dactyl	/ × ×	Prettily

The spondee (′ ′) and the pyrrhic (× ×) are mainly "substitutions" (see p. xxviii), though now and then a line (or a rhythmical group) is characterized by these feet:

And the | *firm soul* | *does the* | *pale train* | *defy*

Seldom do we need to use other "classical" feet in scanning English verse, especially if we admit truncation and the redundant syllable in our analyses; but occasionally it is convenient to use the tribrach (× × ×), the amphi-

---

[10] The usual names for the different-length lines (with respect to number of feet) are as follows:

(*a*)	one-foot verse — monometer	(*e*)	five-foot — pentameter
(*b*)	two-foot — dimeter	(*f*)	six-foot — hexameter
(*c*)	three-foot — trimeter	(*g*)	seven-foot — heptameter
(*d*)	four-foot — tetrameter	(*h*)	eight-foot — octameter

brach (× ´ ×), the cretic or amphimacer (´ × ´), the bacchic (× ´ ´), and the minor ionic (× × ´ ´). Of course any scheme of scansion depends upon the metrical context, and for this reason it is perhaps unwise to illustrate these unusual feet by sporadic or isolated examples. Furthermore, there are often two or more ways of scanning a single line, *e.g.*,

$$\text{A bóy's will is the wind's will,}$$

Or, counting "metrical silences,"

$$\text{A bóy's }_\wedge\text{ will is the wind's }_\wedge\text{ will.}$$

In the four chief rhythms in English verse — iambic, trochaic, anapestic, and dactyllic — each foot must contain one main stress. To be sure, this stress is usually a primary accent, but the secondary accent may be counted as the main stress for the foot, notably in the last foot of iambic rhythm where the rime is on a light syllable; or the secondary accent may be counted as the unstressed element of the foot. In the following line it is so counted three times (though the first foot may be read as a spondee), and once (final syllable) as the stressed element:

$$\text{Sweet twi | light walks | and mid | night sol | itude}$$

Metrical Stresses. The "metrical stress" is frankly a compromise between the two extreme manners of reading poetry: reading it like prose, or exaggerating the pattern by a singsong emphasis of the beats. For example, in blank verse the rhythmical pattern is five unaccented syllables alternating with five accented ones. But in practically any long passage of blank verse, it will be found that some of the syllables occurring in accented positions are prepositions, conjunctions, or other unemphatic and unstressed words. If the passage as a whole is fairly regular, however, the reader will probably feel an inclination to stress the unaccented word or syllable in the *accented position*. In this book such words and syllables are called "metrical accents" (or stresses), and are marked with the symbol (˘), which indicates that the syllable may be read with a degree of stress ranging anywhere from unstressed to secondary accent (and even sometimes to primary accent). A more accurate symbol would be (x̆), but the other is less cumbersome. If the reader prefers to do so, he may regard these "metrical accents" as merely indicating the regular pattern. At any rate, he should regard the degree of stress they represent as variable. In fact all scansions are only approximate, though the value of other symbols is more definitely fixed.

The weak secondary stress (ˏ) is also very roughly approximate, and may often be ignored altogether. But a symbol is needed to indicate what seems normally to be stress ranging somewhere between that of secondary and unaccented syllables. The following line could be read several ways (*e.g.*, emphasizing "my," "own," etc.), but one good way seems to be:

How sweet the west wind sounds in my own trees!

Metrical Licenses. The best poetry is usually not the verse that follows one "set" rhythmical pattern most closely, but that in which speech accents coincide with the pattern sufficiently to keep the rhythmical scheme in the mind of the reader, yet not closely enough to become monotonous.

Substitution. The use of a secondary accent in the position of an unaccented syllable is one common variation, likewise the secondary accent in the position of a primary one. Another variation is what is known as "substitution," which means substituting a trochee for an iamb, etc., where the rhythm is predominantly iambic. This is sometimes called "reversed accent" or "reversed feet." In iambic rhythm the substitution of a trochee is usually made just after the middle of the verse, but practically never in the final foot. Some poets (*cf.* Bryant) make a practice of substituting a trisyllabic foot (an anapest or a dactyl) in dissyllabic rhythm (iambic or trochaic). Usually anapests are substituted in iambic meters and dactyls in trochaic meters, for the former are "rising rhythms" (progressing from unaccented to accented syllables) and the latter "falling rhythms." The substitution of a spondaic foot takes place in all rhythms, and practically anywhere in the line. Since most chapters of this book contain examples of substitutions, illustrations should be unnecessary here.

Extra-metrical Syllables. Aside from substitution, the main metrical licenses are "extra-metrical" or "redundant" syllables and lines that are short one or more unaccented syllables. Of course the insertion of a trisyllabic foot in dissyllabic meters (already discussed) is one way of adding extra unaccented syllables to the line. What is usually meant by the "redundant syllable," however, is found, for instance, in blank verse, where the line has eleven syllables, the last one being unaccented and not counted in the scansion:

Where are | those far | -famed piles | of hu | man gran | deur,

The insertion of an extra syllable at the beginning of the line or just after the cæsura, called an "epic cæsura" (see *The Cæsura,* below), may be scanned either as "extra-metrical" or as trisyllabic substitution, since the terminology does not affect the phenomenon.

Elision. Extra syllables in the line may also be accounted for by elision. This subject is so often misunderstood that it must first of all be explained. Elision is *not* the contraction of syllables; contractions are indicated by an apostrophe, as in *'twas* for *it was,* where the two syllables are contracted to one. In elision all the syllables are pronounced, but pronounced so lightly and quickly that two syllables may be equivalent in weight and time to only one syllable. Therefore, it can take place only under certain phonetic conditions:

(*a*) Elision of "open vowels," where two unaccented vowels come together, either in the same word or in adjoining words: "perpet*ual*," "many *a*," "Arcad*ia*," etc. In scansion the two elided syllables are marked as one unaccented syllable, though both are pronounced (*very lightly*).

(*b*) Elision of "pure *r*," *i.e.*, "*r*" between two unstressed vowels: "num*er*ous," "wand*er*ing," etc.

(*c*) Elision of "pure *l*": "rev*el*er," "per*il*ous," "merr*il*y," etc.

(*d*) Elision of "pure *n*": "op*en*ing," "virg*in*al," etc.

Truncation. There is one very common variety of truncated line which deserves brief discussion. In four-stress iambic couplets, for instance, we often meet lines that contain seven instead of eight syllables. Other lines in the passage may indicate that the pattern is iambic, yet this seven-syllable line begins with an accented syllable. Except for the final foot we could scan it as trochaic, but the most convenient way is to treat it as iambic with the initial unstressed syllable omitted. Lines with initial truncation are frequently called "clipped" or "headless":

Ló! | she walks | upon | the moon,

Lis | tens to | the chim | y tune

The "headless" line is found most often in four-stress couplets, though it may occur in any measure, and in anapestic as well as iambic rhythm. An analogous truncation is the omission of the final unstressed syllable in trochaic or dactyllic verse; but if the majority of the lines end with accented syllables, it is doubtful whether the rhythm should be regarded as "falling."

Syncopation. Sometimes the accentuation of a line of poetry seems to superimpose a second rhythm upon the rhythmical pattern. We may call this "syncopation." [11]

---

[11] This is the common use of the term in textbooks on versification; *cf.* Paull F. Baum, *op. cit.*, p. 18 ff., and J. F. A. Pyre, *A Short Intro-*

Long lines, especially seven- and eight-stress ones, are likely to syncopate. Poe's *Raven* is an outstanding example. The pattern is eight-stress trochaic, with omission of the final light syllable: [12]

$$/ \times \mid / \times \mid / \times \mid / \times \mid / \times \mid / \times \mid / \times \mid /$$

Yet the reader is more than likely to read many, if not all of the lines, in this manner:

Tàke thy béak from òut my heárt, and tàke thy fórm from òff my dóor

Every other accented syllable receives, not the primary stress that the pattern calls for, but a secondary stress. The principle is the same as the piano player's "ragging" a piece of music. Syncopation is often so subtle that it almost defies analysis. It can be carried so far that it produces dissonances, as in the music of a modern jazz orchestra; and dissonance may end with complete annihilation or negation of rhythm.

Masculine and Feminine Rhythm. In addition to classifying the rhythms of verse according to the kinds of feet used, we may also classify them as "masculine" and "feminine." When the ends of words exactly coincide with the divisions of the rhythmical units (that is, with the ends of the feet), we call the rhythm masculine. Feminine rhythm is, of course, the reverse. This distinction is necessary only when the rhythm is so pronouncedly masculine or feminine as to affect the cadence. Bryant's extensive use of monosyllables, for instance, gives a rhythm which is more predominantly masculine than we find in most poetry:

Plod on, | and each | one as | before | will chase

---

duction to *English Versification* (New York, 1929), p. 13. Syncopation in music is different, being similar to "reversed stress" in versification.

[12] We could scan this as a headless line and call it iambic. But Poe himself called it trochaic: see "The Philosophy of Composition."

Feminine rhythm:

Through o | ceans preg | nant with | perpet | ual storms,

The Cæsura.   Most long lines of poetry contain a pause somewhere near the middle.   This is called the "cæsura."   Many four-stress lines have a cæsura, and nearly all five- and six-stress lines have one, while longer lines are likely to have more than one.   This pause may be caused (1) by the punctuation (a comma, most often), (2) by the thought of the line, or (3) by the grammatical structure, such as the beginning of a new phrase or clause ("2" and "3" are likely to coincide).   In the following specimens the cæsura is indicated by the symbol (:).

I like a church; (:) I like a cowl, . . .

A boy's will (:) is the wind's will . . .
When winter winds (:) are piercing chill, . . .

See before us (:) in our journey (:) broods a mist (:) upon
    the ground,

When the cæsura comes at a foot-division, we say that it is masculine; when it divides a foot, we call it feminine, as in:

Lis | ten, my chil | dren, (:) and you | shall hear [13]

Enjambment.   Punctuation and thought also affect the end of the verse in a very important manner.   If the line ends with a comma or a dash, we usually pause there in the reading.   If the punctuation is a period or a semicolon, we make a decided pause, or a "full stop," in the reading.   In either case we say that the line is "end-stopped."   But if there is no punctuation to cause a partial or a full stop at the end of the line, we say that it is "run-on," or *enjambed.*   End-stopped lines are likely to be monotonous, enjambed ones less likely to tire the ear.
    Breath-Sweep.   Enjambment prolongs the breath-

[13] See also *Extra-metrical Syllables.*

sweep, or as we might phrase it, the number of syllables pronounced with one breath or between two pauses. The breath-sweep may extend from one full stop to another, including slight pauses which the reader passes over without stopping to draw a new breath; or it may extend only from one pause of any kind to the following pause of any kind. Blank verse is affected most by breath-sweeps. Part of the grandeur of Milton's blank verse is the result of his tremendously long breath-sweeps. Yet the breath-sweep is an important factor in the rhythms and cadences of any verse. Byron's frequent pauses at irregular intervals make his verse sound nervous. (For further discussion, and illustrations, see pp. 8 and 32.)

Phonetic Recurrence. In addition to the rhythms set up by a succession of stressed and unstressed syllables, which we have defined as "metrical rhythms," there are also rhythms which depend upon similar phonetic repetitions. The most familiar is, of course, rime, the repetition (most often at the end of the line) of similar vowel and consonant sounds in a syllable receiving primary stress. If the vowel and consonant sounds in the rime-words are exactly the same, it is called "identic rime." But the ideal is usually to repeat the vowel sound and final consonants of the riming syllable.

If rime involves only single syllables, it is called "masculine," but if it includes both an accented and an unaccented syllable, it is called "feminine" rime. If two accented syllables are involved (one of which may be a secondary accent), the rime is said to be "double." Occasionally "triple" rimes are used. Sometimes a single final unaccented syllable is made to carry the rime (usually exaggerating the pronunciation), such as when "*eye*" is rimed with "futur*ity*." We call this "light rime." If the rime-word occurs elsewhere than at the end of the line, it is called "internal rime." And if it occurs at irregular intervals within the passage of poetry, it is called "concealed rime."

Some poets are very careful to use perfect rimes, *i.e.*, approximate identity of sounds; but others regard a rough approximation as sufficient. In reading poetry it is never advisable (except where the rimes are obviously intended to be humorous) to distort the pronunciation merely to achieve identity of sound in the poet's rime-words.[14] It is interesting that Poe, who made a fetish of perfect rimes in his criticism, often used very poor ones. But inexperienced students are especially apt to over-emphasize the importance of rime. If so magnificent a poet as John Milton could be careless with his rimes, then we should avoid giving too much weight to this one phonetic embellishment. Before criticizing we should also make sure that we know how the particular rime-words were pronounced at the time the poet used them, and this is often a very difficult matter.

It has already been pointed out that alliteration is a sort of rime. The same is true of consonance and assonance (repetition of similar vowel sounds in accented positions). These are important in the works of certain poets, but can best be discussed in connection with particular poems.

Certain kinds of vowels (those pronounced in the back of the mouth, like broad *a*'s and *o*'s, or front vowels like the *e* in *feet* or *a* in *fate*) often produce a phonetic rhythm and give "tone color" to the line or the passage. Yet this aspect of rime is so subjective that it is difficult to lay down definite principles, and subjective theorizing should be reserved for æsthetics or philosophy. We shall have occasion to refer to "tone color," but with reservations.

Rhetorical Rhythms. Sometimes the main rhythms in poetry cannot be analyzed by any of the methods which we have defined and described. This is true in the case of "parallelism," the main rhythmical principle of biblical poetry, Walt Whitman's verse, and much primitive poetry. Parallelism repeats similar thoughts. Both the syntax and

---

[14] *Cf.* Amy Lowell, *op. cit.*, pp. 17-19.

the sounds of the verse are profoundly affected by these repetitions, though it is usually difficult to scan these rhythms just as we do the ordinary "metrical rhythms." But since these rhythms are analyzed in detail in the chapter on Walt Whitman, it should be sufficient merely to mention them here to indicate that they have a place in the study of prosody and versification.

Reiteration of all types, rhetorical emphases (whether in poetry or oratory), and refrains and repetends are also "rhetorical rhythms." However, their uses are so varied that they cannot be illustrated briefly, and discussions of them will be found in the proper places.

Conclusion. Sometimes vocabulary, syntax, and imagery affect the rhythms and cadences of verse, though these occasions are rare and need not be outlined now. The stanza, or verse-group, is of great importance; but the description must also be given elsewhere. (See the Glossary for a list of the main kinds, with an index of examples.) Nevertheless, it is important to point out here that stanzaic unity depends upon several devices. The most obvious, perhaps, is the unity achieved by a rime-scheme, the repetition of rimes in a set form or pattern. This may give both phonetic and thought unity to the strophe or stanza. Unity of thought, it is true, may be entirely independent of the rime-scheme; yet in the best poetry there is usually either a coincidence or an organic relationship between all of the unities that the stanzas may possess, including thought, rhythm, and grammatical structure, as well as cadence and "tone color."

The object of this outline of terminology and prosodic principles is merely to indicate the prosodic attitudes of the author of this book. It is hoped that enough general information has been given to enable the student to understand the following chapters, but any one interested in the subject of versification should read several of the reliable books on the subject. For this reason, a suggested bibliography will be found at the end of this Introduction.

4. THE ENGLISH BACKGROUND OF AMERICAN PROSODY

From Anne Bradstreet to Freneau, American poets were bound to English prosodic ideals by every tie that connected the two peoples — common language, government, culture, and the colonists' almost total lack of indigenous art. After the Revolution, American poets began theorizing about a native literature; but long after Emerson's declaration of literary independence in *The American Scholar*, American versification conformed to English standards of prosody, frequently those of a generation or two past. And until the time of Walt Whitman technical developments in American poetry probably had little effect on native poets, partly because they were familiar only with English verse and a few contemporary American bards. Thus, for the literary antecedents of Freneau, Bryant, Poe, Whittier, Holmes, and in fact most of the chief American poets, we must search in England, not America. It is very necessary for us, therefore, to know the main trends of English prosody (especially of the eighteenth and early nineteenth centuries) in order to understand the growth of American prosody.

The fifteenth century is the deadest period in all English literature, and the versification is even worse than the literature as a whole, a natural result of the unsettled language. Professor Saintsbury says the versification was in the Slough of Despond. Wyatt and Surrey began the process of pulling it out of the Slough. The effort was continued by Sackville and completed by Spenser, but the final result was a too strict syllabic regularity of meter. It was about this time that George Gascoigne's doctrine that English possesses only one metrical foot, the iambic, gained wide acceptance; that is, in formal poetry, for songs in "triple time" continued, along with some poems not written for music. (*Cf.* Thomas Tusser.)

There are three main types of blank verse: (1) end-stopped lines, adhering strictly to the basic pattern;

(2) lines freely enjambed, with variable cæsuras and trochaic and spondaic substitutions, the unit being not the single line but the passage enclosed by the breath-sweeps; and (3) lines typically enjambed, in which the metrical pattern is treated with great freedom, line division and sentence structure seldom coinciding, and weak endings and redundant syllables being used freely. *Gorboduc* illustrates the first type, *Paradise Lost* the second, and Shakespeare's later plays and Browning's blank verse the third. Shakespeare's versification shows a steady development from the first type (as in *Richard III*) to the third (as in *Cymbeline* and *The Tempest*). Yet Shakespeare never used the final redundant syllable and the light ending with the abandon we find in Fletcher's versification. Milton experimented with blank verse in *Comus* and definitely adopted it for his epics, wherein he achieved a grandeur and sublimity of style unrivaled in the English language. But despite Milton's magnificent success, the eighteenth century turned from blank verse to the heroic couplet, until Thomson's *Seasons* and Cowper's *Task* finally brought the former back into favor. In the nineteenth century, the chief poets — including Coleridge, Wordsworth, Shelley, Keats, Tennyson, and Browning — revived and cultivated the unrimed pentameter, both for dramatic and non-dramatic poems.

The decasyllabic couplet was used little in the fifteenth and sixteenth centuries, except by the Scotch poet, Dunbar, and by Drayton, who employed it in a form like Chaucer's own, neither definitely "end-stopped" nor enjambed. Variety is necessary in narrative heroic couplets (*cf.* Keats and Morris), but the Caroline poets overdid this liberty. Waller is sometimes mistakenly given credit for breaking away from the literary fashions of his age and bringing the classical couplet into prominence, but the "closed" couplet was established as far back as Ben Jonson, and Waller really comes at the end of the period of experimentation. Most of the poets of the middle seventeenth century used both the "stopped" and "run-on" couplet. Waller's were mainly "stopped," though in some of his later and best work he used enjambment. Cowley (1618–1667) practiced both forms. The "stopped" or "closed" couplet gradually prevailed, culminating in the expert handling of Dryden and Pope, whose regularity of versification drove out doggerel.

Among the endless experiments in metrics, a form of the old ballad or common measure was developed by Jonson, Donne, and others. (See Jonson's *Drink to Me Only with Thine Eyes*, which also shows expert fingering of vowels.) And Jonson, too, used the "epode" arrangement, or alternation of shorter and longer lines in the couplet.

The main characteristics of Milton's versification are: (1) the use of verse paragraphs, (2) extraordinarily masterful use of the pause, (3) majestic adaptation of diction to meter, (4) the combination of word-sound and word-connotation, and (5) the perfection of the octosyllabic couplet in *L'Allegro*, *Il Penseroso*, *Arcades*, and *Comus*. Many of Milton's octosyllabic couplets in these poems are "headless," a feature which gives them a special buoyancy and lilt. Butler, Prior, and Swift also used octosyllabic couplets, but theirs were usually strictly eight-syllabled.

Milton had nothing to do with the development of the anapest, yet his *Samson Agonistes* indicates that he could have used this meter with his customary ease and mastery. Tusser, Gifford, and Campion are usually given credit for adopting and developing the anapest, though of course it was found in the folk ballads.

The so-called "Pindaric ode" of Cowley and others (unequal lines with an unequal number of lines to a stanza) was an unfortunate experiment. Dryden was more successful in *Anne Killigrew* and *Alexander's Feast*, the latter in triple time. Swift failed repeatedly with the Pindaric ode.

But the most important development of the latter part

of the seventeenth century [15] was probably Dryden's experiments with the heroic couplet, which he learned to handle in his early heroic plays. The special tricks of Dryden's couplets are: (1) the use of the alexandrine at the end of a passage, (2) the sporadic insertion of a triplet, and (3) repetition of an emphasized word. He was also skilful in preventing a strict iambic line from seeming too iambic. The acme of regularity was reached in Pope. And the second part of his translation of the *Odyssey* showed the danger of this regularity, for it is almost impossible to distinguish Pope's own couplets from those of his two collaborators, Fenton and Broome. But Pope set the prosodic ideals of his age. The main principle of his versification was a restricted line, with the fewest and most jealously guarded licenses, and a very definitely fixed number of syllables. Later critics have often referred to this period as the "syllable-counting age."

The chief measures used by the eighteenth-century English poets were, in the order of their frequency: (1) heroic couplet, (2) octosyllabic couplet, and (3) a few lyrical variations. In many respects, however, the greatest rival of the couplet was blank verse. Milton was the model, though Thomson's *The Seasons* is far more original than imitative. Blank verse was used with different degrees of success; Cowper, for instance, overdid the interior full stop. Johnson disliked blank verse on general principles, but he thought that if it were used at all, it ought to be "tumid and gorgeous." Most eighteenth-century blank verse shows the direct influence of the heroic couplet in the handling of enjambment. Much of it is almost as definitely "couplet moulded" as the heroic itself, and sometimes the blank verse lines so closely approximate the movement of the "closed" couplet that the ear misses the rime at the end of the line.

Imitations of the Spenserian stanza were practically the only stanzaic forms of which the eighteenth century ap-

[15] Dryden died in 1700.

proved. The outstanding imitation is James Thomson's *The Castle of Indolence.*
Most of the lyrics were in "common" or ballad measure (which of course could be classed as a stanza). Other quatrains were the octosyllabics and decasyllabics (for the latter, see Gray's *Elegy*), and a few poets continued to use the old "romance-six" or *rima couée* ($aa_8b_6cc_8b_6$).

In the eighteenth century, prosodic theory assumed great importance. Edward Bysshe published his *Art of Poetry* in 1702, mainly a riming dictionary, with an introduction on "Rules for Making English Verses." Bysshe's work is important because he was the first man to formulate rules for what the eighteenth-century poets were actually doing. Pope's *Letter to H. Cromwell* (1710) shows that he followed Bysshe. Bysshe's principle is strictly syllabic. In addition to (1) insisting upon a strict syllabic count, he (2) barred stanza writing as obsolete, (3) snubbed triple time, (4) demanded middle pauses (cæsuras), and (5) deprecated the overlapping of couplets and lines. And these five points summarize excellently the usual eighteenth-century practice of versification.

Joshua Steele applied musical methods to the notation of meter, and started a troubling of the prosodic waters which survives even yet. He gave metrical time-values to pauses as well as to spoken syllables. Yet most metrists today agree that his scansion is utterly wild.

Gray in his *Metrum* recognized trisyllabic feet in characteristically dissyllabic meter, but he was in this respect in advance of his age. Samuel Johnson believed in strict syllabism, even disapproving of elision, though he admitted that perfect "purity" might become monotonous. Cowper attacked Pope for his "mechanic art" and rote-learned tunes, but he also disliked elision, and criticized Milton for using it. He did believe, however, in shifting pause and cadence perpetually.

Perhaps the number of prosodists shows that something was wrong with eighteenth-century versification. Their great mistake (especially Steele's) was in attacking the problem with *a priori* rules and assumptions. None of them seems to have had any conception of the value of the historical and descriptive method in studying the problems of versification.

The chief forerunners of the nineteenth-century prosodic revolt were *Ossian*, Percy's *Reliques*, and the versification of Chatterton and Blake. *Ossian* and Blake's *Prophetic Books* (especially the latter) were deliberate revolts against the "fetter" and "mechanism" of the poetry of the day. They intentionally discarded the uniformity of meter. Some critics have observed the similarities between the rhythms of *Ossian* and those of Old Testament poetry; and it is probable that its versification could all be explained by the same technique which is used in Chapter VIII in analyzing Walt Whitman's poems, despite the fact that there are portions of conventional meters imbedded in *Ossian*.

The license of substitution (found frequently in ballad meter) was the prosodic lesson of the *Reliques*, yet no one except Chatterton and Blake perceived it until the end of the period. Though Burns used it, he inherited the practice from Scotch originals. But soon after the meeting of Coleridge and Southey at Oxford, both became champions of substitution.

Disgust with the tyranny of the stopped rimed couplet led to experiments in rimeless stanzas, hexameters, sapphics, and Pindarics. The latter form was successfully used in Southey's *Thalabia* and Shelley's *Queen Mab*. However, little good has ever come from attempts to use classical meters in English.

The prosody from 1798 to 1830 may be characterized simply as anti-Bysshe. From Wordsworth to Keats the poets had two definite objects: (1) the liberty to use any form which might suit the poet's subject and temper, and (2) the special selection of forms (and adaptation of them) to appeal to the eye and ear.

Wordsworth allowed himself less freedom than the other poets of the period, but his own range of meter is considerable. In the *Immortality Ode* he constantly, as Saintsbury says, shifted "the values of cadences of the line by alternation of pause, by insertion of words of special weight or colour and the like, against which Johnson had partially protested, but which the joint study of Shakespeare and Milton is, of itself, sufficient to suggest and authorize." [16]

The accent *versus* quantity war was by this time well under way. Coleridge, it is true, took the accent side in the "foot" battle, while Southey indicated a more scientific system than Coleridge's rough and ready indication of accents as all that mattered when he remarked that two syllables may be counted as one when they take up the time of one in pronunciation. Yet the influence of Coleridge's versification was very great. Scott, for instance, acknowledged the influence of *Christabel* on the metrics of his *Lay*. But he, like Burns, was certainly influenced by the Scotch traditions, and Coleridge's own system was not, as he thought, new in English versification.

Scott did not like the stopped heroic couplet, and he made little use of the enjambed form, though he was undoubtedly familiar with it in seventeenth-century poetry. But he admired the Spenserian stanza and employed the form with a skill which is often overlooked by critics and historians.

Moore, a composer and practitioner of music, used the heroic couplet with great mastery, and the influence of music on his poetic technique has been recognized as of great importance. Yet it is difficult to define the exact relationship.

In some respects, Byron's versification is a reversion to eighteenth-century standards. Despite the fact that his

[16] "The Prosody of the Nineteenth Century," *Cambridge History of English Literature*, XIII, 256.

poetry in general is typically nineteenth-century, he could write orthodox eighteenth-century heroic couplets, and he had a fondness and an aptitude for the Spenserian stanza. His Spenserians, however, were more clearly influenced by the Scotch poet Beattie than by Spenser, or even the more recent Thomson. Byron also used *ottava rima* successfully.

After Byron the English prosodic background of American theory and practice becomes more complicated and less important, though Shelley's influence on American versification has never been adequately studied, and is in all likelihood far greater than is ordinarily realized (*cf.* Chapter IX). Certainly by the time "Pre-Raphaelite" prosodic ideals began to influence English poetry, America was becoming more self-reliant. Whitman was Swinburne's American contemporary, yet in most respects the two poets are about as far apart as we could imagine. Browning probably exerted more influence on American versification, but no chief American poet is indebted to him in the same way that Bryant is to Wordsworth or Poe to Coleridge, or even Lowell to Shelley. Tennyson was extraordinarily popular in America, and probably influenced Longfellow; still, we must remember that Longfellow's prosodic antecedents can be found all over nineteenth-century Europe. It seems sufficient, therefore, to end this sketch with Byron. Not because Anglo-American prosodic relations terminate there, but because after Byron American poets were influenced by each other and by various foreign literatures (even including the Sanskrit and the Hindu), with the result that prosodic influence and sources became too complicated for a brief survey.

5. THE RECENT PROSODIC REVOLT

Versification, as defined in this Introduction, means metrical organization of verse. The word is ordinarily understood to include everything that goes into the *tech-*

nique or composition of poetry, but it should not necessarily be considered as a method for testing or determining whether a given piece of writing is *poetry* or not. *Versification* can be defined objectively, and with a certain degree of scientific accuracy; poetry cannot, for poetry is subjective, æsthetic, to some extent merely a psychological "state of mind" (both to the poet and to the reader), and hence elusive.

The exact distinction between poetry and prose has never been satisfactorily made, and probably never can be; yet the differentiation of prose and verse is, for all practical purposes, fairly simple. Both are rhythmical, as Lanier pointed out, but the recurrences of accents, temporal relations, etc., follow more nearly a "pattern" (or a series of patterns) in verse than in prose. If the rhythmical pattern is so elusive that it practically defies analysis, then the composition should not technically be called verse.[17]

It is necessary to state this position with some emphasis because the recent controversy over *vers libre* has constantly become entangled in the vexing but perhaps unsolvable questions of "What is poetry?" and "Is 'free verse' poetry?" We propose to avoid any dogmatic distinctions in the realm of literature and æsthetics and confine our attention to such objective principles of verse analysis as we can discover in the works of the poets who are fairly universally acknowledged to have written *poetry* — moreover, important poetry.

This decision does not deter us from including Walt Whitman's versification in our analyses, since there are definite principles underlying his poetic technique. Emily Dickinson's versification can also be encompassed in such a survey, for her metrical irregularities have been considerably exaggerated and misunderstood.

---

[17] *Cf.* William Morrison Patterson, *The Rhythm of Prose* (New York: Columbia University Press, 1916), especially Chapters I and V (the latter on "Vers Libre").

But the technical characteristics of the bulk of modern "free verse" are such that they cannot be adequately treated under the present linguistic science of versification. Much free verse, of course, does contain fairly simple rhythmical patterns, and often parallelisms, reiterations, assonances, alliterations, "tone colors," and even "concealed rimes" (cf. the "polyphonic prose" of Amy Lowell and John Gould Fletcher); and all of these qualities can be analyzed with a fair degree of success by the methods of this book. However, the prosodic theory which most practitioners of free verse accept and promulgate is a deliberate attempt to evade definite principles. Even the very term *free verse* is, as Professor Pyre points out,[18] a misnomer, because technically *verse* is confined by "laws" — not necessarily the laws of Pope's versification, but laws nevertheless.

Of course free verse is not utterly lawless, yet the rhythmical principles underlying it are so variable that it is almost impossible to deduce generalizations which are accurate and reliable enough to be used in objective analyses. *Vers librists* talk glibly of rhythm and cadence, and scorn meter as old-fashioned and pedantic, though meter, as we have seen, is merely a name for certain sorts of rhythms. Some of the manifestoes of our "modern" poets sound as if they were aimed more at the obstruction of every serious attempt to define accurately the principles of versification than at any genuine expression of literary standards.

To be sure, most of the best free verse poets, such as Amy Lowell and Mr. Fletcher, have been prosodists; that is, they have studied versification earnestly and have then theorized on prosody. Yet, paradoxically, their prosodic thinking has resulted in a revolt against most definite prosodic principles. We must not be misunderstood as condemning them for renouncing the older conventions (since the poets of practically every generation

[18] Pyre, *op. cit.*, p. 53.

do that), but the central doctrine of free verse is that the rhythms must not conform to any patterns at all, except those that naturally express the poet's particular mood of the moment; *i.e.*, no one rhythm is accepted as a basic pattern for any given poem. If the thought or mood of the poet (and individualism is part of the "modern" creed) demands the reiteration of a specific rhythm in different parts of the composition, then the rhythm is repeated, but never in conformance to any preconceived pattern.

The group of modern poets who called themselves the "Imagists" (not all of whom were *vers librists*) did adopt a definite credo, but the principles to which they subscribed [19] are not primarily prosodic, save in so far as vocabulary, style, rhetoric, and subject-matter affect or limit the choice of rhythm. For instance, their resolve "to produce poetry that is hard and clear, and never blurred" refers chiefly to subject-matter and vocabulary; but indirectly it implies compact, concentrated, severely and purposely limited verses, and thus rhythm — no matter how "free" the theory. In short, the famous Imagistic credo is mainly æsthetic, practically the only reference to versification being that its exponents intend to "create new rhythms" and that "a new cadence means a new idea." Above all, they want to free poetry from form. Of course they believe in appropriate symmetry and balance; yet without reference to a specific poem, it is almost impossible to discuss the symmetry of a free verse composition except in vague generalities.

This is not to say that Carl Sandburg, Edgar Lee Masters, Amy Lowell, John Gould Fletcher, Hilda Doolittle, and others have not written poetry (or call it what you will) that is successful and important, or that their literary and æsthetic theories and practices may not eventually revolutionize American prosody, as Amy Lowell in particular believed. But analysis of their compositions

[19] See Amy Lowell, *Tendencies in Modern American Poetry* (Boston, 1917), p. 239.

involves too many principles of æsthetics, music, and modern theories of art to be adequately presented in a brief treatise on American prosody.

If the freedoms of poetic technique continue to increase, a special critique must be developed to explain them. Many people misunderstand versification as a linguistic science, for its sole function should be to explain the technique of poets, never to lay down rules for future poets to follow. Genuine poets always find the laboratory method the only means for working out a technique by which they can express themselves to the world of readers; and they can profit immeasurably by studying and analyzing other poets' technique, though no treatise on prosody can show a young, aspiring poet precisely how *he* ought to write.

Hardly any successful poets are ignorant of the usual principles of versification, yet it is probably also true that most first-rate poets do not themselves completely understand many of the intuitive processes which operate when they write poetry. Indeed, infrequently a poet may seem to develop a "new" technique without ever having set out deliberately to do so. So far as that poet himself is concerned, prosody is superfluous. Ordinarily it is the readers who need the analyses to enable them to understand and appreciate intelligently what the poet has done. Many readers, of course, prefer to appreciate solely in a vague, unanalytical, and intuitive manner. Their common pleas are that analysis crushes the life out of the poem, but teachers of poetry know that this romantic notion often covers ignorance and laziness. As Professor Baum says, "No amount of analyzing can injure the poem. If we think it has injured us, even then we err, and need only recall our natural aversion to hard labor. In nearly every instance it was the work and not the analysis that bothered us."[20]

Recent American scholars have placed more emphasis

[20] Baum, *op. cit.*, p. vii.

on the economics, the sociology, the history, the philosophy, and other significant phases of thought and background in American poetry, than on style, form, and technique. And no doubt versification is only one of the many interesting and important aspects of poetry. But while these other elements are of very great importance, it is to be feared that too often both teacher and student either forget or ignore the fact that, after all, it is primarily *technical form* that separates not only poetry from prose, but one poem from another, and a good poem from a bad one.

SELECTED BIBLIOGRAPHY

NOTE: The books in this bibliography are not necessarily those used in the preparation of this Introduction, nor does the author accept all of their doctrines. Yet all of them are useful to the student of American prosody.

Alden, Raymond MacDonald, *An Introduction to Poetry*. New York: Henry Holt and Company, 1909. xvi + 371 pp.

[This elementary presentation of English versification has been used for many years as a standard textbook.]

Andersen, Johannes C., *The Laws of Verse*. Cambridge University Press, 1928. x + 224 pp.

[Interesting and stimulating exposition of some original theories.]

Baum, Paull Franklin, *The Principles of English Versification*. Harvard University Press, 1924. x + 215 pp.

[Scholarly, reliable, and written in a clear, easy style.]

Bayfield, M. A., *The Measures of the Poets*. Cambridge, England: 1919. viii + 112 pp.

[An attempt to "reform" English prosody on revolutionary principles; not a book for the beginner in prosodic study.]

Hamer, Enid, *The Metres of English Poetry*. London: Methuen and Company, 1930. xi + 340 pp.

[Good presentation of both the principles and some of the main historical developments.]

Jacob, Cary F., *The Foundations and Nature of Verse*. Columbia University Press, 1918. xii + 231 pp.

[A scientific study, valuable for the advanced student.]

Jefferson, Thomas, "Thoughts on English Prosody" [1789?], the Lipscomb edition of *The Writings of Thomas Jefferson.* Washington, D.C. Published under auspices of Thomas Jefferson Memorial Association of the United States, 1903–1905. XVIII, 415–451.

[This treatise is surprisingly sound for 1789, the supposed date of composition. Jefferson came to the conclusion that Dr. Johnson's classical prosody (based on "Quantity") did not adequately explain English versification; consequently he worked out the principles of an accentual system which sounds curiously "modern" to a present-day reader. This essay is of great interest as the first American treatise on English prosody.]

Jespersen, Otto, "Notes on Metre," in *Linguistica, Select papers.* London: Allen and Unwin, 1933. Pp. 249–274.

[One of the best essays on English versification in print, by a great philologist.]

Lanier, Sidney, *The Science of English Verse.* New York: Charles Scribner's Sons, 1880. 315 pp.

[An attempt to reconcile the laws of verse and music. Important historically.]

Liddell, Mark H., *A New English Prosody.* Lafayette, Indiana: 1914. 47 pp.

[An attempt to find a basis for versification in wave-rhythms of thought.]

Omond, T. S., *A Study of Metre.* London: Alexander Moring, Ltd., 1920. xiv + 159 pp.

[Most recent prosodists are indebted to Omond.]

Pyre, J. F. A., *A Short Introduction to English Versification.* New York: F. S. Crofts and Company, 1929. x + 54 pp.

[Merely an outline of the general principles, but a reliable and convenient handbook.]

Smith, Chard Powers, *Pattern and Variation in Poetry.* New York: Charles Scribner's Sons, 1932. 408 pp.

[Easy to read, useful for undergraduates.]

Smith, Egerton, *The Principles of English Metre.* Oxford University Press, 1923. xv + 326 pp.

[Unconventional presentation, but valuable for the student who already has some knowledge of the subject.]

Smithberger, Andrew, and McCole, Camille, *On Poetry.* Garden City, New York: Doubleday, Doran and Company, 1930. 191 pp.

[Popular and elementary.]

Spindler, Robert, *Englische Metrick.* München: Max Hueber, 1927. 229 pp.

[Brief but valuable chapters on some of the chief English poets, Chaucer, Shakespeare, Coleridge, etc.]

Stewart, George R., *The Technique of English Verse.* New York: Henry Holt and Company, 1930. x + 235 pp.

[Uses musical notation, but is simple and fairly reliable.]

Strunk, William, *English Metres.* Ithaca, New York: Cornell Co-operative Society, 1925. 64 pp.

[Excellent summary of the main principles of English versification, with a valuable chapter on the historical development of "The Chief Metres of English Verse." Chap. V.]

Verrier, Paul, *Essai sur les Principes de la Métrique Anglaise.* Paris: Librairie Universitaire, 1909.

Tome premier, Métrique auditoire. xi + 552 pp.
Tome deuxième, Théorie générale du rhythme. 232 pp.
Tome troisième, Esthétique du rhythme. 344 pp.

[Important for the advanced student.]

HISTORIES OF ENGLISH VERSIFICATION (OR PROSODY)

Kaluza, Max, *Englische Metrik.* Berlin: 1909. xvi + 384 pp.

[Gives excellent brief surveys of the different metrical forms, with references to the theories of different scholars. Especially good for the Anglo-Saxon and Middle English periods.]

——, English translation by Dunstan, A. C., *A Short History of English Versification.* London: 1911. xvi + 396 pp.

Omond, T. S., *English Metrists.* Tunbridge Wells, England: R. Pelton, 1903. iv + 120 pp.

[Contains a valuable 54-page essay on the metrists, and an indispensable bibliography of prosodic writings.]

——, *English Metrists (Eighteenth and Nineteenth Centuries).* Oxford University Press, 1907. viii + 274 pp.

Saintsbury, George, *A History of English Prosody.* London: The Macmillan Company, 1906. 3 vols.

[The most exhaustive work of its kind, written in a charmingly personal style that is sometimes more entertaining than instructive.]

CHAPTER I

Philip Freneau

I. INTRODUCTION

PHILIP FRENEAU has been called "the Father of American poetry" so frequently that, whether or not he deserves the title, it is impossible to disregard him in an historical study of American versification. Naturally, some scholars regard him as important and others do not. The late Professor Cairns considered him an inferior poet, whereas Professor Clark has pointed out in a very interesting article that Freneau deserves the title, if for no other reason (though there are others), than that he used fresh imagery and unstilted diction.[1] Indeed, Freneau anticipated Wordsworth in this respect. The truth of the matter seems to be that in the past he has been little studied, but recent anthologies are giving more space to his poems, and all signs indicate that he is on the verge of a revaluation.

Chronology is not especially important in Freneau's poetry, since with the exception of blank verse he used the same forms during most of his poetic career. His technique underwent less growth than we should expect, though of course the poet's interests changed from time to time, with consequently some necessary minor deviations in poetic practices. For example, during the Revolutionary period Freneau wrote chiefly stinging satires in heroic couplets and octosyllabics (many of them containing more anger than poetry), whereas later in life he turned more to light verse and lyrics, in appropriate

[1] Harry H. Clark, "What Made Freneau the Father of American Poetry?" *Studies in Philology* (January, 1929), XXVI, 1–22.

stanzas. Yet he did not abandon the heroic couplet, for he printed poems in this form in 1815 (*The History of the Prophet Jonah* was written in 1768). In octosyllabics we have the *Power of Fancy*, written in 1770; the little Horace translation, printed in 1788; and a number of octosyllabic poems in the 1815 edition. As early as 1774, Freneau wrote one of his best poems, *Pictures of Columbus*, in stanzas. In fact in this poem the poet displayed almost all the devices of versification that he ever used. It even contains a little song, a sort of interlude in anapestics, Freneau's most important contribution to American metrical history.

There are several reasons for beginning a study of Freneau's versification with his blank verse, because if any particular verse form is typical of his early work it is probably unrimed pentameter. And another advantage in beginning our study with his blank verse is that we need to consider only three poems: *The Pyramids of Egypt* (w. 1769), *The Rising Glory of America* (w. 1771), and *Pictures of Columbus* (w. 1774) — Pictures III, IV, V, VIII, X, XI, XII, XIII, XIV, XV, XVI, XVII.

2. BLANK VERSE

The greatest rival of the couplet in eighteenth-century English poetry was blank verse. Milton was the English model, though Thomson's *The Seasons* rises above imitation, and in one aspect is quite different. Thomson's blank verse seems to be "couplet-moulded"; in fact, it so closely resembles the heroic couplet in its movement, its line pauses, and full stops at approximate two-line intervals, that when reading it we miss the rime. Cowper, on the other hand, used the interior stop, but overdid it. This English background is important because Freneau's literary influences were English, not American. And especially is this true of his blank verse, for practically no American blank verse had been written.

The Pyramids of Egypt, The Rising Glory of America,
and *Pictures of Columbus* are all dramatic poems, and if
their versification has any models, we would expect to find
them in the sixteenth-century dramatists or in Milton
rather than in Thomson. A detailed analysis of these
poems shows that this expectation is at least partly justified.

For convenience, we shall begin with an examination of
the single line. *The Pyramids of Egypt* opens with:

> Where are those far-famed piles of human grand | eur,
> Those sphinxes, pyramids, and Pompey's pil | lar, . . .
> Tell me, dear Genius, for I long to see | them.

The first line is noticeably heavy, with a spondee in the
third foot, but there is nothing unusual in this; the line
has no inverted (or reversed feet) and the rhythm is regular enough. Yet all three of the lines have eleven syllables, the final one unaccented (usually called a redundant
syllable). The use of the redundant syllable in blank
verse is found in various places, but it is orthodoxly
regarded as a "Fletcherism" (*cf.* Fletcher's *Rule a Wife
and Have a Wife, Monsieur Thomas,* or even the later
Faithful Shepherdess). There are about twenty lines in
this poem with the redundant syllable, about one-sixth
of the whole composition. This metrical license is also
found in *The Rising Glory of America:*

> He thinks his knowledge far beyond all lim | it, . . .
> To come and have a share in our perdi | tion —

Also in Picture XI of *The Pictures of Columbus:*

> Three well-rigg'd ships to *Christopher Colum* | *bus;* . . .
> Who will not now project, and scrawl on pap | er —
> Pretenders now shall be advanc'd to hon | our;
> And every pedant that can frame a prob | lem,

Somewhat akin to the redundant syllable is the light
ending, *i.e.,* the forcing of a secondary accent on a final
unaccented syllable:

Is strain'd to madness and audac | ity:
>   Picture XII

Launch'd out upon the world's extrem | ities!
>   Picture XIII

Away, away! — friends! — men at li | berty,
>   *Ibid.*

Where beardless men speak other lan | guages,
>   Picture XIV

In all his blank verse Freneau makes free use of this license, which we find in Shakespeare's later plays.

One means of preventing a blank verse line from becoming monotonous is to vary its weight, that is, to use spondees or secondary stresses in unstressed positions. We find both variations in Freneau's blank verse. An initial spondee is not infrequent:

Cape Verd, | Canary, Britain, and the Azores,
>   *The Rising Glory of America*

And occasionally there is a line so heavy as to be unusual:

Hence, old Arcadia — wood-nymphs, satyrs, fauns;
>   *Ibid.*

The light line may range all the way from three primary stresses to four, with the remaining one or two stresses either natural secondary speech accents or "metrical stresses":

Of Af | rica, | to the | Canar | y isles: . . .

Falling | to lee | ward of | her des | tined port, . . .

There strand | ed, and | una | ble to | return,

Forev | er from | their na | tive skies | estranged . . .

And an | imals | to this | vast con | tinent,
>   *The Rising Glory of America*

Yet most important of all is Freneau's tendency to place a "metrical stress" on the third foot — important because he does it so often. Wherever his line has only four natural speech stresses, the chances are about five to one that the extra stress will be forced in the third foot. This stress is not placed there by the metrist merely to make the line scan; Freneau's blank verse lines are sufficiently regular to set up the iambic pattern, thus causing the reader unconsciously to place a secondary accent where the stress is expected. This statement cannot be proved by quoting lines, since the passage must be read in its context. But the following lines indicate the principle:

More new, | more no | ble, and | more flush | of fame . . .

Through o | ceans preg | nant with | perpet | ual storms,

And cli | mates hos | tile to | adven | turous man. . . .

Designed | by na | ture for | the ru | ral reign, . . .

For me | tals bur | ied in | a rock | y waste. —

The Rising Glory of America

Freneau does not use the reversed foot very often in his blank verse line, though it occurs sporadically, usually in the initial foot (as with the spondee):

Digging | the grate | ful soil, | where round | him rise,

Sons of | the earth | the tall | aspir | ing oaks.

Ibid.

Occasionally the third foot is reversed after the cæsura:

First reached | these coasts, | hid from | the world | beside | . . .

'Midst woods | and fields | spent the | remains | of *life*,

Ibid.

Freneau's elisions in his blank verse take place mainly
under three conditions: (1) elision of open vowels (where
two unaccented vowels come together, in the same word
or in adjoining words), and (2) elision of "pure *r*" (where
r is found between unaccented vowels).[2]

Open vowels:

> Now shall th*e* *a*dvent*u*r*o*us muse attempt a theme . . .
> Through oc*ea*ns [3] pregnant with perpet*ua*l storms, . . .
> The tale of Cortez, furi*o*us chief, ordained
> With Indi*a*n blood to dye the sands, and choak, . . .
> Full man*y* *a* league their vent*u*r*o*us seamen sailed . . .
> Allured th*e* *O*lymp*ia*n gods from chrystal skies, . . .
> Hence, old Arcad*ia* — wood-nymphs, satyrs, fauns;
>
> > *Ibid.*

Pure *r* (see vent*u*r*o*us and advent*u*r*o*us above):

> Your northern Tartars, and your wand*e*ring Jews, . . .
> A num*e*r*o*us progeny from these arose, . . .
> For when the gen*e*ral deluge drowned the world.
>
> > *Ibid.*

Occasionally Freneau's blank verse contains a rhetorical
rhythm which the eighteenth-century English poets used
extensively in the heroic couplet, *i.e.*, initial repetition of
word or phrase, the reiteration of sound tending to set
up a rhythm of its own.　In a five-stress line, this rhythm
is likely to syncopate, as for instance in the following,
where the verse is read with only two or three primary
stresses:

> How many generations have decay'd,
> How many monarchies to ruin pass'd!
> How many empires had their rise and fall!
>
> > *The Pyramids of Egypt*

---

[2] Milton also has elision of "pure *n*," but this elision occurs so
infrequently in Freneau's verse that it would perhaps be misleading
to discuss it.　The same is true of "pure *l*."

[3] In the eighteenth century, *ocean* was trisyllabic.

Here there is repetition not only of sounds but also of syntax and parts of speech. "Generations," "monarchies," and "empires," for example, are parallel. But perhaps still more important to the cadence is the fact that this parallelism forces either a full stop or an approximation of one at the end of the line, regardless of the punctuation.

Frequently these reiterations show a tendency to pair off:

How shall I reach the vertex of the pile —
How shall I clamber up its shelving sides?
The Pyramids of Egypt

Like vagabonds and objects of destruction,
Like those whom all mankind are sworn to hate,
The Rising Glory of America

Will stab their prisoners when they cry for quarter,
Will burn our towns, and from his lodging turn
The poor inhabitant . . .
Ibid.

Are there not evils in the world enough?
Are we so happy that they envy us?
Ibid.

Nor shall these angry tumults here subside
Nor murder cease, through all these provinces,
Ibid.

These lines are as "couplet-moulded" as if they rimed, and are in this respect typically eighteenth-century; yet they are characteristic only of particular passages in Freneau's blank verse. His internal full stops are usually punctuated with dashes or interrogation marks, stops which the reader is likely to hasten over, making only a pause of indeterminate length, though these internal pauses help to break the "couplet-mould."

An illustration of Freneau's interplay of the pause and full stop, when the poet is at his best, is the following:

1. But come, / Eugenio, / since we know the past — /
2. What hinders to pervade with searching eye
3. The mystic scenes of dark futurity! //
4. Say, / shall we ask what empires yet must rise, /
5. What kingdoms, powers and states, / where now are seen
6. Mere dreary wastes and awful solitude, /
7. Where Melancholy sits, / with eye forlorn, /
8. And time anticipates, when we shall spread
9. Dominion from the north, and south, and west, /
10. Far from the Atlantic to Pacific shores, /
11. And people half the convex of the main! — //
12. A glorious theme! — // but how shall mortals dare
13. To pierce the dark events of future years /
14. And scenes unravel, / only known to fate? //

The Rising Glory of America

It will be observed that nearly one-third of these lines
are enjambed. There are only four full stops in the fourteen lines (the one in line twelve can be modified to a
pause); and while the breath-sweeps are far from Miltonic, they do definitely give the cadences of blank verse
rather than those of the heroic couplet. In every technical aspect, this passage is good blank verse, and it makes
us regret that Freneau forsook that form for other media
of poetic expression.

3. THE HEROIC COUPLET

Practically all the metrical characteristics of Freneau's
blank verse are found in his heroic couplets, the differences
being more quantitative than qualitative. His couplets
are mainly end-stopped. Where he uses enjambment, it
usually extends over only four lines, occasionally six,
with no internal stops at all; completely unrestricted
enjambment almost never extends over two lines. The
following extract, from *The History of the Prophet Jonah*
(w. 1768), is a fair illustration of Freneau's early heroic
couplets:

"Aríse! | and ó'er | the ìn | tervén | ing wáste,
"To Nín | evèh's | impér | ial túr | rets háste;
"That mígh | ty tówn | to rú | in Í | decreé,
"Procláim | destrúc | tion, ànd | procláim | from mé:
"Too lóng | it stánds, | to Gód | and mán | a fóe,
"Withóut | one vír | tue léft | to shíeld | the blów;
"Gúilt, bláck | as níght, | their spéed | y rú | in bríngs,
"And hót | test vén | geance fròm | the Kíng | of Kíngs."

Canto I

In these eight lines there are three definitely light or "under-weighted" verses, one with a "metrical stress" in the second foot and two with similar stresses in the third foot, as in Freneau's blank verse. One line has an initial spondee, the heavy line contrasting with the following light one. We also have elision.[4] Every line is partly stopped, every couplet is completely stopped, and reversed feet are used in the same manner as in the blank verse:

"Hígh on | the sea | -beat prow | will I | ascend, . . .

To plunge | me head | lòng from | that gid | dy steep

After about 1785 Freneau used the heroic couplet more than before for short poems, such as *Florio to Amanda,* *On a Book Called Unitarian Theology, Elegiac Lines,* and *Jack Straw.* In these short poems we might expect more metrical variations than in the earlier and longer poems, but such is not the case. For instance, less than half of the twenty-six lines of *Jack Straw* are entirely regular. This merely bears out the statement at the beginning of

---

[4] In addition to elision of "open vowels" and "pure *r*," there is also elision of "pure *n*," as in "And ever | y threat | *eni*ng surge | lay hush'd | in peace."

this chapter that there are no especially important chronological developments in Freneau's versification.

One other difference between Freneau's blank verse and his heroic couplet is the much greater use he makes of parallelism in the couplet, which is the more appropriate place for it. *The British Prison Ship* (w. 1780) has extensive parallelism of various kinds, but especially epanaphora, *i.e.*, initial reiteration of word or phrase:

> Strike not your standards to this miscreant foe,
> Better the greedy wave should swallow all,
> Better to meet the death-conducted ball,
> Better to sleep on ocean's deepest bed . . .
>
> Canto II

Such parallelism seldom extends over two or four lines, though occasionally we have a catalog anticipating Walt Whitman's style. Notice the "grammatical rhythm" in the following, where a parallel adjective plus noun is followed by another adjective plus noun. They are held together by the initial reiteration of "the" and the internal reiteration of "and the":

> Hunger and thirst to work our woe combine,
> And mouldy bread, and flesh of rotten swine,
> The mangled carcase, and the batter'd brain,
> The doctor's poison, and the captain's cane,
> The soldier's musquet, and the steward's debt,
> The evening shackle, and the noon-day threat.
>
> Canto II

In *The American Village*, written earlier (printed 1772), the parallelism is frequently in groups of three lines, skilfully distributed at appropriate intervals throughout the poem:

> To clear the forest, or to tame the soil;
> To burn the woods, or catch the tim'rous deer,
> To scour the thicket, or contrive the snare.

This passage, however, illustrates not only triplet parallelism but also the balance or antithesis of half-line against half-line, resulting in a cæsural pause so emphatic that it divides the verse into two metrical units, each with two stresses. It is practically impossible to avoid reading such a line as four-stress, with an anapestic substitution in the third foot and an amphibrach ($\times$ / $\times$) or an epic cæsura (whichever one prefers to call it) in the second foot:

$$\times / \,|\, \times / (\times) : | \times \times / \,|\, \times /$$

> The howling forest, and the tiger's den,
> The dang'rous serpent, and the beast of prey,

We have already observed that one of Freneau's favorite devices in his blank verse is a "metrical stress" in the third foot, though the verse-pattern there is usually sufficient to superimpose the five-stress rhythm. But parallelism in *The American Village* [5] may be responsible for such a line as:

> Made fertile by the labours of the swain,

which definitely has a pæonic swing and is not altogether fortunate.

In general, the important contrast between Freneau's heroic couplet and his blank verse is the greater enjambment in the latter. Characteristic are the eighty-five "run-on" lines out of six hundred and forty, or about thirteen per cent in *The British Prison Ship*, as opposed to thirty-one per cent in *The Rising Glory of America*. This one contrast is probably explained by the fact that couplet rime tends to band the verses together, rhythmically and syntactically. The accompanying rhetorical and thought parallelism, which we find more pronounced in the couplet than in blank verse, is probably a natural concomitant.

It is well to remember, however, that the closed couplet had been handed down to Freneau fully developed and rigidly standardized by the eighteenth-century English

[5] This poem, as the title suggests, owes much to Goldsmith's *Deserted Village*.

poets. And like Dryden, Freneau knew how to keep his iambic pentameter from becoming too iambic. A rough estimate is that only about forty per cent of his heroic couplets have ten syllables with five normal accents, *i.e.*, lines neither "light" nor "heavy" with neither substitution nor redundant syllables. Whether forty per cent is well on the side of metrical freedom is questionable, but there is certainly no doubt that it is quite sufficient to prevent the reader from losing the pattern.

Freneau's heroic couplet is at its best when he is telling a story, or a story combined with lyric expression, as in *Florio to Amanda;* and at its worst when he is pointing a moral or indulging in personal invective, as in parts of *The British Prison Ship*, with its over-rhetorical style. Never, it must be admitted, do Freneau's couplets attain the polish of Pope's school or the rugged strength of Dryden's, yet at times they reach sonorous grandeur, as in:

> When round the bark the howling tempest raves
> Tossed in the conflict of a thousand waves,
>
> To a Concealed Royalist

4. OCTOSYLLABICS

Freneau used the octosyllabic couplet in both lyrics and satire, but he was more successful in the lyrics. In the four-stress couplet he adopted the usual metrical devices of reversing the initial foot, balancing a light-stress line against a following heavy line, etc. But his most important and successful variation is the seven-syllable or "clipped" line, a form widely used by the "Miltonic school" in England in the eighteenth century. About three-fourths of *The Power of Fancy* is in the "clipped" line,[6] of which the following is a fair illustration:

---

[6] This percentage is much higher than Milton's. *Comus* contains fifty-six per cent of "headless" lines, *L'Allegro* fifty-eight per cent. Fletcher's *Faithful Shepherdess*, with its seventy-three per cent, is nearer Freneau's average.

Lo! | she walks | upon | the moon,
List | ens to | the chim | y tune
Of | the bright, | harmon | ious spheres,
And | the song | of an | gels hears;
Sees | this earth | a dis | tant star,[7]
Pen | dant, float | ing in | the air;

Since the subject-matter of *The Power of Fancy* is akin to that of *L'Allegro*, it is to be expected that Freneau was influenced by Milton.

In *The Citizen's Resolve* we have the octosyllabic and the heroic couplet used for a skilful contrast of two moods:

So spoke *Lysander*, and in haste
His clerks discharg'd, his goods re-cased,
And to the western forests flew
With fifty airy schemes in view;
His ships were set to public sail —
But what did all that change avail? —
In three short months, sick of the *heavenly train*,
In three short months — he moved to town again.

On the whole, Freneau's use of the short couplet for satire [8] is not very effective, since it lacks the appropriate exaggeration of rime and meter; but sometimes he makes his point by antithesis:

Some court the great, and some the muse,
And some subsist by mending shoes —
The Silent Academy

One effective piece of light verse is *To Zoilus*, arranged in six-line stanzas. This poem provides an interesting contrast to his Horace translation, *Horace, Lib.* I, *Ode* 15, which is arranged in four-line stanzas. Technically, the two pieces are very much alike, though *To Zoilus* gives

[7] Milton's *Paradise Lost*, B. II, v. 1052 (Note, in the Clark edition of *Poems of Freneau*).
[8] *Cf.* the octosyllabic couplet satires of Swift, Prior, and Gay, who almost certainly influenced Freneau in this practice.

the impression of being more "couplet-moulded" (actual count does not altogether bear out the impression) than the Horace translation, which has couplet rime but quatrain thought-movement. The Horace poem, incidentally, is a very close and commendable translation, a fact which may account in part for the qualities of the versification. *To Zoilus* is also different in that it seems to work up to a sort of climax in each stanza, the turn in thought coming after the fourth line. Compare the following:

> The monster comes, severe and slow,
> His eyes with arrowy lightnings glow,
> Takes up the book, surveys it o'er,
> Exclaims, "damn'd stuff!" — but says no more:
> The book is *damn'd* by his decree,
> And what he says must gospel be!
>
> *To Zoilus*

> As 'cross the deep to Priam's shore
> The Trojan prince bright Helen bore,
> Old *Nereus* hushed each noisy breeze
> And calmed the tumults of the seas.
>
> *Horace, Lib.* I, *Ode* 15

Freneau wrote many trite poems in the octosyllabic couplet, such as *The Seasons Moralized*, yet on the whole it was his happiest lyric measure and is perhaps characteristic of his latest (1815) poems. The eight-syllable line is also used in many of the stanzaic poems, such as the famous *On a Honey Bee* (see p. 20).

5. THE ANAPEST

The eighteenth-century English poets used the anapest to some extent, but it was Freneau who popularized this meter in America. With the possible exception of regular dactyl, the anapest is the most unnatural rhythm in normal speech of any modern English meter and is, therefore, inappropriate except for satire, where the exaggerated movement in itself produces a comic effect, or for certain syncopated lyrical effects.

Freneau deserves credit not only for starting the anapest on its American career but also for having used the measure so appropriately. He used it in several combinations, including couplets, quatrains, and various stanzas (see pp. 19–21), yet the couplet predominates in the satire. An early example is *A Political Litany* (w. 1775), the versification of which resembles Goldsmith's *Retaliation* and illustrates the main characteristics of Freneau's anapestics:

From the caitiff, lord *North*, who would bind us in chains,
From a royal king Log, with his tooth-full of brains,
Who dreams, and is certain (when taking a nap)
He has conquered our lands, as they lay on his map.

This is very regular; the only variations from the strictly correct model are, first, a substitution of an iamb in the initial foot (Freneau very seldom uses it elsewhere in the line), and second, a suppressed secondary accent in the second foot of the first two lines. Both of these variations, however, are scarcely worth mentioning; for since the iambic and the anapestic are rising rhythms, one missing initial unaccented syllable retards the metrical flow very little, and the fact that the line does gallop, with an almost inevitable syncopation, causes a foot accented in ordinary speech ($\times \diagdown \diagup$) to become a regular anapest in the line. The secondary accent is still stressed lightly but is pronounced so rapidly that it is felt as an unstressed syllable.

Sometimes the secondary accent comes on the first syllable of the foot ($\diagdown \times \diagup$), if the foot is interior. This makes the line a little more irregular than in the case of secondary accent on the second syllable of the foot ($\times \diagdown \diagup$)

but does not greatly alter the rhythm.   In the following line we have what really amounts to a final redundant syllable, though it is the rime word (pronounced "ŭm" to rime with "freedom"):

Who still | follow on | where delu | sion shall lead them.

To the Public has regularly eleven syllables to the line, the initial foot being iambic.   The metrical scheme of the first stanza is:

× / | × × / | × × / | × × /   a
× / | × × / | × \ / | × \ /   b
× / | × \ / | × × / | × × /   a
× / | × × / | × × / | × \ /   b
× / | × × / | × × / | × × /   c
× / | × × / | \ × / | × × /   c

To a Deceased Dog is a more amusing poem in precisely the same scheme (except that it is in quatrains and the initial foot is not always iambic).

In *The New England Sabbath-Day Chace*, Freneau anticipates Browning[9] in using the anapest to suggest the actual gallop of a horse.

> By this time the deacon had mounted his poney
> And chaced for the sake of our souls and — our money:
> The saint, as he followed, cried — "Stop them, halloo!"
> As swift as he followed, as swiftly we flew —

Undoubtedly the connotation of swiftness has something to do with the surprising rapidity of the last line, but the repetition and balance of one half-line against the other is typical of many of Freneau's anapestic verses. The cæsura is also more pronounced than in an iambic meter, giving the line a tendency to split up into a 2 + 2 movement.

Is it more than three shillings, / the fine that you speak on;

What say you good Darby — / will that serve the deacon.

[9] *Cf. How They Brought the Good News from Ghent to Aix.*

Here we also have more exaggerated rimes than in any other of Freneau's metrical forms; "speak on," for instance, rimes with "deacon." In *The Political Balance* "Britain" rimes with "spit on."

But sometimes Freneau's anapestics are almost as rough as the versification of a limerick and are hardly more than doggerel. *To Shylock Ap-Shenkin* contains such verse as:

Now preaching and screeching, then nibbling and scribbling,
Remarking and barking, and whining and pining,
    And still in a pet,
From morning 'til night, with my humble gazette.

At other times, even the limerick-effect is especially appropriate, as in Picture IX of *The Pictures of Columbus*, the interlude between the sailor Thomas and Susan his wife, which is an effective comic song:

SUSAN

If I was a maid as I now am a wife
    With a sot and a brat to maintain,
I think it should be the first care of my life,
    To shun such a drunkard again:
Not one of the crew
Is so hated by Sue;
    Though they always are bawling,
    And pulling and hauling —
Not one is a puppy like you.

The meter of the often-quoted *To a Caty-did* (published in 1815) may possibly be an outgrowth of Freneau's experiments with the anapest, though the poem can be scanned as anapestic only by questionable juggling of the accents. The following are typical lines:

In a branch of a willow hid

Sings the evening Caty-did: . . .

Caty-did, Caty-did, Caty-did!

Here the amphimacer seems to be the typical foot, giving
an interesting metrical balance: [10]

$$/ \times / \,|\, \times \times \quad | / \times /$$
$$/ \times / \,|\, \times \times \quad | / \times /$$
$$/ \times / \,|\, / \times / \,|\, / \times /$$

By 1815 the lyrics of Moore and Byron were undoubtedly
available to Freneau as models, and are very likely the
metrical sources of this excellent lyric.

6. STANZAS

A couplet is hardly a form of stanza but since a line
analysis fails to reveal several important characteristics
of Freneau's versification, it is convenient to use the subject of couplet paragraphs as a transition to the discussion
of his stanzas. Though, as we have noticed, the majority
of Freneau's couplets are closed, the full stop may be
punctuated by a semicolon, a colon, an interrogation
point, an exclamation point, or a dash. The poet's usual
method is to paragraph after each period. In *America
Independent*, these sentence-paragraphs run from four to
thirty lines; and in *George the Third's Soliloquy*, one paragraph extends over forty lines.

The British Prison Ship (in many respects an inferior
poem) is skilfully paragraphed, the length of the sentence
being indicative of the moods of the poem. In the first
part of Canto I (the capture), which is mainly descriptive,
the sentence-paragraphs extend over about six or eight
lines; but the latter part of the canto, composed of narration and conversation, has longer periods, around ten or
sixteen lines. The boatswain's prayer (or curse?) covers
about sixteen lines. In Cantos II (the prison ship) and
III (the hospital ship), the longer paragraphs of realistic

---

[10] The accentuation of "in" (first line) may vary from unstressed
to primary stress, and "evening" (second line) could have an elision
of the unaccented syllables.

descriptions are interspersed with short, impassioned, declamatory periods. In all his heroic couplets, Freneau keeps a dexterous balance between his long and short paragraphs. An excellent example is *Lines Addressed to Mr. Jefferson,* or the anapestic couplet, *Royal Consultations.* A real stanzaic form is Freneau's favorite device of the octosyllabic couplet quatrain (*aabb*). Two typical examples are *On the Death of Dr. Benjamin Franklin* and *Epistle from Dr. Franklin,* the one elegiac in subject-matter and the other humorous. Sometimes, however, the couplet and not the quatrain is the unit of thought, the four-line groups being merely a convenient arrangement. Such is *To Sylvius: On the Folly of Writing Poetry.* In *The Drunkard's Apology* each quatrain is built around a "conceit" in the Elizabethan sense.

We find the elegiac stanza (*abab*), in both five- and four-stress iambic rhythms, used in a number of poems. In Freneau's pentameter verse the subject-matter ranges all the way from the elegy — as in *Stanzas to the Memory of Two Young Persons,* or *The Deserted Farm House* (in the manner of Gray) — to the satire, as in *To Shylock Ap-Shenkin;* while the four-stress stanzas are elegiac or lyric, as in *The Vanity of Existence,* or *The Indian Burying Ground,* one of Freneau's most famous poems.

Freneau did not use the ballad stanza proper (*i.e.,* *abcb,* 4 + 3), but we find a number of slight variations. An $a_4b_3a_4b_3$ stanza is used, as in *Reflections on the Mutability of Things,* and the anapestic *Elegy on the Death of a Blacksmith.* We also find the *abcb* stanza in iambic pentameter (*cf. The House of Night, Scandinavian War Song,* etc.), and in tetrameter (*cf. The Wanderer*). *May to April* has internal rime in the first verse (*a*) $abcb_4$. Other quatrains are *aaab,* as in the "clipped" octosyllabic *The Volunteer's March.* The form *aaaB* (the *B* is a repetend) is used in *The Battle of Stonington.*

The triplet (*aaa*) is found only in a few poems, such as

the four-stress *To a Night Fly* and *On Amanda's Singing Bird*, as well as the five-stress *On Passing by an Old Churchyard*.

The "Venus and Adonis" stanza (*ababcc*) seems to have been a favorite with Freneau. In the regular five-stress form we have *To Sylvius on His Preparing to Leave the Town* and Picture XVIII of *Pictures of Columbus;* yet the octosyllabic form seems to have been more adapted to Freneau's tastes and abilities, for in this stanza he celebrated George Washington's arrival in Philadelphia (title: *Occasioned by . . .*), and wrote *The Anniversary of the Storming of the Bastille, The Wild Honey Suckle, Amanda in a Consumption, Tobacco,* etc. *On a Honey Bee* and *The Wild Honey Suckle* are usually included in all the anthologies and are probably unequalled in lightness and delicacy anywhere else in Freneau's poetry. The "Venus and Adonis" rime-scheme is also used in four-stress anapests and in 4 + 3 iambics.

Other six-line stanzas are *abcabc*$_4$ (see *Amanda's Complaint*); *abcbdd,* "rime-skip" (see *The Dying Elm*); *aa*$_4$*b*$_3$*cd*$_4$*b*$_3$ (see *The Dish of Tea*); and *abaa*$_4$*b*$_3$ "tail-rime" (see *On Retirement*). A more frequent rime-skip is *aabbcdee*$_4$. Tail-rime stanzas are found in various combinations, but two examples are *Battle of Lake Erie* (*aaabcccb*$_4$) and *Prophecy of King Tammany* (*ababccca*$_4$).

In the eight-line stanza we find *Prayer of Orpheus* and *Hatteras* (*ababcdcd,* 4 + 3). *Neversink* has nine lines, riming *abcbdeffe,* 4 + 3.

Freneau's "odes," like those of most of his English contemporaries, are simply long stanzas with lines of different lengths; but he did not allow himself even the liberties that the form permits. Of the Pindaric ode, with its turns, counter turns, and stands, he apparently had no conception. In fact Freneau simply concocted a stanza with a combination of couplet and quatrain rimes, using lines of two lengths. *Ode to Liberty* is a translation of a French ode, but it does not follow altogether the original meter or rime; for the French poem contains three stanzas of ten octosyllabic lines to the stanza, whereas Freneau's translation has twelve, eleven, and eight lines. His rimes are $abcbddeeffgg_4$, $abaabccded_4e_3$, and $a_4b_5a_4b_5cdc_4d_5$.

On the Symptoms of Hostilities rimes $abab_4cc_2dd_4$ (except the first stanza, the first quatrain of which is questionable, being either abcc or abaa). The meter is anapestic. But perhaps Freneau did not intend this poem for an ode.

7. CONCLUSION

Freneau did not introduce any new stanzas, and the forms that he borrowed were, for the most part, precisely those which we might expect from his contact with eighteenth-century English poetry. He was also conservative in using the conventional stanzas, permitting few variations and never letting the thought run over from one stanza to another. The manner in which he used the four- and six-line stanzas shows that he was never very far away from the conventional closed couplet. A study of his stanzas reveals more convincingly than anything else could that Freneau was not a pioneer in American versification, even if we may justifiably call him the Father of American Poetry. He was not, of course, unoriginal, but his claim to originality must rest upon his unstilted diction and fresh imagery rather than his poetic form — no small claim to fame, when we remember that he began writing thirty years before the world heard of Lyrical Ballads.[11]

[11] The question of Freneau's indebtedness to the eighteenth-century English poets is too complicated for adequate treatment in a discussion of this kind and no attempt has been made to indicate more than the most obvious and undebatable sources and parallels. Joseph M. Beatty, Jr., has written an informative article on "Churchill and Freneau" in American Literature (May, 1930), II, No. 2. Other studies of this kind are needed.

8. MINOR AMERICAN POETS OF THE SEVENTEENTH AND EIGHTEENTH CENTURIES

The history of seventeenth- and eighteenth-century American versification is largely a history of imitation of English poetry, in both subject matter and form; consequently, the versification before Freneau (or possibly even Bryant) is relatively unimportant. Some knowledge of these imitations, however, helps to give perspective to the accomplishments of Freneau and Bryant. Even the earliest colonists' experiments with meter prepared the way for later American prosodic traditions. Governor Bradford's rimed economic facts, the popular political jingles of Nathaniel Ward's *Simple Cobler*, and William Wood's catalogs of native fauna and flora in *New England's Prospect* are significant as attempts to find metrical media for the expression of emerging national thoughts and ideals.

The first book printed in America was a volume of poetry, if *The Bay Psalm Book* may be called poetry. This paraphrase of the Psalms in a very rough and awkward ballad meter was printed at Cambridge in 1640. The ideal of the translators was to preserve as closely as possible the biblical diction, apparently regarding rhythm as unimportant; and of course they succeeded only in destroying the sonority of the King James Version. The most popular book of the age was Michael Wigglesworth's *Day of Doom* (1662), a poem as ridiculous as the Puritans' attempt to paraphrase the Psalms. The meter may be arranged either as quatrain "fourteeners" or broken up as double-stanza ballad meter with internal rime. The result is naturally a singsong jingle which is wholly inappropriate for the serious subject matter, *e.g.:*

Not we, but he ate of the Tree, whose fruit was interdicted:

From this time until the end of the seventeenth century (and during part of the eighteenth) the most popular type of verse in America was memorial poems. The elegy on Reverend Thomas Shepard by Reverend Urian Oakes illustrates one of the most successful examples of the type, but even it is in doggerel pentameter couplets and quatrains, with atrocious rimes and a style of elaborate conceits and allusions, a fashion preserved by John Norton. The best extant American elegy of the seventeenth century is *Bacons Epitaph, Made by his Man* (c. 1676). Who the "Man" was is not known, but he was evidently no novice with the pentameter couplet, which is freely enjambed, with varied pauses and internal full stops used daringly, and the whole skilfully cadenced. But this unknown Virginia poet was an anomaly in seventeenth-century America. The thousands of other elegiac verses are a dead waste of New England pentameter couplets in awkward rhythms and ill-matched rimes imitating Quarles and other English poets now forgotten.

The most remarkable American versifier of the seventeenth century was Ann Bradstreet. She was admittedly influenced by Du Bartas and she made adaptations from Sylvester. Her couplets may be called typically Sylvesterian — looser than the heroic, with poor rimes, and cæsuras that slide around to fit the thought. Her best poem, *Contemplations* (1678), has the rime-scheme $ababcc_5c_6$, and suggests interesting influences, perhaps Spenser and Giles Fletcher. She never learned, however, to control either her rhythms or her diction. Even her most lyrical passages have such awkward lines as:

I heard the merry grasshopper then sing,

The turning point in early American versification was the year 1699, when Dr. Benjamin Colman brought back from England the poems of Blackmore and Waller, which he admired, imitated, and influenced others to read. From this time until the nineteenth century American versification followed closely in the footsteps of the best known English poets. Dr. Colman later imitated Dryden in his

Elijah's Translation (1707), and his daughter, Jane Turell, imitated Pope.

In 1715 Francis Knapp addressed a poetical epistle to Pope. From this time until the end of the century Pope was the chief prosodic influence in America. Reverend Mather Byles corresponded with him, enclosing in his letters copies of his own poems. Byles also boasted a correspondence with Watts, whose hymns he imitated. Reverend John Adams, a friend of Byles, also imitated Pope, but his *Address to the Supreme Being* (c. 1745) shows some Miltonic influence. By the third quarter of the eighteenth century the American poets were turning for guidance to other English poets, though Pope still remained the favorite. Thomas Coombe's *Peasant of Auburn* (1775), for instance, is an obvious imitation of Goldsmith's *Deserted Village.* Many American imitations of Thomson's *Seasons* appeared soon after the first American edition in 1777.

This is not the place for a review of the numerous Columbiads, the "glory of America" vogue for which Freneau was responsible, and the countless patriotic songs and ballads inspired by the Revolution. The versification of these pieces is largely imitative and conventional. The ballad meter with internal rime of Francis Hopkinson's *The Battle of the Kegs,* however, is an interesting echo of *The Day of Doom* versification, though of course the spirit and subject-matter are utterly different.

Perhaps the two most imaginative poets before Freneau were Thomas Godfrey and Nathaniel Evans, both of Pennsylvania. Godfrey's *Court of Fancy* (1763) is strictly syllabic, in closed couplets, but there is an ease and grace in the handling not found in other minor poets of the period. Godfrey acknowledged his indebtedness to Chaucer and Pope. The blank verse of his tragedy, *The Prince of Parthia* (the first native blank verse drama to be performed on the American stage), is significant because, unlike the English blank verse of the last half of the eighteenth century, it is not couplet-moulded. The chief prosodic influence upon it appears to have been Shakespearean. But Godfrey, like his contemporaries, was imitative of the English, of Dryden in his odes, of Gray and Young in his elegiacs, and of Shenstone, Prior, Collins, and others in his songs. Nathaniel Evans is known chiefly for his graceful and forceful *Elegy* (1763) to the memory of his friend Godfrey, but the versification is the conventional pentameter couplet of the times.

The list of the imitations of Butler's Hudibrastic octosyllabic couplets is too long to record here, but one of the most famous examples is the mock-heroic *McFingall* (1777–1782) of John Trumbull. The lines, however, are more regularly syllabic than Butler's; and although Trumbull uses some feminine and double rimes we do not find the exaggerated rimes of *Hudibras*.

The clipped octosyllabic couplet is found in parts of Timothy Dwight's *Greenfield Hill* (1794), which is written in heroic couplets, Spenserian stanzas, blank verse, and octosyllabics. Dwight used the Popian couplet in *The Conquest of Canaan* (1785) and *The Triumph of Infidelity* (1788), the latter a "philosophical" poem. Joel Barlow's *The Hasty Pudding* (1793) offers additional evidence that the conventional closed couplet was still popular near the end of the century. It is thus obvious that Pope remained the greatest prosodic influence upon American versification of the eighteenth century, and that the American poets of the century were almost wholly imitative.

SELECTED BIBLIOGRAPHY

PHILIP FRENEAU

TEXT

Freneau, Philip, *Poems*, ed. by Harry Hayden Clark. New York: Harcourt, Brace and Company, 1929.
[This edition contains the best of Freneau's work. The Introduction is excellent.]

Freneau, Philip. *Poems of Philip Freneau, Poet of the American Revolution*, ed. by Fred Lewis Pattee. Princeton University Press, 1902–1907. [Complete.]

CRITICISM

Beatty, Joseph M., Jr., "Churchill and Freneau," *American Literature* (May, 1930), II, No. 2, 121–130.

Clark, Harry H., "Literary Influence upon Philip Freneau," *Studies in Philology* (January, 1925), XXII, 1–33.

——, "What Made Freneau the Father of American Poetry?" *Studies in Philology* (January, 1929), XXVI, 1–22.

——, "Philip Freneau," *Encyclopædia Britannica*.

Hustvedt, S. B., "Phillipic Freneau," *American Speech* (October, 1928), IV, 1–18.

More, Paul Elmer, "Philip Freneau," *Shelburne Essays*, fifth series. Boston: Houghton Mifflin Company, 1908.

MINOR POETS

Onderdonk, James L., *History of American Verse (1610–1897)*. Chicago: A. G. McClurg and Company, 1901.

Otis, William Bradley, *American Verse 1625–1807*. New York: Moffat, Yard and Company, 1909.

Tucker, Samuel Marion, "The Beginnings of Verse, 1610–1808," *Cambridge History of American Literature*. New York: G. P. Putnam's Sons, 1917. Chapter IX, I, 150–184.

Tyler, Moses Coit, *A History of American Literature During the Colonial Times*. New York: G. P. Putnam's Sons, 1897. Esp. "New England: The Verse-Writers," I, 264–292. [Vol. I, for period 1607–1676; Vol. II, for 1676–1765.]

Wegelin, Oscar, *Early American Poetry, 1650-1799*. [A bibliography.] New York: Peter Smith, 1930. Sec. ed.

CHAPTER II

William Cullen Bryant

I. INTRODUCTION

It would be misleading to call William Cullen Bryant the "father of American prosodists" in the same sense that Freneau is known as the "Father of American Poetry"; yet it would not be altogether untrue. He was unmistakably a prosodist in both meanings of the term; that is, he was both a critic and theorizer of the linguistic science of prosody and a practitioner of metrical theory. And it is not an exaggeration to say that by both example and precept he pointed the way for at least the American poets of his generation. Furthermore, whether or not his poetry is better than Freneau's (and most critics agree that it is), it has always been more widely recognized, thus making his versification more influential than Freneau's.

Bryant's essay *On Trisyllabic Feet in Iambic Measure* was not published until 1819, but most of it seems to have been written as early as 1811, the year in which he composed the middle portion of *Thanatopsis*. This essay and certain portions of his *Lectures on Poetry* are, strictly speaking, his only direct contributions to the history of American prosodic theory; yet other essays and reviews (including *Nostradamus's Provençal Poets, Moriscan Romances, Female Troubadours, Oldham's Poems, Abraham Cowley,* and his Introduction to the anthology called *A New Library of Poetry and Song*) indicate that Bryant was a competent student of prosody during practically his whole lifetime, and give him some claim to being the first American prosodist. Thomas Jefferson, to be sure, wrote his *Thoughts on English Prosody* around 1789, but few people ever had the privilege of reading it before the twentieth century (see bibliography at the end of the General Introduction). At one time Bryant, too, seems to have contemplated writing a book on prosody.[1]

2. BRYANT'S PROSODIC THEORY

"On Trisyllabic Feet in Iambic Measure"[2] introduces no revolutionary doctrine, for the substitution of the trisyllabic foot had been slowly gaining ground in English prosody since the publication of Percy's *Reliques* (1765), and more rapidly since the publication of *Lyrical Ballads* (1798). But in Bryant's day the war for this freedom had not yet been won, especially in America. Bryant blamed this conservatism on habit: "Where the ear is inured to the regular iambic, and to pauses at the end of every couplet, and, whenever it is possible, at the end of every line, it perceives nothing but harshness and irregularity in more varied pauses and a greater license of prosody."[3]

The only feet, he observes, that can be substituted in English iambic verse are the anapest and the tribrach (three unaccented syllables). First he shows that a certain use of the anapest and the tribrach "has been allowed from the very beginnings of English poetry" under several circumstances, namely:[4]

(1) ". . . when the first two syllables in these feet are vowels or diphthongs."

"To scorn | delights | and live | labo | rious days,"

(2) ". . . when the letter *r* only is interposed between the vowels . . ."

---

[1] See Parke Godwin, *A Biography of William Cullen Bryant* (New York, 1883), I, 275 (letter to Richard H. Dana).
[2] *Prose Writings*, ed. by Parke Godwin (New York, 1884), I, 57–67.
[3] *Ibid.*, p. 59.   [4] *Ibid.*, p. 61.

"And ev | ery flower | that sad | embroid | ĕr̆y wēars,"

(3) ". . . when the consonant *n* comes between the vowels, and the vowel preceding this letter is so obscurely or rapidly pronounced as to leave it doubtful whether it may be considered as forming a distinct syllable."

"Under | the op | ĕn̆ing ey̆e | lids of | the morn."

(4) "Sometimes the liquid *l*, in a like position, gives the poet a like liberty . . ."

"Wafted | the trav | ĕl̆lĕr tō | the beau | teous west."

Note that these *elisions* are common in most English poetry (except during part of the eighteenth century), and are usually called elisions of "open vowels," "pure *r*," "pure *n*" and "pure *l*." (See p. xxvi.)

Bryant next takes up what he calls "pure trisyllabic feet" — "where the first two syllables will not admit of a contraction, or, which is nearly the same thing, refuse to coalesce in the pronunciation,"[5] as in this line from Shakespeare:

Thou ever young, fresh, loved, and *delicate wooer*,

"For my part," he writes, "when I meet with such passages, amid a waste of dissyllabic feet, their spirited irregularity refreshes and relieves me, like the sight of eminences and forests breaking the uniformity of a landscape." Yet his main concern is simply "to show that it is an ancient birthright of the poets which ought not to be given up."

This statement is very significant, since it prepares us to expect in his poetry no new innovations, experiments,

[5] Under "pure trisyllabic feet" Bryant includes some examples that come under the rules of elision which he himself lays down. *E.g.*, "the river of bliss" is not "the riv̇er ȯf bliss," but "the riv*er* of bliss" — elision of pure *r* between two unaccented vowels. He also fails to recognize an elision of two unaccented vowels in "cit*y* of Minos," or the "pure *l*" in "per*ilous* flood."

or unorthodox practices. And it is the key to Bryant's whole prosodic theory. In *Lecture Fourth*, "On Imitation and Originality," or "the studying and copying of models of poetic composition," he says that "to slight the experiences of our predecessors on this subject is a pretty certain way to go wrong." Indeed, "At the present day . . . a writer of poems writes in a language which preceding poets have polished, refined, and filled with forcible, graceful, and musical expressions. He is not only taught by them to overcome the difficulties of rhythmical construction, but he is shown, as it were, the secrets of the mechanism by which he moves the mind of his reader; . . ." He thinks, however, that the poet would do well "to take no particular poem nor poet, nor class of poets, as the pattern of poetic composition, but to study the beauties of all."

The introduction to *A New Library of Poetry and Song* [6] includes all the main points of Bryant's prosodic theory, which may be conveniently summarized as follows:

X　(1) He believes that only "poems of a moderate length, or else parts of the greater works" give the highest imaginative and intellectual pleasure — thus anticipating Poe.

(2) He again stresses the prosodic debt of one age to another.

(3) He dislikes affectations of all kinds, especially of style and "novelties of expression."

(4) But he prefers freedom of manner (apparently including technique).

(5) He is glad to see that hackneyed phrases and rime tags are no longer much used by contemporary poets.

(6) And he is especially pleased that blank verse is dropping its Latinisms and "awkward distortions resorted to by those who thought that by putting a sentence out of its proper shape they were writing like Milton."

Simple as these points appear to be, they are as compre-

[6] "Poets and Poetry of the English Language," *Prose Writings*, I, 147–160.

hensive as Wordsworth's famous reforms; in fact they resemble Wordsworth's ideas on prosody and make us wonder how deeply Bryant was influenced by the tenets in the Preface of *Lyrical Ballads*.[7] How closely Bryant followed his own theories will appear throughout the remainder of this chapter.

3. BLANK VERSE

Hardly any discussion of Bryant's poetry or versification can avoid beginning with his first and most famous poem, *Thanatopsis*, published in 1817, the main part of which is claimed to have been written in 1811, when the poet was only sixteen years old. The poet wrote other blank verse very nearly as good as *Thanatopsis* (such as *Inscription for the Entrance to a Wood* with its long breath-sweeps and varied pauses, though less sonorous), but this poem illustrates most of the characteristics of Bryant's blank verse, and is the poem which every one knows.

Since the introduction and conclusion were added perhaps six years after the middle portion was written, every student of versification should be interested in comparing the earlier and later portions. It is obvious that the transitions in thought are weak, but a close examination will also reveal certain differences in versification, which are mainly three. First, there are more monosyllables in the earlier part, giving a preponderantly masculine rhythm. Second, the rhythm is as a result more regular. Third, the pauses and breath-sweeps (the most important factors in blank verse cadences aside from accentuation)

[7] This question has never been sufficiently investigated, but see Carl Van Doren, "The Growth of Thanatopsis," *The Nation*, October 7, 1915. Bryant read *Lyrical Ballads* in 1811. *Cf.* Parke Godwin's *Life*, I, 104. Professor William Ellery Leonard (see his chapter on Bryant in the *Cambridge History of American Literature*, I, 260 ff.) does not find very important similarities between Wordsworth's thought and Bryant's.

are different, being somewhat longer and more varied in the 1817 additions.   These differences are easier to feel than to analyze, but the following extracts illustrate the point:

> To him who in the love of Nature holds
> Communion with her visible forms, she speaks
> A various language; // for his gayer hours
> She has a voice of gladness, and a smile
> And eloquence of beauty, and she glides
> Into his darker musings, with a mild
> And healing sympathy, that steals away
> Their sharpness, ere he is aware. // . . .

That seven of these eight lines are enjambed and that they contain only two full stops, every one will agree, but the minor pauses will be managed differently by different readers.   No one, however, is likely to pause very decidedly for the comma.   Bryant's commas are never a sure indication of pauses, anyway.   Yet notice the short pauses in this extract from the early version:

> As the long train
> Of ages glides away, / the sons of men, /
> The youth in life's fresh spring, and he who goes
> In the full strength of years, / matron and maid, /
> The speechless babe, / and the gray-headed man — /

In general, the long breath-sweeps of the first lines of this poem are not typical of the bulk of Bryant's blank verse, though he used them occasionally in later years. A skilful fingering of pauses, however, is characteristic of most of his blank verse, and is one of his most distinctive achievements. It is also significant that in this poem over twice as many periods end within the line as terminate at the end of the verse, probably a representative average for Bryant. A full stop is so often placed at the end of the initial foot, or somewhere between the end of the third and fourth feet, that it is almost a mannerism. The cæsura is likewise variable.

Returning to the two quoted passages, we notice in the first that only two lines have five natural speech accents (and in each line one of these is secondary), but there are no metrical stresses in the second passage. This difference is also fairly characteristic of the remainder of the earlier as opposed to the later portions of the poem.

Taken as a whole, Bryant's blank verse rhythm is fairly regular, yet he very successfully uses several variations to avoid monotony. These variations are principally:

(1) The spondee —

Fáir fórms, | and hoar | y seers | of a | ges past, . . .

Óf the | gréat tómb | of man. | The gol | den sun, . . .

In théir | lást sléep | — the dead | reign there | alone. . . .

Plód ón, | and each | one as | before | will chase . . .

And make | their bed | with thee. | As the | lóng tráin

(2) The foot preceding a spondee is often a pyrrhic, or practically so.[8] (See lines two, three, and five above.) Also:

In all his course; nor yet | in the | cóld gróund, . . .

In the | fúll stréngth | of years, matron and maid . . .

The speechless babe, | and the | grày-héad | ed man —

---

[8] This metrical device is found in the verse of Chaucer, Shakespeare, and Milton; but rarely in the eighteenth century. In fact, it disappeared from English versification during the dictatorship of Pope. But it returned with Wordsworth and Coleridge, and is found extensively in Byron, Shelley, and Keats.

(3) The reversed foot (trochee for iamb) is so common in all blank verse that it need not be illustrated (but see "matron | and maid" above).

(4) The light verse is of no special importance either, since Bryant uses it with sufficient economy to prevent its ever disturbing the pattern; but it will be noticed that his metrical stresses usually occur where the phonetic environment is such that the syllable receives at least a light secondary stress when the line is read naturally.

> Shall one by one be gathered to thy side,
>
> By those, who in their turn shall follow them.

Unusually light:

> Their mirth and their employments, and shall come

Though Bryant uses the trisyllabic foot extensively in other measures, it is found much more rarely in his blank verse. The second line of *Thanatopsis* does, however, contain an example:

> Communion with her vis | ible forms, | she speaks

The elisions are the same as those explained by Bryant himself in his essay *On Trisyllabic Feet in Iambic Measure*.

We also find a considerable number of alliterations in this first poem: "*m*ake the *m*eadows green," "*s*un *s*hall *s*ee no more," "*m*atron and *m*aid," "*S*courged to his dungeon, but *s*ustained and *s*oothed."

Part of the sonorous effect of the poem is probably due to the connotations of the monosyllabic vocabulary, the masculine rhythm aiding the sententious didacticism. The vowels also unmistakably give tone color. And while it is perhaps unsafe to generalize on tone color, one line in particular illustrates what the student should listen for in reading the poem. The line is: "Where rolls the Oregon, and hears no sound," with its back vowels and rolling *r*'s. Sometimes a line has a predominance of front vowels: "In s*i*lence from the l*i*ving and no fr*i*end." [9]

One stylistic trait is important in Bryant's blank verse. The first part of *Thanatopsis*, for instance, is characterized by dependent clauses and phrases preceding the main statement. "To him who in the love of Nature holds Communion with her visible forms, *she speaks a various language.*" Or "while from all around — Earth and her Waters, and the depths of air — *Comes a still voice.* —" But a still better example is this serpentine sentence from *A Winter Piece:*

> . . . When shrieked
> The bleak November winds, and smote the woods,
> And the brown fields were herbless, and the shades,
> That met above the merry rivulet,
> Were spoiled, *I sought, I loved them still;* . . .

Hymn to Death is one of Bryant's least successful poems in blank verse; and it is interesting, therefore, to inspect its technical characteristics. We have discovered the key when we find that it is predominantly oratorical, with, as we might expect, (1) apostrophes; (2) interrogations and exclamations; (3) appositives and antitheses, balancing of phrase against phrase; and (4) reiterations of word, phrase, and grammatical construction.

Parallelism and reiteration, however, are not necessarily bad. In fact, they are used successfully in most of Bryant's later blank verse. This, no doubt, is partly because his later verse in this form is used extensively for lyric purposes, as in *A Rain-Dream*, which is lyric not only in treatment but also in subject-matter. In the following passage the reiterations and alliterations are italicized, and the reader will have no difficulty in discovering the parallelisms:

[9] Phonetically, the *i* in "silence" is a diphthong and is pronounced in neither the front nor the back of the mouth exclusively. It is a "glide," beginning with the back vowel *a* (as in *father*) and advancing toward the position of the front vowel *e* (as in *see*).

Now *s*lowly falls the dull blank night, and *s*till,
All through the starless hours, the mighty Rain
Smites with perpetual *s*ound the forest-leaves,
And beats the matted grass, and still the earth
Drinks the unstinted bounty of the clouds —
Drinks for her cottage *w*ells, her *w*oodland brooks —
Drinks for the springing *t*rout, the *t*oiling bee,
And *b*rooding *b*ird — *drinks* for her tender flowers,
Tall oaks, and all the *h*erbage [10] of her *h*ills.

In other poems Bryant also uses the strongly accented three-stress phrase followed by a lighter two-stress phrase, which seems merely to echo the first cadence. Or we may call it thesis and arsis, the thesis representing the heavier stress and the arsis the lighter:

thesis	arsis
Drinks for her cottage wells,	her woodland brooks —

In his blank verse Bryant uses the changing figure almost as extensively as Walt Whitman does. (There is no question of influence, for Bryant was using it as early as 1830 — and there is also this difference: Whitman's figure is usually confined to the single verse, whereas Bryant's runs over freely into succeeding lines). This use of the changing figures is metrically important because it frequently sets the pattern of the line; and it is at least partly responsible for Bryant's tendency to repeat the same cadence throughout a whole passage, as in *The Prairies:*

Breezes of the South!

Who toss the golden and the flame-like flowers,

And pass the prairie-hawk that, poised on high,

Flaps his broad wings, yet moves not — ye have played

---

[10] "Herbage" appears to alliterate with "hills," but it is impossible to be sure whether Bryant pronounced the "h" in "herbage."

Among the palms of Mexico and vines
Of Texas, and have crisped the limpid brooks

Repeating the cadence does not become monotonous when we have the minor variations illustrated here: the inverted initial foot, secondary accents in different positions, and a totally different cadence in the last line.

Sometimes the parallelistic changing figures produce a short, compact phrase, with frequent pauses and full stops, as in the story of *Sella:*

The morning came, / and Sella was not found. //
The sun climbed high; // they sought her still; // the noon, /
The hot and silent noon, / heard Sella's name,
Uttered with a despairing cry, to wastes
O'er which the eagle hovered. //

Or in *The Flood of Years:*

There are they who toil, /
And they who strive, / and they who feast, / and they
Who hurry to and fro. // The sturdy swain — /
Woodman and delver with the spade — is there, /
And busy artisan beside his bench, /
And pallid student with his written roll. //

Bryant's translation of Homer, about 1865–1870, shows practically all the metrical devices of his early blank verse, except for perhaps less ingenuity in the variation of his pauses. And this translation also shows how little genuine growth there was in his blank verse between 1811 and 1870. Aside from the later tendency to use this measure for lyric subjects, as we have seen, there are few chronological differences.

But the 1811–1817 standard was very high. Though Bryant's verse never reached the sublimity of *Paradise Lost* or Wordsworth's *Lines Above Tintern Abbey*, it does not suffer in comparison with the best of Thomson or Cowper, and its versification has much in common with Wordsworth's.

4. OCTOSYLLABICS

Bryant's next favorite measure, after blank verse, was the four-stress iambic quatrain, yet he also wrote some octosyllabic couplets and several four-stress anapestic quatrains. Chronologically, the four-stress quatrain (*cf. The Yellow Violet*, w. 1814) precedes the octosyllabic couplet ("*Oh Fairest of the Rural Maids,*" 1820), but it is simpler to consider the couplet first.

Despite the fact that "*Oh Fairest of the Rural Maids*" is in couplet rime, it is grouped in four-line stanzas, always ending with a period. Most of the verses contain four regular speech accents, and consistently eight syllables, though about one-fifth of the lines contain only three speech accents, as in the first stanza:

> Oh fairest of the rural maids!
> Thy birth was in the forest shades;
> Green boughs, and glimpses of the sky,
> Were all that met thine infant eye.

All the other important variations are represented by the following specimens:

> The twilight of the trees and rocks
> Is in the light shade of thy locks; . . .
> On their young figures in the brook.

Here, as in the blank verse, a spondee is likely to be preceded or followed by two light syllables, giving us a foot that often scans as a minor ionic. As a rule, Bryant's couplets are more regular than his four-stress quatrains, and, incidentally, inferior as poetry.

The first important metrical trait of the $abab_4$ quatrain is the frequent use of a cadence composed of a primary-secondary-primary accentuation. In *The Yellow Violet*, we discover the blúe bìrd's wárble knów

and in *The Hunter of the West* we find

the dáy-dàwn cóld and cléar . . .

snów-shòes láced.

It is a typically compound construction, accentuated according to the "ancient law of compounds," [11] but the words are not necessarily hyphenated. *The West Wind* contains the most successful use of this cadence and affords the greatest number of examples:

Whose bránching pínes rìse dárk and hígh, . . .

Do nòt the bríght Jùne róses blòw, . . .

The lòose whíte clòuds are bórn awáy. . . .

And thére the fúll broàd ríver rúns,

And mány a fóunt wèlls frésh and swéet,

The actual number of speech stresses may range all the way from three, as in:

Wórn with the strúggle and the strìfe,

from a *Summer Ramble*, to five, as in:

Séven lóng yéars of sórrow and páin; . . .

Áll níght lóng I tálk with the déad,[12]

from *The Maiden's Sorrow*, with its onomatopoetic effects. Bryant also makes much greater use of alliteration in his four-stress lyrics. *A Day-Dream* depends largely upon this device for its unworldly effect:

[11] *I.e.*, in noun, adjective, and adverb compounds the chief stress is placed on the first element of the compound, but in verb compounds the stress always falls on the root syllable.

[12] In both of these examples the second stress may be secondary, but primary stress on "long" and "night" gives a more dramatic reading.

> A *d*ay-*d*ream by the *d*ark-blue *d*eep;
> Was it a *d*ream, or something more?
> I *s*at where Posilippo's *s*teep,
> With its gray *s*helves, o'erhung the *s*hore.

There seems to be no special significance in the particular consonants used for alliteration, but this poem provides a fair illustration of their frequency. Altogether there are twenty-eight alliterations, in the following order: *s*, 8; *w*, 5; *l*, 3; *f*, 3; *d*, 3; *b*, 2; *c*, 2; *r*, 1; *o*, 1.[13] Sibilant alliterations are undoubtedly a favorite, sometimes extending to all the accented syllables, as illustrated by this line from *Abraham Lincoln:*

> Oh, *s*low to *s*mite and *s*wift to *s*pare,

In such a poem as *The Twenty-Second of December*, Bryant's utterly bare, unadorned style, with its simple vocabulary and regular meter, is exceedingly appropriate and impressive. For instance:

> Wíld was the dáy; the wíntry séa
>
> Moáned sádly on Nèw-Englánd's stránd,
>
> When fírst the thóughtful ănd the frée,
>
> Our fáthers, tród the désert lánd.

The only metrical dexterities here are the initial inversions in the first two lines and the heavy-syllabled second line, both of which are onomatopoetic.

5. THE TRISYLLABIC FOOT

We have already observed that Bryant occasionally substitutes the trisyllabic foot in his blank verse, and the second line of *Thanatopsis* has already been cited as an example. Other instances are:

---

[13] This is not counting the frequent single repetitions of an initial consonant (in a stressed position) used alliteratively in the preceding line. (*Cf.* the second line of the above quotation from *A Day-Dream.*)

Should tempt the loitering moth and dil | igent bee.

The Twenty-Seventh of March

By the road | -side and the borders of the brook.

Summer Wind

A playmate of her young and in | nocent years,

Monument Mountain

The shining ear; nor when, | by the riv | er's side,

Ibid.

She talked with mus | ical voice | and sweetly laughed.

Sella

In the four-stress iambic couplet, the trisyllabic substitution is also found, as in *The Hurricane*, where there is at least one anapestic foot to each verse, occurring anywhere in the line:

Lord of the winds! I feel thee nigh,

I know thy breath | in the burn | ing sky!

And I wait, | with a thrill | in every vein,

For the coming of the hurricane!

An anapest in the last foot is infrequent, but when it does appear, the line usually contains at least one other anapest:

And the for | ests hear and an | swer the sound. . . .

With the ver | y clouds! | — Ye are lost | to my eyes.

The trisyllable is seldom found in the stanzaic poems, but an example from *To a Waterfowl* is:

While glow | the heavens | with the last | steps of day,

But in other poems, like *Green River*, one or two anapests are substituted in each line and become part of the verse-pattern:

When bréez | es are sóft | and skíes | are fáir,

I stéal an hóur from stúd | y and cáre,[14]

And híe | me awáy | to the wóod | land scéne,

Where wán | ders the stréam | with wá | ters of gréen,

This substitution later develops into a greater freedom, similar to Coleridge's versification of *Christabel*, which contains four accents without regard to their position in the line. *Rizpah* is perhaps the best example:

Héar what the désolate Rízpah sáid,

As on Gíbeah's rócks she wátched the déad.

The sóns of Míchal befóre her láy,

And her ówn fáir chíldren, déarer than théy:

By a déath of sháme they áll had díed,

And were strétched on the báre róck, síde by síde.

In this scheme the number of trisyllabic feet to the verse may range all the way from one to four:

Í have máde | the crágs my hóme, and spréad . . .

In the bláze | of the sún | and the wínds | of the ský.

Finally, the trisyllable may dominate completely, so that we have anapestic rhythm with iambic substitutions. Such a poem is "*I Cannot Forget with What Fervid Devotion*,"

$$ \times \diagup \mid \times \times \diagup \mid \times \times \diagup \mid \times \times \diagup (\times) $$

which monotonously gallops away. *The Gladness of Nature* and "*When the Firmament Quivers*" are other examples — the latter being saved from monotony by the use of the spondee and secondary accents, as in:

[14] The "–y and" may be regarded as an elision of open vowels.

When the firmament quivers with daylight's young beam,

And the woodlands awaking burst into a hymn,

And the glow of the sky blazes back from the stream,[15]

It is obvious that Bryant carried the use of the trisyllabic foot much farther than did the poets he quoted
in his 1811 essay on this subject. At times he inserts it
into his line so frequently that it no longer remains a
substitution, a metrical freedom, but becomes an important part of the verse-pattern. His most successful use
of the trisyllabic foot is probably in the free manner of
his *Rizpah* poem, which shows that he is not an eighteenth-
century poet and metrist but a typically nineteenth-
century poet.

6. RIMED IAMBIC PENTAMETER

Aside from the Spenserian stanza, Bryant's rimed pentameter verse need not be discussed in detail. The heroic
couplet did not appeal to him at all, and only four of his
poems are in five-stress quatrains — *The Child's Funeral,
The Future Life, The Life That Is,* and *October.* The
"Venus and Adonis" stanza, however, is used more often
in Bryant's poetry (see *Lines on Revisiting the Country,
To a Mosquito, A Meditation on Rhode Island Coal, The
Journey of Life, Spring in Town,* and *To the Apennines,*
written between 1825 and 1835).

Practically all of Bryant's usual poetic devices are found
in the five-stress line, including the extensive use of the
(/ \ /) cadence, though his pauses are less skilfully managed here than in his blank verse, and there is far less
enjambment. His rimes, as always, are correct. But the
rhythm is often too monotonously regular.

[15] Note: "sky blazes back" is much more dramatic than "sky
blazes back."

7. THE SONNET

Bryant was not a sonneteer, for he published only ten sonnets in all, and scarcely any of these are comparable to his better known poems in other forms. He seems, however, to have passed through two stages of sonnet writing in his life: the first beginning in 1824 and lasting through 1827, the last covering the years 1876 and 1877 (the undated translation from the Portuguese may have been written a little earlier, but probably not). Unimportant as these sonnets are as a whole, their chronological development is very interesting.

The first sonnet, *To —*, is strictly English (*i.e.*, *ababcdcdefefgg*), and is fairly successful; yet his next attempt, *Mutation*, written in the same year (1824), is in the Spenserian form (*i.e.*, *ababbccdcdee*), and is probably the best sonnet he ever wrote — best not only metrically but also imaginatively. *November*, also written in 1824, is English except for the final couplet, which returns to the *b*-rime, thus: *ababcdcdefefbb*.

The second half of Bryant's first period of sonnet writing (1826–1828), the least successful of all, includes *Midsummer, October, William Tell*, and *To Cole, the Painter, Departing for Europe*. These are in a form which is a mixture of the English and Italian forms, riming *abbacddceffegg*. The first quatrain is strictly Italian, the second and third use new rimes in the Italian manner, and the whole mélange ends with a typical English couplet. Full stops occur at the end of the first and second quatrains (in the Italian manner) and just before the final couplet (in the English manner).

Bryant's last original sonnets are in still another form. His Portuguese translation, merely called *Sonnet*, is conventionally Italian (*i.e.*, *abbaabbacdcdcd*), and is smooth in rhythm and structure. Yet the two sonnets of 1876–1877, *A Sonnet, To —* and *In Memory of John Lothrop Motley*, are in a contaminated Italian form, riming *abab*

abab cdcdcd. The first quatrain rimes are English, but, like the Italian, the second repeats the rimes of the first, though still in the English order; the sestet is, of course, strictly Italian, and the total, final effect is more Italian than English. This mongrel is less unfortunate than the earlier one, since Bryant's last two sonnets are nearly as successful as his first two, though hardly the equal of the Spenserian *Mutation.*

8. THE SPENSERIAN STANZA

Bryant used the Spenserian stanza ($ababbcbc_5bc_6$) in only two poems, *The Ages* (w. 1821) and *After a Tempest* (w. 1824), but these two poems are exceptionally good. So harsh a critic as Edgar Allan Poe wrote, "The cadences [in *The Ages*] . . . cannot be surpassed. There are comparatively few consonants. Liquids and the softer vowels abound, and the partial line after the pause at 'surge,' with the stately march of the succeeding alexandrine is one of the finest conceivable finales." [16] He was referring specifically to Stanza VI:

Look on this beautiful world, and read the truth

In her fair page; see, every season brings

New change, to her, of everlasting youth;

Still the green soil, with joyous living things,

Swarms, the wide air is full of joyous wings,

And myriads, still, are happy in the sleep

Of ocean's azure gulfs, and where he flings

The restless surge. Eternal Love doth keep,

In his complacent arms, the earth, the air, the deep.

[16] Poe's *Works*, edited by Woodberry and Stedman, VI, 138–139.

Poe especially commended the cadences at "page," "swarms," and "surge." To be noticed, too, are the skilful variations achieved with secondary accents. In this passage we also meet again the changing figures, commented upon elsewhere. The preparation for the alexandrine in the preceding half-line prevents the six-stress line from dragging, as it is so likely to do in unskilful hands. Bryant's handling of the alexandrine is, in fact, perhaps the greatest difference between his use of this stanza and Spenser's. In the *Faerie Queene* the last two lines are usually complete in thought as well as in rime, summing up the thought of the stanza or adding some final description, and often, for this very reason, drawing out and slowing up the narration. Spenser's seventh line is therefore likely to be end-stopped. Bryant's seventh line, on the contrary, is usually enjambed, and never end-stopped. A full stop may be used internally in line seven, but there is nearly always a short phrase or fully enjambed preceding line to assimilate the final alexandrine and break up the last two lines into pauses which disguise the fact that they are of unequal length. Yet the alexandrine usually does express a concluding thought or sentiment.

After a Tempest is mainly descriptive, and in some ways the Spenserian stanza is used even more appropriately here than in *The Ages*. The fifth stanza rather curiously anticipates the thought of that famous stanza of Tennyson's *Locksley Hall*, beginning, "For I dipped into the future . . .":

> I looked, and thought the quiet of the scene
> An emblem of the peace that yet shall be,
> When o'er earth's continents, and isles between
> The noise of war shall cease from sea to sea,
> And married nations dwell in harmony;

9. THE ALEXANDRINE

Bryant's use of the alexandrine is a special subject in itself. He not only used the single-line alexandrine in the Spenserian stanza and in his own modification of the "Venus and Adonis" stanza ($ababc_5c_6$), as in *A Walk at Sunset* and *The Old Man's Funeral*, but he even wrote whole poems in the alexandrine measure. Before analyzing these, it is necessary to define the modern and Middle-English alexandrine.[17]

The modern English alexandrine (1) has nearly always exactly twelve syllables; (2) it is usually divided into two equal parts by a cæsura after the sixth syllable; (3) in each half-line the second, fourth, and sixth syllables are regularly accented, the others remaining unstressed; (4) the initial syllable may not be omitted; and (5) the line ordinarily has a masculine ending.[18]

Bryant wrote two poems in the pure alexandrine form [19] of which the following extracts are representative: [20]

Beside a massive gateway [:] built up in years gone by, . . .

I mark the joy, the terror; [:] yet these, within my heart,

Can neither wake the dread [:] nor the longing to depart;

And, in the sunshine streaming [:] on quiet wood and lea,

I stand and calmly wait [:] till the hinges turn for me.

Waiting by the Gate

[17] The alexandrine is rarely found in modern English poetry, but some examples are Drayton's *Poly-Olbion* (1613), in couplets, and Browning's *Fifine at the Fair* (1872), in alternate rime.

[18] This summary is a paraphrase of Kaluza's definition. See Max Kaluza, *Englische Metrik in historischer Entwicklung* (Berlin, 1909), § 155.

[19] The alexandrine first appeared in English poetry in the couplet-rimed chronicle of Robert Mannyng of Brunne (early 14th century), which is a translation of a French psalm in alexandrines, which are different from those of both Middle and Modern English.

[20] There are some resemblances between the versification of *The Third of November* and Meredith's *Love in a Valley*.

Softly breathes the west-wind [:] beside the ruddy forest, . . .
Dreary are the years [:] when the eye can look no longer
    With delight on Nature, [:] or hope on human kind;
Oh, may those that whiten [:] my temples, [:] as they pass me,
    Leave the heart unfrozen, [:] and spare the cheerful mind!

The Third of November, 1861

We notice (1) that the first passage and over half of the second have not twelve but *thirteen* syllables; (2) that the cæsura comes *after* the fifth, sixth, or seventh syllables; (3) that the first syllable is stressed in three of these lines, thus (4) omitting the initial *unstressed* syllable; and that (5) several lines have *feminine endings*. Plainly Bryant's alexandrines do not fit the above definition on any of the five counts.

In the Middle-English alexandrine the number of stresses and not the number of feet are counted. The line is divided by a cæsura with exactly three stresses to a half-line. An anacrusis may precede the first stress (or beat) of each half-line, and an unstressed syllable may occur at the end of each half-line. The scheme is, therefore, as follows:

$$(\times) \diagup \mid \times \diagup \mid \times \diagup (\times) \mid : (\times) \diagup \mid \times \diagup \mid \times \diagup (\times)$$

And this is precisely the pattern of Bryant's alexandrines — with one very minor difference: his cæsura sometimes comes before two unstressed syllables instead of between them, as indicated above. Thus:

Drear | y are | the years | [:] when the eye | can look | no
    longer

But we also have the exact Middle-English pattern in:

I mark | the joy, | the terror; | [:] yet these, | within | my
    heart, . . .

A development from the Middle-English alexandrine is a couplet with six stresses (twelve syllables) in one line and seven (fourteen syllables) in the next, referred to by metrists as "poulter's measure," [21] because in England a dozen eggs used to be either twelve or fourteen, depending upon their size.

The main part of Bryant's *The Lament of Romero* (1828) is in this form. Trisyllabic substitution sometimes gives the long line fifteen syllables, yet the rhythm is unmistakably the old "poulter's measure."

"Fair — fair | — but fall | en Spain! | 'tis with | a swell | ing

heart,

That I think | on all | thou mightst | have been, | and look | at

what | thou art;

But the strife is over now, and all the good and brave,

That would have raised thee up, are gone, to exile or the grave.

Thy fleeces are for monks, thy grapes for the convent feast,

And the wealth of all thy harvest-fields for the pampered lord

and priest. . . ."

"When the spirit of the land to liberty shall bound,

As yonder fountain leaps away from the darkness of the ground:

And to my mountain-cell, the voices of the free

Shall rise as from the beaten shore the thunders of the sea."

Another interesting experiment of Bryant's, related to "poulter's measure" (for it has regularly fifteen syllables),

---

[21] "Poulter's measure" was much used in the 16th century drama, and in one long poem by Arthur Brooke, *Romeus and Juliet*, the main source for Shakespeare's *Romeo and Juliet*. Macaulay revived the measure, printing it as long lines in *Virginia* and short lines in *Horatius*.

is his eight-stress line in *The Cloud on the Way*. The verse has one very pronounced cæsura which divides it into two equal parts with four stresses each; and unless read very fast, there are also two other lighter cæsura pauses, dividing the line into four sections with two stresses each. In the examples below the main cæsura is marked [:], the lighter (:).

This poem is also a good illustration of the fact that marking and naming feet is sometimes entirely arbitrary. The line begins with an accented syllable and ends with one. We may regard the initial foot as "clipped" or the last one as incomplete; either way, we have a perfectly symmetrical and satisfactory scheme, in spite of the fact that in one case we mark the line as iambic and in the other trochaic. The rhythm does, however, seem to have a trochaic lilt, and is so scanned below; but if it is trochaic, it is the only one of Bryant's poems in this meter:

See, be | fore us, | (:) in our | journey, | [:] broods a | mist (:)
    u | pon the | ground;

Thither | leads (:) the | path we | walk in, | [:] blending | with
    (:) that | gloomy | bound.

Never | eye (:) hath | pierced its | shadows | [:] to the | mys-
    ter | y (:) they | screen;

Those who | once (:) have | passed with | in it | [:] never | more
    (:) on | earth are | seen. . . .

Passest | down (:) the | rocky | valley, | [:] walking | with me |
    (:) hand in | hand, . . .

"Here," thou | sayst, (:) "the | path is | rugged, | [:] sown
    with | thorns (:) that | wound the | feet;

The stanza $ababcdcd_4$ is simply the eight-stress verse with internal rime arranged differently, though it has sixteen instead of fifteen syllables and is unmistakably iambic. Examples are *To the River Arve* and *The Hunter of the Prairies*. The $aabb_4c_2c_4$ stanza is another variation (see "*Oh Mother of a Mighty Race*").

Some prosodists [22] have an interesting theory that the ballad stanza ($abcb$, $4 + 3$) is a development from the old "fourteener" (seven-stress), which in turn developed the alexandrine. Whether or not this theory is well founded, Bryant's *The Stress of Life* ($abcbdebe$, $4 + 3$) is definitely composed of seven-stress couplets.

10. OTHER STANZAS

Bryant's most important stanzas have been discussed; so it should be sufficient merely to list his other stanzas. Some variations of the $abab$, $4 + 3$ quatrain are a $3 + 5$ arrangement in *The Past*, and the addition of two short lines ($abab_4cc_2$) in "*The May Sun Sheds an Amber Light*." The hymns are mostly in straight octosyllabic couplets and quatrains rather than, as we might expect, the ballad stanza. Other quatrains are $abab_3$ in *A Sick Bed* and $abcb_3$ in *My Autumn Walk*. In *The Brighter Day* the quatrain is expanded into $a_3b_5aa_3b_5$.

In six-line stanzas we have: $a_4b_3a_4b_3a_2a_4$, in *Song for New Year's Eve*; $ababCC_4$, in *Not Yet*; and $ababBB_4$, in *The Wind and Stream*. The "Venus and Adonis" stanza has already been discussed. The eight-line stanza $ababcdcd_4$ is used in *Our Country's Call*, and the same quatrain in pentameter in *The Return of Youth*; $ababcccb$ ("tail rime") in *The Winds*; $a_3b_3c_4b_3d_3e_3f_4e_3$ in *Song*, "*These Prairies Glow with Flowers*"; and $abab_4cc_2dd_4$ in *Italy*.

Death of Slavery is in a twelve-line stanza, $abba_5cc_3dedeff_5$, which is as irregular as an ode. *The Song of the*

[22] *Cf.* Johannes C. Andersen, *The Laws of Verse* (Cambridge, England, 1928), Chapter III.

Sower is an actual ode, the rime-scheme of the first three stanzas being as follows (the three-stress lines are italicized — the others are four-stress):

I. aba*bcccb*ddee;   II. aabbb*c*dedeffgghhi*ji*j;   III. aabb-cdcdeeffgegg*e*gehh*e*ii*e*jjkk.

In none of these forms, however, does any of Bryant's best poetry appear. They are listed here merely to show the extent of his stanzaic practices. And they demonstrate, unmistakably, that Bryant's poetic fame does not rest on his ingenuity in the invention of stanzas, or in any sort of rime-scheme dexterity. Yet we have seen that he did very successfully adapt some old stanzas (such as the Spenserian and the "Venus and Adonis") to his own abilities in versification.

In the shorter stanzas his greatest achievement is perhaps *To a Waterfowl*, a quatrain riming $a_3b_5a_5b_3$. Some of Bryant's most ardent admirers claim to see in this stanzaic arrangement the symbolism of the flight of the bird, and as a matter of fact, the poem does give the sensation of gliding. But the stanzaic form does not deserve all the credit.

II. BRYANT'S CONTRIBUTIONS

Conservative in the use of stanzaic devices, careful with his rimes, and an adapter of such old meters as the alexandrine, poulter's measure, and the eight-stress line, Bryant was, nevertheless, abreast of the times in his defense and use of trisyllabic substitution, in his breaking away from the tyranny of the heroic couplet, and in his deliberate attempt to work out a versification which fitted his needs rather than to shape his message to conform to an inherited verse technique. He is eminently important in the history of American versification because his technique was finished, effective, and truly artistic. Of all American poets, his achievement is most nearly comparable to and worthy of Wordsworth himself.

But Bryant is particularly important in the history of American prosody because he was the first American to publish important criticism and theories on purely prosodic subjects. And it is also significant that in his most important prosodic essay, *On Trisyllabic Feet in Iambic Measure*, he argued for a newly recognized freedom. He can scarcely be called an innovator or "radical" in his practices, but this attitude of alertness to new developments and general prosodic independence started American prosodic history on the path which eventually led to a truly epoch-making "revolution." Kreymborg speaks of "Forefather Bryant" [23] with specific reference to his poetry, but he was even more truly the forefather of American prosody.

12. PROSODIC EVENTS OF THE TIMES

Since so few years separated Bryant's poetic apprenticeship from Poe's, the minor poets of the time may be discussed in either chapter. For convenience we shall outline here some important prosodic events that were taking place during the later days of Freneau and the youth of Bryant, leaving for the Poe chapter the consideration of the minor American poets of about the first third of the nineteenth century.[24]

Freneau perfected his versification too early to be seriously influenced by the rising tide of Romanticism, but Bryant was learning to write poetry during the most exciting and stimulating poetic activities that had taken place in English literature for many years. Three years after Bryant's birth (1794) Southey published his volume of poems containing accentual "Sapphics" and "Dactylics." In 1798–1799 Coleridge published his *Sibylline*

[23] Title of chapter on Bryant in Alfred Kreymborg's *Our Singing Strength* (New York: Coward McCann, 1929), pp. 27–40.

[24] For a discussion of the main principles of the English background of the period see General Introduction, pp. xxxvi–xliii.

Leaves, containing several poems in hexameters. Controversy over these "classical meters" did not subside for
many years. But the most important prosodic event of
this period was the 1800 Preface to *Lyrical Ballads.*[25]   In
1805 Scott published his *Lay of the Last Minstrel,* based on
Coleridge's new accentual principle. In all there were
five movements in English poetry which could not fail to
influence American versification in one way or another:
(1) The revival of blank verse and the creation of a new
poetic style, as in Thomson's *Seasons;* (2) the related
"Miltonic school," with the revival of interest in the
octosyllabic couplet and blank verse, as practiced by
Parnell, Young, Blair, and others; (3) the "imitators of
Spenser," in the work of Shenstone, Akenside, Beattie,
and others; (4) the work of the "antiquaries," notably
Percy's *Reliques,* Macpherson's *Ossian,* and Chatterton's
Rowley Poems; and (5) finally, *Lyrical Ballads.* It was
an age of feverish experimentation with new forms and
principles.[26]   And naturally the theory of English and
American prosody was being reforged on many anvils, by
both poets and metrists.

SELECTED BIBLIOGRAPHY

TEXT

Bryant, William Cullen, *Poetical Works,* ed. by Parke Godwin.   New
York: D. Appleton and Company, 1883.   2 vols.

——, *Prose Writings,* ed. by Parke Godwin.   New York: D. Appleton
and Company, 1884.   2 vols.

——, *William Cullen Bryant,* ed. by Tremaine McDowell.   (American
Writers Series.)   New York: American Book Company, 1934.

[Selections of the best of Bryant's poetry and prose, with a critical
introduction.]

---

[25] *Thanatopsis* appears to have been written before Bryant saw
Lyrical Ballads.   See William Ellery Leonard's "Bryant and the
Minor Poets," in *Cambridge History of American Literature* (New
York, 1917), I, 262.

[26] See T. S. Omond, *English Metrists, 18th and 19th Centuries,* Oxford
University Press, 1907.

CRITICISM

Kreymborg, Alfred, "Forefather Bryant," *Our Singing Strength.* New York: Coward-McCann, 1929. Pp. 27–40.

Leonard, William Ellery, "Bryant," *Cambridge History of American Literature.* New York: G. P. Putnam's Sons, 1917. Vol. I, pp. 260 ff.

Saintsbury, George, "American Poets and Prosodists," *History of English Prosody.* New York: The Macmillan Company, 1910. Vol. III, Chapter 5, p. 481.

CHAPTER III

Edgar Allan Poe

I. INTRODUCTION

"EVEN when poets such as Mr. Woodberry and Mr. Hervey Allen have written of Poe," says Professor Werner in his interesting article on "Poe's Theories and Practices in Poetic Technique," "they have discussed his poetry largely in generalities with little mention of technical details.

"The result has been a handing down of four conventional statements about his theories of verse: that all poems must be short; that poetry is close to music; that beauty is the chief aim of poetry; and that 'The Raven' was the result of a logical process. All these ideas can be found by looking no farther than two of Poe's best known critical essays, 'The Poetic Principle' and 'The Philosophy of Composition.' These conventional opinions may be correct, but they are merely repetitions of Poe's own generalizations. They treat no problems of meter or of rime and other repetitions; they say nothing of inversions, archaisms, contractions, stanza forms, or any other items in which a short, musical, beautiful poem by Poe differs from a short, musical, beautiful poem by Longfellow or Whitman or Edna Millay." [1]

Professor Werner adds that Poe in his own criticism was very seriously concerned with the technical problems of prosody. Poe was, indeed, the first American author to publish a real treatise on English and American pros-

[1] W. L. Werner, "Poe's Theories and Practices in Poetic Technique," *American Literature* (May, 1930), II, No. 2, 157–165.

ody;[2] yet it is not altogether surprising, inexcusable as it may seem, that *The Rationale of Verse* should have been so little studied, and still less understood. For it is exceedingly confusing on certain fundamental prosodic facts, almost totally wrong in regard to some linguistic facts (those of the English language in particular), and contradictory on several minor points. A thorough discussion and analysis of the treatise is, therefore, impossible here because it would be both too complicated and too long.[3] But some understanding of Poe's prosodic theory is indispensable to the student of either his poetry or the general history of American prosody.

2. THE RATIONALE OF VERSE

Clement Wood has called *The Philosophy of Composition* Poe's greatest hoax, and *The Rationale of Verse* has some of the same qualities; in both, Poe carries "rationalism" *ad absurdum*. Still, he was probably sincere in his attempt to reduce the composition and the analysis of poetry to definite, tangible principles — a laudable purpose. He does not deny artistic and intuitive principles, but he feels that they have been over-emphasized; and it is for this reason that he stresses and over-stresses the rational.

Yet it is just here that *The Rationale of Verse* is weakest. In the attempt to deduce definite principles, Poe endeavors to solve the fundamental metrical problems with mathematical precision. In fact so misleading is Poe's doctrine that we find so eminent a poet and scholar as E. C. Stedman making the following statement in his introduction to Poe's criticism: "He simply might have said [in *The Rationale of Verse*] that English verse is character-

[2] Thomas Jefferson's excellent little essay was not published until 1905. See bibliography following the General Introduction.

[3] The author expects soon to publish an article giving a thorough analysis and discussion of the prosodic and linguistic questions raised by *The Rationale of Verse*.

istically accentuate instead of quantitative — the reverse
being true of classical; that, although it is often the more
melodious when the more quantitative, its quantity is
incidental and derives from the gift of the poet, while
stress of accent, so different from syllabic length, deter-
mines its metrical system; that in one line of a couplet
there may be twice, even thrice, as many syllables as in
the other, and yet, if each contains only the given number
of accented syllables, they are 'equal to each other.'" [4]

But that is not what Poe does say, or, apparently,
mean. He fails to realize that English verse is accentual
rather than quantitative, else why the attempt to define
length (duration) of syllables? *Quantity* depends upon
time; *accent* merely upon expiratory stress. Poe's system
takes into account only time, and he even makes fun of
Coleridge's "scanning by accents" (*cf.* Preface to *Christabel*). No, all that Poe's theory says is that every line of
poetry has (or should have) a characteristic rhythm, and
that each foot of this rhythm covers an equal duration of
time in the pronunciation; some of the feet have more
syllables than others, but these extra syllables are simply
pronounced with sufficient rapidity to preserve the time
of the characteristic foot. That Poe did not understand
all the implications of such a theory is shown by his
insistence that he believes in *natural* pronunciation,
whereas this theory would force us to read poetry to the
ticking of a metronome. The mistake probably arose
from Poe's belief that poetry is "an inferior or less capable
music." [5] *The Rationale of Verse* may, indeed, apply to
words that are actually sung, but it makes no allowances
for rhetorical stress, subtle onomatopoetic effect, and
other *time-variations* within the line.

It is very likely, however, that Poe did attempt to read
poetry according to his theory (though no *natural* reading

[4] *The Works* of Edgar Allan Poe, edited by E. C. Stedman and
G. E. Woodberry (New York, 1914), VI, xvi.
[5] *Ibid.*, p. 70.

could be consistent with it), for Hervey Allen reports one of Poe's auditors at a lecture which the poet gave in Lowell, Massachusetts, in 1848, as saying that Poe was careful to stress the regular beat, "measuring the movement as if he were scanning it." He always maintained that "hard unequally stepping poetry had better be done in prose." [6]

For the present study, the best way to deal with Poe's prosody seems to be merely to summarize as briefly as possible the most important points of his doctrine, both those in *The Rationale of Verse* and several additional and correlative ones from his book reviews and other criticism.

3. BRIEF SUMMARY OF POE'S PROSODIC THEORY

(The Rationale of Verse)

(1) Strictly regular *alternation* of syllables differing in quantity forms no part of any prosody.

(2) The "cæsura" (a foot composed of one "long" syllable) is one of the most important feet "in all verse." This "cæsura," "a variable foot," may occur either at the end or in the middle of a line.[7]

(3) "The *natural* long syllables are those encumbered . . . with consonants . . . [*i.e.*, pronounced with lingual difficulty]." "*Accented* syllables are of course always long, but, where *un*encumbered with consonants, must be classed among the *unnaturally* long." [8]

(4) The "principle of equality" demands that each foot in a line of poetry be pronounced in a period of time uniform with that of every other foot in the line, regardless of the number of syllables.

(*a*) This principle (with respect to balance and uni-

---

[6] Hervey Allen, *Israfel* (New York, 1926), II, 763.

[7] This use of the word "cæsura" is extremely confusing; it usually means, "A rhythmic break, usually a sense pause, about the middle of a verse." (Webster's Collegiate Dictionary.)

[8] Poe's *Works*, VI, 72.

formity) also applies to rime, stanza, alliteration, and refrain.[9]

(b) The equal-time rule applies only to single lines; all lines of a stanza need not conform to one time-pattern.

(c) But the "loose" stanza is "ineffective." [10]

(5) Time being the essential feature of "equality," there should be no "blending," i.e., substitution of an anapest or a dactyl for an iamb or a trochee, or vice versa, because three-syllable and two-syllable rhythms have different time-units.[11]

(6) Contractions or elisions are not permissible, because natural speech demands the pronunciation of all syllables; but in "bastard feet," [12] additional light syllables are permissible if they may be pronounced with sufficient rapidity to maintain the regular time-unit of the line. (Cf. footnote 12.)

(7) The Greek hexameter has never been successfully used in English because natural English spondees are rare; the English hexameter is a dactylic rhythm.[13]

(Reviews and Criticisms)

(8) The poet "should limit his endeavors to the creation of *novel moods* of beauty in *form*, in color, in *sound*, in sentiment." [14] (The italics are not Poe's.)

(9) The "indefinite" is an important element in true poetry — "a suggestive indefiniteness of meaning, with

---

[9] This application of the principle is ambiguous; Poe does not illustrate or fully explain it.

[10] "Loose" as applied to stanza is also ambiguous, but we should expect it to mean looseness of structure, i.e., rime scheme, length of lines, and possibly thought.   [11] Poe, *op. cit.*, VI, 86.

[12] Poe uses the term "bastard" for a foot with an extra unaccented (very light) syllable; e.g., a bastard trochee is ($/ \times \times$). But a "double quick" trochee is ($/ \times \times \times$), occurring in an otherwise regular trochaic line. *Ibid.*, pp. 105–106.

[13] *Ibid.*, VI, 123 ff.

[14] *Ibid.*, p. 156. (Review of Longfellow's *Ballads and Other Poems.*)

the view of bringing about a definiteness of vague and therefore spiritual *effect.*" (Poe first applied this doctrine to music and later to poetry in general.[15])

(*a*) General, indefinite imagery is more poetic (*i.e.*, in "Ideality" and "Poetic Sentiment") than specific, concrete imagery.[16]

(*b*) "Similes . . . are never . . . strictly in good taste . . . except when naturally arising from the subject in the way of illustration — and, when thus arising, they have seldom the merit of novelty." [17]

(10) The music of the line should never be disturbed by "harsh consonants." [18]

(11) Rimes should not be (*a*) identic, (*b*) light (*i.e.*, rimes on *–dy, –ty, –ly,* etc.) or (*c*) inexact.[19]

(12) In diction the poet should avoid archaisms, contractions, and inversions. (*Cf.* 6, above.)

Most critics agree that Poe's own poetry is the best illustration of his theories, and Professor Foerster even goes so far as to say, "He was right in making his theory and practice harmonious; he was wrong in allowing them absolutely to coincide." [20] Whether or not his theory and practice were harmonious we must postpone for further consideration, but that they did not absolutely coincide we shall soon see.

4. THE CHRONOLOGICAL DIFFICULTY

The first difficulty that the student of Poe's versification meets is a purely chronological one. During his lifetime, Poe published four collected editions of his poems (known as the editions of 1827, 1829, 1831, 1845), and

[15] Poe's *Works*, VI, 309–322. (Reviews of *The Culprit Fay* and Moore's *Alciphron.*)   [16] *Ibid.*   [17] *Ibid.*, VI, 319.

[18] Both Bryant (in "William Cullen Bryant") and Miss Barrett (in "Miss Barrett's 'A Drama of Exile and Other Poems'") are criticized for their "harsh consonants." *Ibid.*, VI.

[19] See Werner, *op. cit.*, p. 160.

[20] Norman Foerster, *American Criticism* (Boston, 1928), p. 5.

after his death his literary executor brought out a fifth
edition (1850). Most of these poems were first published
in magazines and newspapers. The difficulty referred to
above arises from the fact that most of these poems were
revised not once but several, often many, times. Professor Woodberry says, "There is no such example in
literature of poetic elaboration as is contained in the suc-
cessive issues of [Poe's] poems." [21]

Professor Killis Campbell tells us in the Introduction
to his edition of Poe's poems: "Of the forty-eight poems
collected by Poe or by his literary executor, no fewer than
forty-two were republished or were authorized to be republished at least once; and of these all but one (Sonnet —
To Zante) were subjected to some sort of verbal revision
upon republication. Six of the poems appeared in two
different forms, thirteen in three different forms, nine in
four different forms, eleven in five different forms, one
(Lenore) in eight different forms, and one (The Raven) in
fifteen different forms. Three of the six poems that were
published only once, survive in manuscript versions that
differ in some respect from the published versions.
Twenty of the poems underwent a change of title, and
five changed title twice.

"Among the earlier poems one (A Dream within a
Dream) emerged from its several recastings an entirely
different poem, no single line, no part of a line, of the
original being retained in the final draft." [22]

These revisions are important for the versification in
two respects. First, the revisions often change the
rhythm of the line and almost always change its melody
(a point to be considered later in this chapter); and
second, the different versions are sometimes in an entirely
new metrical form. For example, the beginning of Al
Aaraaf in the 1829 version (Poe's final choice) is in octosyllabics, mainly couplets, and is as follows:

---

[21] Poe, op. cit., II, 411.
[22] The Poems of Edgar Allan Poe (Boston, 1917), pp. xxxv–xxxvi.

O! nothing earthly save the ray
(Thrown back from flowers) of Beauty's eye,
As in those gardens where the day
Springs from the gems of Circassy —
O! nothing earthly save the thrill
Of melody in woodland rill —

Yet in the 1831 versions these lines were changed to:

Mysterious star!
Thou wert my dream
All a long summer night —
Be now my theme!
By this clear stream,
Of thee will I write;
Meantime from afar
Bathe me in light!

Sometimes the different line arrangements keep the same words and meter, as in *Lenore*, but this illustration from *Al Aaraaf* is characteristic of many of Poe's best poems. Though it would be possible to classify and discuss Poe's poems by types of meter and stanzas (as in the chapters on Freneau and Bryant), such a discussion, with its complicated references to different versions of the same poems, would be exceedingly confusing to all readers except Poe specialists. A more convenient (if less thorough) scheme is to center the discussion around those poems which are usually considered Poe's best. Fortunately, these poems do represent Poe's most important metrical forms, and may be analyzed in chronological order.

5. *AL AARAAF* (1829), "THE HEROIC COUPLET"

Al Aaraaf is composed of octosyllabic groups, heroic couplets, and songs of two- and three-stress lines. Of these forms, the heroic couplet is the most characteristic of Poe's early versification. He used it in only one other poem, *Dreams* (1827). The following extract from *Al Aaraaf* is a fair sample of the versification:

"What tho' | in worlds | which sight | less cy | cles run,
Link'd to | a lit | tle sys | tem and | one sun —
Where all | my love | is foll | y, and | the crowd
Still think | my ter | rors but | the thun | der cloud,
The storm, | the earth | quake, and | the o | cean wrath
(Ah! will | they cross | me in | my an | grier path?) —
What tho' | in worlds | which own | a sin | gle sun
The sands | of time | grow dim | mer as | they run,
Yet thine | is my | resplen | dency, | so given
To bear | my se | crets thro' | the up | per Heaven.

This passage, isolated from its context, seems fairly regular. Only twice is the initial foot inverted to a trochee; and the line has ten syllables, with the single exception of the trisyllable "angrier," where we may have an elision of open vowels "i" and "e" (an elision often made in conversational speech). The lines, however, are characteristically light, seven out of the ten having a "metrical stress" in the third or fourth foot to bring the accents up to five; and the spondee ("one sun") is not undubitably a spondee. Furthermore, only three lines are enjambed; yet the pauses are so placed that we feel that at any moment the heroic couplet pattern may be lost. In a later passage short phrases do almost completely disguise the pattern, though the meter is, technically, still that of the heroic couplet:

But what is this? — it cometh — and it brings
A music with it — 't is the rush of wings —

A paúse — and thèn a sweéping, fálling stráin,
And Nèsace is ìn her hálls agáin.

Why Poe never used the heroic couplet again is obvious:
it is not sufficiently lyrical. And in those instances in
which he had already used it, the result was too lyrical
to be a typical heroic couplet.

The few lines that run over ten natural syllables may
be accounted for by ordinary elisions, such as open vowels,
in "many a" (II, 5), or pure *r*, in "tow*e*ring" (II, 7);
by contractions, as in "th' unburthen'd" (II, 12), or
"'t is" (II, 49); by double rime, as in "holy" and "melancholy" (II, 188–189); and by the alexandrine as in:

Apárt from Heáven's Etérnity — and yét how fár from Héll!

(II, 173) [23]

Unguíded Lóve hath fállen — 'mid "teárs of pérfect moán."

(II, 181)

These alexandrines close the passage in which they occur,
but the following one occurs toward the middle of a "paragraph":

And scówls on stárry wórlds that dówn beneáth it líe.

(II, 193)

It is interesting to notice that some of Poe's contractions are not necessary, the vowel omitted being silent
anyway, as in "unburthen'd" (II, 12) and "opal'd" (I,
41). We also find light rime, as in "bee" — "reverie"
(I, 58, 59) and "bent" — "firmament" (II, 194, 195).
The Rationale of Verse, however, was not written until
fourteen years later (first version, 1843).

[23] The line may be scanned as a "fourteener" with a "metrical
stress" on the final syllable of "Eternity."

6. FOUR-STRESS VERSE

The four-stress couplet seems to have been Poe's favorite metrical form, for he wrote nearly three times as many poems in this measure as in any other one single form. We find him using it in *Spirits of the Dead* (1827) and in the *Dream-Land* (1844).

The fifteen-line introduction to Part I of *Al Aaraaf* is very regular, beginning:

> O! nothing earthly save the ray
>
> (Thrown back from flowers) of Beauty's eye,
>
> As in those gardens where the day
>
> Springs from the gems of Circassy —
>
> O! nothing earthly save the thrill
>
> Of melody in woodland rill —

The parenthesis in the second line is rather awkward, and the rime in the fourth line ("Circassy" — "eye") is absurd, as Poe himself would later have reminded other poets. But much more important are the uses that the poet makes of rime and refrain in this fifteen-line passage. He begins with alternate rime in the first four lines, then shifts to couplets except for the triplet composed of the eleventh, twelfth, and thirteenth lines. The refrain, "O! nothing earthly save the ray," "O! nothing earthly save the thrill," and "Oh, nothing of the dross of ours," occurs in lines one, five, and eleven, and is an interesting embryonic promise of the mature Poe refrain.

The first lines of the *City in the Sea* (1831) are practically free stress, each line containing four accents but with the syllables ranging from seven to twelve:

> Lo! Death has reared himself a throne
>
> In a strange city lying alone

Far down within the dim West,
Where the good and the bad and the worst and the best
Have gone to their eternal rest.

As the poem progresses, it becomes more regular in rhythm, partly as the result of reiteration and alliteration:

Up domes — up spires — up kingly halls —
Up fanes — up Babylon-like walls —
Up shadowy long-forgotten bowers
Of sculptured ivy and stone flowers —
Of many and many a marvelous shrine
Whose wreathéd friezes intertwine
The viol, the violet, and the vine.

Poe once said that he considered *The Sleeper* (1831) his best poem. It is more regular than the *City in the Sea*, and a great deal more alliterative:

At midnight, in the month of June,
I stand beneath the mystic moon
An opiate vapor, dewy, dim,
Exhales from out her golden rim,
And softly dripping, drop by drop,
        .   .   .   .
The lily lolls upon the wave;
        .   .   .   .
Looking like Lethe, see! the lake

Here meter, alliteration, and vowel color combine to produce the mood of voluptuous drowsiness.

7. *TO HELEN* (1831) AND *ISRAFEL* (1831), "FREE STRESS"

Despite the fact that *To Helen*, rated by many critics as Poe's best single poem, has an octosyllabic basis, the final effect of the stanza is practically "free stress." The lines do average about four stresses, and the rhythm is approximately iambic, but the effect that the poem gives when read aloud is no one certain metrical foot, so often and subtly are the accents varied. The number of syllables to the line also varies from eight in the first line to four in the last, though most have seven or eight. The first stanza is the most regular:

> Helen, thy beauty is to me
>
> Like those Nicean barks of yore,
>
> That gently, o'er a perfumed sea,[24]
>
> The weary, way-worn wanderer bore
>
> To his own native shore.

The second stanza ends with the famous lines:

> To the glory that was Greece
>
> And the grandeur that was Rome.

"Greece," incidentally, rimes with "face," hardly more than a weak consonance. And except for the rime on "which," the last two lines of the poem could be scanned with only four accents, and are likely to be so read:

> Ah, Psyche, from the regions which
>
> Are Holy Land!

[24] The verb is ordinarily "perfúmed," but here this pronunciation so obviously spoils the rhythm that it would seem the poet intended the accentuation indicated in this scansion.

We must read this poem straight through, however, to get the full effect of its metrical freedom. The enjamb-ment and the slight pauses are partly responsible for the freedom within uniformity of rhythm. The poem is not too heavily laden with alliteration, and the recurrence of back vowels, in such phrases as "long wont to roam," produces a pleasing melody. Each stanza is an expanded metaphor.

But it is in *Israfel* that the poet becomes "melody mad," with its fourteen rimes to eight stanzas (51 lines), and a predominance of *l*'s, *u*'s, and *o*'s. The lines range from four-stress to two-stress, the two-stress lines throwing the rimes into greater prominence:

In Heaven a spirit doth dwell
    "Whose heart-strings are a lute";
None sing so wildly well
As the angel Israfel,
And the giddy stars (so legends tell),
Ceasing their hymns, attend the spell
    Of his voice, all mute.

Tottering above
    In her highest noon,
    The enamoured moon
Blushes with love, . . .
    .   .   .   .

The ecstasies above
    With thy burning measures suit —
Thy grief, thy joy, thy hate, thy love,

With the fervour of thy lute —
Well may the stars be mute! . . .

. . . .

If I could dwell
Where Israfel
Hath dwelt, and he where I,
He might not sing so wildly well
A mortal melody, . . .

The Conqueror Worm, often praised by the critics, shows some of the same metrical freedom that we have observed in *To Helen* and *Israfel*, though it is by no means as good as *To Helen*. The *b*-rime of each stanza is repeated four times, the scheme being *ababcbcb*.

The Bells (1848–1849) is, of course, Poe's most famous and most extreme example of almost complete metrical freedom coupled with incessant reiteration. In this poem, in fact, we have repetition, or phonetic recurrence, of almost every imaginable kind. The rimes reiterate the same sounds; alliteration and assonance repeat both consonant and vowels within the line; words are repeated in all sorts of positions; there are parallelisms of words, phrases, and clauses; and we discover numerous refrains and repetends. Words almost lose their meaning in the "tintinnabulation" of jingling, chiming, clanging, tolling sound. For pure onomatopoetic effect, the poem is unsurpassed in the English language, and probably in any language; but it is all onomatopœia — an out and out *tour de force*. The four sections of the poem represent four moods: jolly sleigh bells, "mellow wedding bells," "loud alarum bells," and the solemn tolling bells.

8. *LENORE*, "SEVEN-STRESS"

Though *Lenore* is arranged in seven-stress lines, in its final and accepted version, the fundamental rhythm is that of the ballad, 4 + 3, *abab*. There are three main versions of the poem. *A Pæan* opens:

> How sháll the búrial ríte be réad?
>
> The sólemn sóng be súng?
>
> The réquiem for the lóveliest déad,
>
> That éver díed so yóung?

These verses do not begin *Lenore* but are shifted to line ten,

How *shall* the ritual, then, be read — the requiem how be sung

Another version, *Pioneer*, gives us the opening lines of *Lenore:*

> Áh, bróken is the gólden bówl!
>
> The spírit flówn foréver!
>
> Let the béll tóll! — A saíntly sóul
>
> Glídes dówn the Stýgian ríver!
>
> . . . .
>
> And, Gúy De Vére,
>
> Hast *thóu* no téar?
>
> Weep nów or névermore!

These short lines are simply grouped together into a "fourteener":

Áh, bróken is the gólden bówl! — the spírit flówn foréver!

Let the béll tóll! — a saíntly sóul floáts on the Stýgian ríver: —

Etc.

While the rhythm and rime remain precisely the same, the subjective effect on the reader is surprising, the longer line seeming to have a different "swing" from the shorter ones.

9. THE COLISEUM, "BLANK VERSE"

Poe's one attempt to write dramatic blank verse, *Politan* (1835–1836) was not very successful, though it is difficult to judge whether the failure is due more to the versification or the bathos of the melodramatic subject-matter. But the style as well as the form is unmistakably bombastic:

> MONK.   Thy words are madness, daughter,
> And speak a purpose unholy — thy lips are livid —
> Thine eyes are wild — tempt not the wrath divine!
> Pause ere too late! — oh, be not — be not rash!
> Swear not the oath — oh, swear it not!
> LALAGE. 'T is sworn!

Short breath-sweeps, exclamations, brief phrases punctuated with dashes (though Poe's dashes sometimes do not mean anything, or conversely, *may* mean anything) are characteristic of the whole drama.

Poe handled blank verse as a lyric measure with more skill, though he used it in this manner only four times:[25] in *The Coliseum* (part of *Politan*, written 1833), in *To M.L.S—*, in *To — —*, and in *To Helen* (not the famous *To Helen* of 1831). But *The Coliseum* contains his best work in this measure. The following extract, taken from three sections, illustrates the versification:

> Type of antique Rome! Rich reliquary
>
> Of lofty contemplation left to Time
>
> By buried centuries of pomp and power!
> . . . .

---

[25] C. Alphonso Smith wrongly says three, counting *The Coliseum,* too. See his *Edgar Allan Poe* (Indianapolis, 1921), p. 214.

But stay! these walls — these ivy-clad arcades —
These mouldering plinths — these sad and blackened shafts —
These vague entablatures — this crumbling frieze —
These shattered cornices — this wreck — this ruin —
These stones — alas! these grey stones — are they all —
All of the famed and the colossal left
By the corrosive Hours of Fate and Me?

"Not all" — the Echoes answer me — "not all!
.   .   .   .
We are not impotent — we pallid stones.
Not all our power is gone — not all our fame —
Not all the magic of our high renown —
Not all the wonder that encircles us —
Not all the mysteries that in us lie —
Not all the memories that hang upon
And cling around about us as a garment,
Clothing us in a robe of more than glory."

The bombastic declamation and the verbal reiteration
of this quotation are characteristic of Poe's blank verse
style. Both make utterly impossible the long, sonorous
breath-sweeps that we usually associate with great blank
verse. And the reiteration, especially, is proof that Poe's
blank verse, like his heroic couplet and in fact all other
measures, is lyrical rather than dramatic or expository.

The blank verse stage of Poe's versification is important,
however, mainly because in it he used parallelism and repetition extensively. This form of verse may not have en-
couraged his use of reiterative devices in other measures,
yet it is at least evidence that the reiterative style was
growing on the poet. It is important, too, to notice that
he repeats not only thoughts, constructions, and words,
but also certain approximate vowel sounds: "sad and
blackened shafts," "Clothing us in a robe of more than
glory."

In certain scenes of *Politan* words are also carried over
from one speech to another and reiterated in a way that
affects the thought and melody but not especially the

meter, as in *The Coliseum*.   Scene III has some good
examples:

> BALDAZZAR.   Politan, it doth *grieve* me
> To see thee thus.
> POLITAN.   Baldazzar, it doth *grieve* me
> To give thee cause for *grief*, my honored friend.
>
> . . . .
> POLITAN.   Alas! alas!
> There is an imp would *follow* me even there!
> There is an imp *hath* [26] *followed* me even there!
> There is — what *voice* was that?
> BALDAZZAR.   I *heard* it not
> I *heard* not any *voice* except *thine own*,
> And the echo of *thine own*.
> POLITAN.   Then I but *dreamed*.
> BALDAZZAR.   Give not thy soul to *dreams:* . . .
>   . . . thou wilt not hear
> In hearkening to imaginary sounds
> And *phantom voices*.
> POLITAN.   It *is* [26] a *phantom voice!*

Here the reiteration is stilted and fantastic, but it marks
the transition stage in the poet's experimentation with
repetition as a rhythmical device.

10.   THE RAVEN (1845), "EIGHT-STRESS," "SYNCOPATION"

The Raven is much less onomatopoetic than *The Bells*,
but the technique [27] of the two poems shows a number of
resemblances in the repetition of suggestive sounds, refrains, and repetends.   Poe's own explanation of his use
of the sonorous long *o* is too well known to deserve comment here.   Yet the effect the poet achieves is due fully

---

[26] Italicized by Poe.

[27] Poe has been accused of borrowing (or plagiarizing, as some
hostile critics have put it) the meter from Chivers.   Professor Damon
says Poe merely "adapted" the meter from Chivers.   For a full discussion, see: S. Foster Damon, *Thomas Holley Chivers, Friend of Poe*
(New York, 1930), pp. 207–214.

as much to his alliterative pairs as to his use of certain
vowels. A few specimens are, "weak and weary," "While
I nodded, nearly napping," "surcease of sorrow," "rare
and radiant," "dreaming dreams," "dared to dream,"
"Ghastly grim," "Bird or beast," etc. But the alliteration is aided, of course, by the double rimes — effective
not only because they are double but because they are
both double and internal.

Once upon a midnight *dreary*, while I pondered, weak and *weary*
Over many a quaint and curious volume of forgotten lore —
While I nodded, nearly *napping*, suddenly there came a *tapping*,
As of some one gently *rapping, rapping* at my chamber door.

Metrically, the poem is composed of eight-stress trochaic lines, the sixth line of each stanza (containing the
refrain "nothing more" or "nevermore," etc.) being four-
stress. The cæsura divides the line equally into two
parts of four-stresses, eight syllables each (except where
the occasional masculine rime cuts the count to seven).
The rhythmical pattern, however, is not simple trochaic octameter, for the length of the line and the alliterative pairs syncopate the rhythms, so that it becomes
(almost despite the reader's attempt to avoid it):

$$\diagdown \times \diagup \times \diagdown \times \diagup \times [:] \diagdown \times \diagup \times \diagdown \times \diagup \times$$

Isolated lines do not always appear to be syncopated, as in:

What this grim, ungainly, ghastly, gaunt, and ominous bird
    of yore,

but the syncopation is so insinuating, beginning with the
very first line of the poem, that it is scarcely possible for
the reader to escape it when he reads the whole poem.

Once upon a midnight dreary, while I pondered, weak and
    weary, . . .
Ah, distinctly I remember it was in the bleak December; . . .

"Prophet!" said I, "thing of evil! — prophet still, if bird or
    devil! . . ."[28]
Take thy beak from out my heart, and take thy form from off
    my door!"
        Quoth the Raven, "Nevermore."

Of the three causes of this syncopation (the length of
the line, double rime, and alliteration), the rime and alliteration seem to be most influential; since the poem still
has the syncopation when arranged in four-stress lines —
an experiment the student should try.

11. *ULALUME* (1847), "ANAPEST," "APPOSITIONAL
REITERATION"

Many isolated lines of Poe's poems are anapestic, but
we seldom find him using this measure even for several
consecutive lines. The whole of *Ulalume — A Ballad*,
however, is regular three-stress anapestic. This poem is
also interesting as a culmination of Poe's experimentation
in reiteration. The pleonastic construction, commonly
found in genuine ballads, is one of the repetitions:

> The skies, they were ashen and sober;
>   The leaves they were crispéd and sere —

The other reiteration resembles the refrain in *The Raven*
or *The Bells*, yet it is different in that it is an appositional
statement. Sometimes most of the words are repeated,
as in:

> The leaves they were crispéd and sere —
> The leaves they were withering and sere:

> Of cypress, I roamed with my Soul —
> Of cypress, with Psyche, my Soul

[28] This line and some others will not be accented the same by all
readers. Some will read it with primary accents where others have
secondary stress; but the line is syncopated in either case.

These reiterations are found in the second and third lines of each stanza. The last four lines of the stanza have a different sort of parallelism and reiteration, fewer words being repeated and the appositional statements being interwoven, in *abab* sequence:

> It was hard by the dim lake of Auber,
> In the misty mid region of Weir —
> It was down by the dank tarn of Auber,
> In the ghoul-haunted woodland of Weir.

Some stanzas have the construction and parallelism of the first three lines repeated in the following three. These stanzas have ten lines, riming in different combinations, but the second rimes *abbaccdcdc* and the eighth *abbabbabbb*. The fifth stanza has twelve lines, with a second parallelistic couplet in the seventh and eighth lines; and the ninth stanza has thirteen lines. This variation of the stanza pattern prevents monotony of a stanza form which would undoubtedly be tedious if repeated consecutively. The first stanza is typical of the rhythms of the whole poem:

> The skies they were ashen and sober;
>
> The leaves they were crispéd and sere —
>
> The leaves they were withering and sere:
>
> It was night, in the lonesome October
>
> Of my most immemorial year:
>
> It was hard by the dim lake of Auber,
>
> In the misty mid region of Weir —
>
> It was down by the dank tarn of Auber,
>
> In the ghoul-haunted woodland of Weir.

The poem has many double and even identic rimes. Aside from repeating sounds, the sequence of rimes in the stanza seems to have no particular significance (*i.e.*, such as binding the strophe together, indicating a change in thought, etc.). In none of Poe's verse does he succeed in coming nearer writing mere music, mere melody, than in *Ulalume*. This is not to say that the poem is without thought, but everything is subordinate to *sound* and *mood*. *Eulalie — A Song* (1845) is very similar in technique, though less complicated in stanza formation.

12. *ANNABEL LEE* (1849), "THE CULMINATION OF POE'S LYRIC STYLE"

Annabel Lee is in many ways a culmination of Poe's lyrical versification, with its parallelism, reiteration, internal rime, concealed rime (rime at irregular intervals), vowel melody and consonant alliteration. The first stanza has several of the same kinds of repetitions that we observed in *Ulalume*, *e.g.*, the pleonastic construction:

> And this maiden she lived with no other thought

Also the parallel couplet:

> Of those who were older than we —
> Of many far wiser than we —

The interwoven parallelism is likewise used:

> But we loved with a love that was more than love —
> I and my Annabel Lee —
> With a love that the wingéd seraphs of Heaven
> Coveted her and me.

Yet the parallelism of: "*She* was a child and *I* was a child," with the balancing of the pronouns as well as the repetition of "child," is a sort of reiteration we have not so far observed. The repetition of a phrase, as "In this kingdom by the sea," has also been commented upon, especially where it forms a refrain for a certain line in the stanza; but in *Annabel Lee* we find a single word being repeated and interwoven throughout the two stanzas, as with "love" in the first and second stanzas:

It was man | y and man | y a year ago,

   In a kingdom by the sea,

That a maiden there lived whom you may know

   By the name of Annabel Lee; —

And this maiden she lived with no other thought

   Than to love and be loved by me.

She was a child and *I* was a child,

   In this kingdom by the sea,

But we loved with a love that was more than love —

   I and my Annabel Lee —

With a love that the winged seraphs of Heaven

   Coveted her and me.

The stanzas vary from six to eight lines, with of course corresponding changes in the rime schemes. Three examples of internal rime are:

> That the wind came out of the cloud, *chilling*
> And *killing* my Annabel Lee.

> For the moon never *beams* without bringing me *dreams*
>   Of the beautiful Annabel Lee;
> And the stars never *rise* but I see the bright *eyes*
>   Of the beautiful Annabel Lee;

The stanzas are unified by one single thought, expressed in a single sentence, ending with the last line. There is also a balancing of parallel stanzas, or rather the rhythmical occurrence of thoughts. For instance, in the second stanza, "But we loved with a love that was more than love —" occurs again as the theme of the fifth stanza, "But our love it was stronger by far than the love."

The poem is, in practically every respect, the realization of Poe's ideal: a poem with sense wedded to sound, the result being primarily music; a poem of an unearthly mood or "atmosphere" achieved by every sort of reiteration of which Poe was capable; and, above all, a poem which is suggestive rather than definite, beautifully unreal with its generalities.

13. OTHER STANZA FORMS

Poe's most important stanza forms have already been illustrated in the discussions of his most important poems, but several other stanzas that he used should be commented upon briefly.

First of all, under this head, should come the sonnet, of which Poe wrote five, none comparable to his poems in other forms. The *Sonnet to Science* is usually regarded as his best. It forms a sort of preface to *Al Aaraaf*. The rime-scheme is *ababbcbcdedeff*, somewhat similar to the Spenserian form (*ababbcbccdcdee*). A later sonnet, called *Sonnet — To Zante*, is strictly English (*ababcdcdefefgg*). The remaining three are hybrids. *Sonnet — Silence* is not, correctly, a sonnet, for it has fifteen lines. The rime-scheme is mainly English, *ababcddccefefgg*. *An Enigma* rimes *ababcddceffcgg;* and *To My Mother*, *ababcdcdececff*.

The rimes of *Bridal Ballad* are especially curious. The scheme is mainly "tail-rime," *viz.*, *abaab, cbcccb, dbddddb, ebeeebeb, fbffbb.* But the unusual feature is, of course, the use of six rimes for the twenty-nine lines, five stanzas. And *Evening Star*, in 3 + 2 measure, has the most complicated set of rimes in the whole canon of Poe's poems — *abcbdefegghiihjjhkkbllb.*

The simple *abab* stanza does not seem to have appealed to Poe, yet one example is " *The Happiest Day, The Happiest Hour.*" Another is the 1827 *Song.* (A stanza of a discarded version of *Lenore*, called a *Pœan*, has already been quoted.)

This is about the extent of Poe's use of stanzas sufficiently regular to record. In practically all of his best poems he regarded the stanza as simply a paragraph, varying not only in length but also in rime-schemes. In fact, as we have seen, his stanzas do not always have the same rhythm throughout; and his later stanzas are the freest. It is difficult to understand, therefore, what Poe meant in his *Rationale of Verse* by saying that the "loose" stanza is always "ineffective." Certainly it is unlikely that he would have agreed that his stanzas were ineffective, nor would perhaps most of his readers; but the fact remains that many of them are so free that they almost defy analysis.

14. SOME COMPARISONS OF POE'S THEORY AND PRACTICE

An attempt has been made in the discussion of Poe's most important poems merely to point out the main technical characteristics in a purely objective manner. This attempt (along with the necessity for economy of space) has made it impossible to discuss in satisfactory detail some questions on which it is necessary to pass judgments. Not even Walt Whitman affects different readers more diversely than does Poe. And in versification as well as in æsthetics, it is always possible with Poe to make out a very good case for either side.

We have already paid some attention to Poe's criticism of the liberties taken by other poets with rime, and we have noticed that he violates his own criticism. In *Marginalia* ("Inversion"), Poe says that, "The true artist will avail himself of no 'license' whatever. The very word will disgust him." We have already seen that Poe does regard light, identic, and inexact rimes as undesirable "licenses." In a recent article, Professor Pettigrew [29] reports that an examination of Poe's principal poems reveals fifty-three instances of light rime, an average of

[29] Richard C. Pettigrew, "Poe's Rime," *American Literature* (January, 1933), IV, 150–159.

one to every two pages in the Mabbott text; imperfect vowel identity in eighty rimes and imperfect identity of consonants in thirteen; and seven identic rimes. But, as he goes on to say, "Much more certainly objectionable than any characteristic of Poe's rime . . . is the fundamental poverty of it. I doubt that any other important poet is so repetitive in his riming as is Poe. This distressing limitation — which is only one more intimation that he could never have been more than a comparatively minor poet — is made all the more conspicuous by his essential emphasis on verbal melody in his rimes, which consequently force themselves upon our attention. Not only that, but almost all of his rimes are entirely too obvious — already too threadbare before he rendered them more so — to bear the merciless repetition to which he subjects them." [30]

For example: "Night (twice as to-night) appears in twenty-six rimes, in thirteen of which it is associated with *light*, and once each with *delight*, *twilight*, and *starlight*. *Light* itself occurs in twenty-two rimes . . . Love is employed in twelve rimes, in nine of these being coupled with *above*." [31] And Professor Pettigrew's whole list is very interesting.

Another severe critic of Poe's rimes is Mr. Aldous Huxley, who objects especially to Poe's use of proper names (three-fourths of which have two or more syllables): "These proper-name rhyme-jewels," he declares, "are particularly flashy in Poe's case because they are mostly dissyllabic. Now, the dissyllabic rhyme in English is poetically so precious and so conspicuous by its richness that, if it is not perfect in itself and perfectly used, it emphatically ruins what it was meant emphatically to adorn." [32]

Professor Pettigrew defends Poe on this count, however, when he asks whether the prominent position does not rather "enhance their suggestive potentialities and lend atmosphere to the entire line? Grant that necessity was

[30] Pettigrew, *op. cit.*, p. 156.   [31] *Ibid.*, p. 157.
[32] Aldous Huxley, "Vulgarity in Literature," *The Saturday Review of Literature* (September 27, 1930), VII, 158–159.

the mother of Poe's inventiveness in the names *Auber,
Weir, Yaanek, Ulalume* — are not these words of the very
essence of the weird, and is not this sufficient compensa-
tion for their questionable parentage?" [33]

But this debate dwindles down to whether or not
"rich rime" is desirable. It need not concern us here,
since it has nothing to do with Poe's prosody, except, of
course, in so far as it affects his doctrines on melody and
novel mood and sound. In regard to the other characteristics of Poe's rimes, though, we must agree that his
theory is at strange variance with his practice.

We have noticed that Poe's rimes, alliterations, and
reiterations all help to produce the music for which this
poet's verse is famous, yet Professor Werner [34] finds another
reason, namely, the greater frequency of certain consonants in Poe's verse. This is best illustrated by Professor
Werner's table, based on an examination of 500 lines of
verse from five major American poets.

	First in Frequency	2nd	3rd	4th	5th	6th	7th	8th
Poe	N	R	T	L	S	Th	D	M
Average of next four poets	R	N	S	T	D	L	Th	M
Whittier	R	N	D	S	T	L	Th	M
Longfellow	R	N	T	S	D	Th	L	M
Lowell	R	N	S	T	D	L	Th	M
Whitman	R	N	T	S	D	L	Th	M
Dr. Rickert's list [35]	R	N	T	S	L	D, K	Th	M

[33] Pettigrew, *op. cit.*, p. 155.

[34] Werner, *op. cit.*, p. 158.

[35] "Based on a much larger number of sounds, in Edith Rickert,
New Methods for the Study of Literature (Chicago, 1927), p. 238."

The higher frequency of *n* over *r* is, of course, most surprising, first because the greatest frequency is the most important and second because *r* ranks first in all the other counts. The greater frequency of *l* in Poe's verse is to be expected, partly because one poem, *The Bells*, would be sufficient to bring the total up considerably. It is regretable that no one has made a frequency score of the initial consonants in the verse of these poets. A study of the alliterative consonants used by Poe, Longfellow, and Bryant might reveal some interesting results.

In general, Poe followed his own theory regarding diction, especially in regard to archaisms and inversions; and most of his contractions occur in the earlier poems, though as late as 1848 we find him still using "'t is" (*cf. Ulalume* and *To — —*). In the *To Helen* of 1828 the unnecessary contraction "upturn'd" is also used five times.

The theory regarding *equal time* in pronunciation of each foot in a line cannot be examined thoroughly here, but it may be observed that almost any line could be *forced* into such a scheme. Numerous examples, however, might be found in which one part of a line in Poe's verse is pronounced more rapidly than other parts. One of the most convincing instances is *The Raven*, where the syncopation makes the reader hurry through every other foot.

Take thy beak from out my heart, and take thy form from off

my door!

The syncopation may be reversed:

Take thy beak from out my heart, and take thy form from

off my door!

but the line still has the same number of primary and secondary accents, with a corresponding tendency to hurry over the lighter stresses.

Poe's meter, as we observed, becomes practically "free

stress" in such poems as *To Helen* (1831), *Israfel, The Conqueror Worm*, and *The Bells*. Yet on the whole it is fairly regular, or at least regular enough to conform to his theory; for in theory he permits different rhythms in different lines of the same stanza.

But Poe appears to follow his own theory most closely in the doctrine which we summarized as rule number 8 at the beginning of this chapter: The poet "should limit his endeavors to the creation of *novel* moods of beauty in form, in color, in *sound* . . ." All of Poe's experimentation with rime, alliteration, "indefinite" imagery, and even meter, progresses toward the attainment of this one ideal, and is realized most successfully in such poems as *Ulalume, Lenore*, and *The Raven*. Here we have the "essential" Poe (at any rate in versification); here his theory and practice most unmistakably converge. And it is for this reason that Andrew Lang said: ". . . Some foolish old legend tells of a musician who surpassed all his rivals. His strains were unearthly sad, and ravished the ears of those who listened with a strange melody. Yet his viol had but a single string, and the framework was fashioned out of a woman's breast-bone. Poe's verse — the parallel is much in his own taste — resembles that player's minstrelsy . . ." [36]

15. VERSIFICATION OF THE MINOR POETS

The two most important minor poets of the period were Joseph Rodman Drake and Fitz-Greene Halleck. Drake's most famous poem, *The Culprit Fay* (1816), antedates some of Bryant's poetry, though he was apparently not a significant formative influence on Bryant. But the versification of this poem is typical of the age of Poe because the meter is very similar to that of *Christabel*. The first stanza begins:

[36] Quoted from Andrew Lang by Alfred Kreymborg in *Our Singing Strength* (New York, 1929), p. 65.

'Tis the mid | dle watch | of a sum | mer's night —
The earth | is dark, | but the heav | ens are bright;
Nought | is seen | in the vault | on high
But the moon, | and the stars, | and the cloud | less sky,
And the flood | which rolls | its milk | y hue,
A riv | er of light | on the wel | kin blue.

The basic meter is iambic, with free substitution of anapests; but the main principle, like that of *Christabel*, is that each line has four primary stresses (or "beats") irrespective of the number of syllables. Thus the line may be strictly iambic, as in:

The stars | are on | the mov | ing stream,

Or trochaic:

Fairy! | Fairy! | list and | mark,

Or anapestic:

But the moon, | and the stars, | and the cloud | less sky,

This adaptation of Coleridge's principle is Drake's most important contribution to American prosodic history.

Drake and Halleck were close friends, and even collaborated on *The Croakers*, but on the whole Halleck's versification represents other influences, especially those of Byron and Campbell. The latter was apparently the more potent influence, though one of Halleck's best poems, *Marco Bozzaris* (1825), is particularly Byronic in technique. *On the Death of Joseph Rodman Drake*, in ballad meter, is universally recognized as Halleck's best poem, but the technique is significant only for its grace and ease. Perhaps his most typical versification is in *Fanny*, which uses a modification of Byron's *ottava rima* (the stanza of *Beppo* is used without modifications in *Connecticut*). Although on the whole *Fanny* shows considerable skill in verse technique, it is written in an easy conversational style which at times becomes almost slovenly in its looseness. One significant feature of this style is the use of mid-line full stops. The whole technique is even more free and natural than Bryant's blank verse; but it is a freedom which is often on the verge of descending to doggerel, like much of the verse of the "master" Byron himself.

Bryant said, "Halleck's poetry . . . is remarkable for the melody of numbers. It is not the melody of monotonous and strictly regular measurement. His verse is constructed to please an ear naturally fine, and accustomed to a wide range of metrical modulations." [37] But George L. Lathrop correctly observed that his love of irony, contrast, and "an abrupt alternation of mood" often lead to "a break in the tune." [38]

During this period several poets wrote some American songs which have since become a part of our national heritage — such songs as Frederick A. Woodworth's *Old Oaken Bucket* and John Howard Payne's *Home Sweet Home*. Edward Coote Pinkney's songs are not so familiar, but some of them are charming, as are also a number of George P. Morris's. But these songs merely carry on the traditions of the whole history of English songs. If they influenced the development of American versification at all, it was merely a further popularizing of such freedoms as we find in Bryant's prosodic theory, increasing the use of double rime, and possibly encouraging the use of lyric measures — contributions which in no way altered the general trends of American prosodic developments.

Most of the minor poets of the period were still using the closed couplet, *e.g.*, Woodworth in his comic *Battle of the Comets* (1834) and N. P. Willis in *The Belfry Pigeon*. Willis is important, however, for his mastery of Wordsworthian blank verse. In his 1827 poem delivered at Yale

---

[37] *New York Mirror*, Sept. 24, 1836, Vol. 14, p. 97.
[38] *Atlantic Monthly*, June, 1877, Vol. 39, p. 724.

College his lines still tend to march in pairs, but even here there are traces of the later ease. A few years later, in *The Widow of Nain*, we find blank verse as skilfully and easily manipulated as Bryant's though without Bryant's sonorousness — and sententiousness. Notice especially the phrasing and the breath-sweeps:

> The Roman sentinel stood helm'd and tall
> Beside the gate of Nain. // The busy tread
> Of comers to the city mart was done, /
> For it was almost noon, / and a dead heat
> Quiver'd upon the fine and sleeping dust, /
> And the cold snake crept panting from the wall, /
> And bask'd his scaly circles in the sun. //
> Upon his spear the soldier lean'd and kept
> His idle watch, / and, / as his drowsy dream
> Was broken by the solitary foot
> Of some poor mendicant, / he raised his head
> To curse him for a tributary Jew, /
> And slumberously dozed on. //

Other minor poets of the period may be dismissed briefly. James Kirke Paulding wrote conventional couplets, a few of James Gates Percival's poems have a small degree of amateurish lyricism, and Charles Fenno Hoffman's songs have catchy musical lilts.

In England, meantime, the romantic movement was triumphant. Wordsworth had edited his collected works in 1836. Coleridge was in his dotage, but his criticism was still being read on both sides of the Atlantic. Keats had died in 1821, Shelley in 1822, and Byron in 1824, but their prosodic influences were just beginning to affect seriously American versification. And the "Victorian Age" was now only a few years off.

SELECTED BIBLIOGRAPHY

Edgar Allan Poe

Text

Poe, Edgar Allan, *Works*, ed. by E. C. Stedman and G. E. Woodberry. New York: Charles Scribner's Sons, 1914. 10 vols.

——, *Poems*, ed. by Killis Campbell. Boston: Ginn and Company, 1917.
[Excellent introduction and notes.]

——, *Edgar Allan Poe*, ed. by Margaret Alterton. (American Writers Series.) New York: American Book Company, 1934.
[Selections of the best of Poe's poetry and prose with a critical introduction.]

Criticism

Foerster, Norman, "Poe," *American Criticism*. Boston: Houghton Mifflin Company, 1928. Chapter I.

Huxley, Aldous, "Vulgarity in Literature," *The Saturday Review of Literature* (September 27, 1930), VII, 158–159.
[Prejudiced discussion of Poe's rime.]

Markham, Edwin, "Poe," *American Writers on American Literature*, ed. by John Macy. New York: Horace Liveright, 1931. Chapter XI, 135–152.
[Most of the important facts discovered by Poe scholars are included, but without acknowledgments.]

Pettigrew, Richard C., "Poe's Rime," *American Literature* (January, 1933), IV, 151–159.

Saintsbury, George: "American Poets and Prosodists," *History of English Prosody*. New York: The Macmillan Company, 1910. Vol. III, Chapter 5, 483–487.

Smith, C. Alphonso, "The Critic" and "The Poet," *Edgar Allan Poe*. Indianapolis, Ind.: The Bobbs-Merrill Company, 1921. Chapters III and IV.

——, "Repetition in the Poems of Edgar Allan Poe," *Repetition and Parallelism in English Verse*. New York: University Publishing Company, 1894. Chapter IV.

Werner, W. L., "Poe's Theories and Practices in Poetic Technique," *American Literature* (May, 1930), II, No. 2, 157–165.

Minor Poets

Text

Drake, Joseph Rodman, *The Culprit Fay and other Poems*. New York, 1835.

Halleck, Fitz-Greene, *The Poetical Writings of . . .*, ed. by J. G. Wilson. New York, 1869.

Morris, George P., *Poems*. With a memoir of the author. New York, 1860.

Willis, Nathaniel Parker. *Poems, Sacred, Passionate, and Humorous.* 1846.

Woodworth, Samuel, *Poetical Works*, ed. by his son. New York, 1861. 2 vols.

Criticism

Adkins, Nelson Frederick, *Fitz-Greene Halleck*. Yale University Press, 1930.
[Contains much information on the period.]

Bryant, William Cullen, "Early American Verse," in *Prose Writings*. New York, 1884. Vol. I, 45–46. (First printed as "An Essay on American Poetry," *North American Review*, July, 1818, p. 198 ff.)

——, "Fitz-Greene Halleck," in *Prose Writings*, I, 369–393.

Leonard, William Ellery, "Bryant and the Minor Poets," *Cambridge History of American Literature*. New York, 1917. Vol. I, pt. 2, Chapter 5, 260–283.

Poe, Edgar Allan, "The Literati," and "Minor Contemporaries," in *Works*, ed. by E. C. Stedman and G. E. Woodberry. New York, 1914. Vol. 8.

——, "Marginalia," *Works*, Vol. 7, p. 253 *passim*.

Stedman, E. C., "Growth of the American School," in *Poets of America*. New York, 1885. Chapter II, 31–61.

CHAPTER IV

Ralph Waldo Emerson

I. THE TRANSCENDENTAL THEORY OF PROSODY

CRITICS and literary historians seldom mention Emerson's poetry without referring to its metrical irregularities. "His verse," says Professor Gay in a recent biography, ". . . is spasmodic, and it contains, moreover, elementary faults that Macaulay's boy of fourteen could have patched and mended — forced rhymes, arbitrary inversions, lapses of taste." [1]

It is usually assumed that Emerson violated the established rules of versification either because he did not know better or because his ear was unable to detect his lapses from the established rhythms, and Lowell's testimony may be cited to support the assumption: "I never shall forget," said Lowell in a letter, "the good-humoredly puzzled smile with which he once confessed to me his inability to apprehend the value of accent in verse." [2]

That Emerson did make such confessions, more than once, is undeniable, but they testify more to his modesty than to his ignorance. Though Sanborn's explanation may not be altogether acceptable, it starts off on the right track. Emerson, he says, "lamented his imperfect use of the metrical faculty, which he felt all the more keenly in contrast with the melodious thoughts he had to utter and the fitting words in which he could clothe these thoughts. He would have written much more in verse if he had been content with his own metrical expression

---

[1] Robert M. Gay, *Emerson* (New York, 1928), p. 193.
[2] *Letters of James Russell Lowell*, edited by Charles E. Norton (New York, 1893), II, 275 (letter to James B. Thayer).

as constantly as he was delighted with it sometimes. But it is also true that he purposely roughened his verse, and threw in superfluous lines and ill-matched rhymes as a kind of protest against the smoothness and jingle of what he called 'poetry to put round frosted cake.'" [3]

Not only did Emerson have a definite prosodic theory to guide his practice, but he also expressed it on numerous occasions. Most critics have failed to take it into account, first, because it is in revolt against established prosodic traditions, and second, because it is intricately bound up with Emerson's philosophy, and is usually expressed philosophically.

Jean Gorely gives an excellent summary of Emerson's whole poetic and prosodic doctrine: "Emerson, then, believed that poetry is mystical; that it comes into being as the result of inspiration. In that moment the poet sees the very essence of things. But vision is beyond his will. It comes to him unawares. Moreover, it is sudden and inconsecutive. It is advancing. Health, rest, human intercourse, solitude of habit, and a life in the open are all favouring circumstances. The poet makes the unseen visible by means of language. But he is not here the conscious creator. Vision, also, shows him the symbols and the thought takes its own form in language that is rhythmical. Because of this, there is a certain indwelling beauty in poetry and we measure its greatness by its cosmical quality. In such a theory, *poetry is spiritual and forms a link between the visible and invisible worlds.*" [4]

At first thought, such a theory as this does not seem to be, strictly speaking, a theory of prosody at all. It says nothing about meters, rimes, and the usual principles of versification. But it does, as we shall see, include definite *attitudes* on such technical problems.

[3] Franklin Benjamin Sanborn, *The Genius and Character of Emerson* (Boston, 1898), p. 211.

[4] Jean Gorely, "Emerson's Theory of Poetry," *Poetry Review* (July–August, 1931), XXII, 272–273.

"The transcendentalist worships the symbol. He believes that the writer's principal power is the effective use of figures of speech. So deep and far-reaching, indeed, is his devotion that there is hardly anything of good repute connected with or a part of writing that is not intimately associated with the symbol. Reason, the noble mental faculty, embodies its reflections emblematically. Imagination is the power to symbolize. The man of genius is such because of his control of the symbol. Poetry presupposes the trope." [5]

Figures of speech represent spiritual truth symbolically. Furthermore, prose is the expression of the actual, whereas poetry expresses the ideal.[6] In other words, the chief difference between prose and poetry is not necessarily a matter of rhythm but of imagery. However, "Words are signs of natural facts" and "material appearance." [7] Emerson means that the word-symbols that the poet uses to express his thoughts represent material objects, or "things." At best, the word-symbol merely *suggests*. The word and the thing should be one, or as nearly harmonious as possible; yet language is inadequate.

> We cannot learn the cipher
> That's writ upon our cell;
> Stars taunt us by a mystery
> Which we could never spell.
>
> *The World-Soul*

> Wandering voices in the air
> And murmurs in the wold
> Speak what I cannot declare,
> Yet cannot all withhold.
>
> *My Garden*

[5] Emerson Grant Sutcliffe, "Emerson's Theories of Literary Expression," *University of Illinois Studies in Language and Literature* (1923), VIII, 17.

[6] *Cf. Journal*, III, 492.

[7] *Nature, Addresses and Lectures*, "Language," p. 24.

This doctrine is further complicated by Emerson's mystical philosophy of the unity of plurality; *i.e.*, each individual material fact, thing, or image represents one all-pervading spiritual unity. Therefore: "not only may the same symbol be used in differently figurative ways, but the same idea may be typified by an indefinite number of symbols . . ." [8]

Emerson's prosodic theory concerns first, style, the qualities of which have been satisfactorily summarized by Professor Sutcliffe in these words: "On the one hand, fidelity to fact and common sense moderation — conveyed by a language generally simple in character, and thus involving the use of elements drawn from everyday experience, popular speech, compression, and understatement. On the other hand, elevation and intensity — conveyed by the symbol. It must be, then, that the symbol, the ideal expression, will partake of these same characteristics which mark the expression of the actual; the ideal, too, must be communicated simply: in a style which has as its substance ordinarily human event and circumstance, which is idiomatic, and which is free from the inaccuracies of excess." [9]

The relation of this theory to Wordsworth's (as expressed in the preface to *Lyrical Ballads*) is of course obvious. Yet equally important is the fact that Emerson's poetics also contain the text for Walt Whitman's famous 1855 Preface. This Preface was highly important not only because it was undoubtedly instrumental in the development of Whitman's "new" free-verse style but also because it was Whitman and not Emerson who came nearest to realizing Emerson's prosodic and poetic ideal, as expressed for example, in *The Poet*.

"We have yet had no genius in America, with tyrannous eye, which knew the value of our incomparable materials, and saw, in the barbarism and materialism of the times, another carnival of the same gods he so much

[8] Sutcliffe, *op. cit.*, p. 51.   [9] *Ibid.*, p. 57.

admires in Homer; then in the Middle Age; then in Calvinism. Banks and tariffs, the newspaper and caucus, Methodism and Unitarianism, are flat and dull to dull people, but rest on the same foundations of wonder as the town of Troy and the temple at Delphi, and are as swiftly passing away. Our logrolling, our stumps and their politics, our fisheries, our Negroes and Indians, our boats . . . the northern trade, the southern planting, the western clearing, Oregon and Texas, are yet unsung. Yet America is a poem in our eyes; its ample geography dazzles the imagination, and it will not wait long for metres." [10]

Emerson's use of "realistic" words, *i.e.*, words with unpoetic associations, is accounted for by this phase of his theory. In fact, theoretically, he would even include profanity. "I confess to some pleasure," he says, "to some titillation of my ears, from the stinging rhetoric of a rattling oath in the mouth of truckmen and teamsters. How laconic and brisk it is by the side of a page from the North American Review." [11]

The stylistic and vocabulary aspects of Emerson's prosodic theory are not only easy to perceive, but they are rather explicitly enunciated; yet just how, we may ask, do they stand with regard to rhythm and meter? These points Emerson never fully or clearly discussed, but the rhythmical implications of the theory may be deduced.

First, the great emphasis on the symbol and the image includes more than mere diction. The compression necessary to make the image stand out effectively is itself a trait of versification and always affects the rhythm if used over several consecutive lines. Furthermore, this style of writing compels attention to phrases and lines rather than strophes or stanzas. It is not surprising, therefore, that Emerson should say, "The poem is made

[10] *Essays*, II, *The Poet*, pp. 37-38.
[11] *Journal*, V, 419.

up of lines each of which filled the sky of the poet in its turn." [12] As Professor Sutcliffe adds, "each of which . . . momentarily epitomized eternity for him." [13] That this was Emerson's own method of composition is well known. He found value, to quote Professor Sutcliffe again, "in the mere collection of meteoric particles, since the ability to create astronomic systems or even constellations was denied him." [14]

The meter itself, to follow out the logical implications of this theory, should be only those rhythms suggested to the poet by his subject and the mystical forces playing upon him during his period of "inspiration." Such rhythms would be as free as those of nature — though not, however, altogether "free," since nature obeys laws of her own. Hence, we should not be surprised to find Emerson writing what we today call "free verse." And we do find him coming nearer to free verse than is usually realized, yet it remained for Walt Whitman to demonstrate what Emerson's prosodic doctrine really means. It is significant that Emerson was the first to greet Whitman on the threshold of a new poetic career, thus demonstrating that he could recognize the realization of his ideals when he saw it.

But Emerson himself remained the blazer of trails. For this reason, his verse technique is somewhere between the old versification and the new — and, therefore, was perhaps more puzzling to his contemporaries and later critics than the theories and practices of the *vers librists* themselves.

2. BLANK VERSE

There are three excellent reasons for beginning a study of Emerson's versification with an examination of his blank verse: (1) It is used in more poems of his youthful period (*i.e.*, from 1826–1834) than any other measure, not

[12] *Journal*, X, 464. [13] Sutcliffe, *op. cit.*, p. 123.
[14] *Ibid.*, p. 124.

even excepting his life-long favorite, the four-stress couplet. (2) Blank verse demands more regularity than any other measure Emerson ever used. (3) Some of Emerson's notes in his *Journal* enable us to form a conception of how he composed his blank verse.

The Summons (w. 1826) is one of the earliest dated blank verse poems, and it seems to be representative of Emerson's youthful unrimed pentameter. Most of the poem has regularly ten syllables to the line, but the shifting of accents is freer than in the average blank verse. The fourth line, for example, has a pyrrhic in the fourth and a spondee in the fifth foot.

To leáve | my woóds | and streáms | and the | sweét slóth

At times, the use of secondary accents gives the line a different cadence:

To leáve the rúdeness of my woódlànd lífe,
Sweét twilìght wálks and mídnìght sólitùde . . .
And the glad héy-dày of my household hoúrs,

Seldom outside *Paradise Lost* do we find a blank verse line like:

Boóks, Múses, Stúdy, fíresìde, fríends and lóve.[15]

With one exception the ordinary rules of elision [16] account for all extra syllables, holding the count down to ten. However, the elision of "th*e* *u*neasy" in the following line is not altogether fortunate because the "un–" receives a weak secondary stress:

Has quénched | the uneás | y blúsh | that wármed | my cheék;

[15] *Cf.* "Rocks, Caves, Lakes, Fens, Bogs, Dens, and shades of death," *Paradise Lost*, II, 621.
[16] See General Introduction, § 3, p. xxix–xxx.

Yet no recognized rule permits the elision of "innocent" into a dissyllable, though the tongue may trip over the last two syllables very quickly and lightly:

The ín | nocent mírth | which sweet | ens dail | y bréad,

The following extract, with its metrical stresses on final light syllables, reversed feet (often two to a line), extra syllable in the middle of the line (which may be accounted for by elision), meager enjambment, and general awkwardness, is typical:

I was | a boy; | boyhood | slid gay | ly by
And the | impa | tient years | that trod | on it
Taught me | new les | sons in | the lore | of life.
I've learned | the sum | of that | sad his | tory
All wom | an-born | do know, | that hoped | -for days,
Days that | come dan | cing on | fraught with | delights,
Dash our | blown hopes | as they | limp heav | ily by.
But I, | the bant | ling of | a coun | try Muse,
Aban | don all | those toys | with speed | to obey
The King | whose meek | ambas | sador | I go.

"I've learned the sum of that sad history All woman-born do know, that hoped-for days," is unpardonably awkward syntactically, and unsuccessful in all respects. Nevertheless, we should not condemn the poet too severely for a boyhood poem which he himself never placed in his collected verse. *The River*, written the next year, is much better:

And I behold once more
My old familiar haunts; here the blue river,

The same blue wonder that my infant eye
Admired, sage doubting whence the traveller came, —

With the exception of a redundant syllable which may appear anywhere in the line and a rather unusually free substitution, *A Letter* (1831), *Self-Reliance* (1833), and *Written in Naples* (1833), are fairly conventional blank verse. But in the eccentric blank verse of *Hamatreya* we have, as Alfred Kreymborg has pointed out,[17] a precursor of the technique of Edgar Lee Masters in his *Spoon River Anthology:*

Bulkeley, Hunt, Willard, Hosmer, Meriam, Flint,
Possessed the land which rendered to their toil
Hay, corn, roots, hemp, flax, apples, wool and wood.
Each of these landlords walked amidst his farm,
Saying, ''T is mine, my children's and my name's.
How sweet the west wind sounds in my own trees!
How graceful climb those shadows on my hill! . . .'
Earth laughs in flowers, to see her boastful boys
Earth-proud, proud of the earth which is not theirs;
Who steer the plough, but cannot steer their feet
Clear of the grave.

Admirable as this poem is, these lines deserve to be called blank verse only because they have an average of ten syllables and do not rime. The catalog line is, of course, the greatest peculiarity, apropos of which Kreymborg says: "Another contemporary poet, Marianne Moore, shows a love for building an image through rising

[17] Kreymborg, *op. cit.,* p. 74.

substances in the line: 'hemp, rye, flax, horses, platinum, timber and fur.' It does not follow that Masters and Miss Moore plagiarized Emerson, but that each, along with many other poets since Whitman, owe part of their inspiration to the Concord bard. He is in the blood of every American original." [18]

The catalog also forms part of the rhythms of *Blight* (1843):

> Rue, cinquefoil, gill, vervain and agrimony,
> Blue-vetch and trillium, hawkweed, sassafras,
> Milkweeds and murky brakes, quaint pipes and sundew,

And again, we find it woven in somewhat differently in *The Adirondacs*, Emerson's longest poem in blank verse:

> In Ádiróndac lákes,
> At mórn | or nóon, | the gúide | róws báre | héaded:
> Shóes, flánnel shírt, and kérsey tróusers máke
> His bríef toilétte: at níght, or ín the ráin,
> He dóns a súrcoat which he dóffs at mórn:
> A páddle ín the ríght hánd, ór an óar,
> And ín the léft, a gún, his néedful árms.

On the whole, the rough meter of *The Adirondacs* is different from Emerson's other blank verse only in its greater dependence upon such rhetorical devices as parallelism and repetition.

> The séasons cháriot him fróm his exíle,
> The raínbow hóurs bedéck his glówing cháir,
> The stórm-winds úrge the héavy wéeks alóng . . .
> The fórtunate stár that róse on us sánk nót;

The prodigal sunshine rested on the land,
The rivers gambolled onward to the sea,

Only the parallel imagery holds such poetry together, though of course the syntactical structure molds the rhythm, or rather bends it this way and that from the regular blank verse pattern. Each line has a separate image, which (according to Emerson's own theory) is practically a poem in itself.

Seashore is especially interesting because it grew out of a notebook record jotted down on the spot. Emerson's nephew's note to this poem reads in part: "The day after our return to Concord, he [Emerson] came into our mother's room, where we were all sitting, with his journal in his hand, and said, 'I came in yesterday from walking on the rocks and wrote down what the sea had said to me; and to-day, when I open my book, I find it all reads as blank verse, with scarcely a change.'

"Here is the passage from that journal, as he read it to us: July 23. 'Returned from Pigeon's Cove, where we have made acquaintance with the sea, for seven days. 'Tis a noble, friendly power, and seemed to say to me, Why so late and slow to come to me? Am I not here always, thy proper summer home? Is not my voice thy needful music; my breath thy healthful climate in the heats; my touch thy cure? Was ever building like my terraces? Was ever couch so magnificent as mine? Lie down on my warm ledges and learn that a very little hut is all you need . . .'"

And here is the first part of the poem:

I heard or seemed to hear the chiding Sea
Say, Pilgrim, why so late and slow to come?
Am I not always here, thy summer home?
Is not my voice thy music, morn and eve?

My bréath thy héalthful clímate ín the héats,

My tóuch thy ántidote, my báy thy báth?

Was éver búilding líke my térraces?

Was éver cóuch magníficent as míne?

Líe on the wárm róck-ledges, and thére léarn

A líttle hút suffíces líke a tówn.

Why Emerson wrote down "what the sea seemed to
say to him" in blank verse is an interesting psychological
question, as is also the fact that this part of the poem is
unusually regular blank verse for Emerson.　But more
important for the present discussion is the fact that the
subject-matter did suggest to the poet a rhythm, which
he unconsciously followed.　We could not ask for a better
illustration of Emerson's poetic theory in practice.

3. HEROIC COUPLET

Emerson wrote very few poems in the heroic couplet
measure, and none of these are of any special importance.
It is worth noticing, however, that his earliest heroic
couplets are his most regular ones.　*To-day* was written
in 1824:

I ráke | no cóf | fined cláy, | nor púb | lish wíde

The ré | surréc | tion óf | depár | ted príde.

Sáfe in | their án | cient crán | nies, dárk | and déep,

Let kíngs | and cón | querors, sáints | and sóldiers sleep —

The only metrical variations here are the substitution of
a trochee in one initial foot and the use of one metrical
stress in a third foot, both very common in heroic couplets.
The poem does not even have a redundant syllable, for
"conquerors" may be counted as a dissyllable by elision
of "pure *r*."

The 1827 portion of *Prayer* contains only one couplet, the other lines riming alternately. This trick of mixing couplet and alternate rimes soon becomes characteristic of a great portion of Emerson's verse, especially in the four-stress measure. But whether or not we are justified in regarding the heroic couplet as the pattern for this part of *Prayer*, we may analyze it as iambic pentameter. Some of the lines are exceedingly awkward, as:

> And my | unser | vicea | ble limbs | forego,

which has only three natural speech accents, "unserviceable" being drawn out to five syllables with a metrical stress on "–a–." Or was it intended to be scanned at all? Another line begins with three trochees:

> Yet I | think on | them in | the sil | ent night,

Still another line has two pyrrhics and two trochees:

> And the | firm soul | does the | pale train | defy

While the final line is an alexandrine:

> And bid | each aw | ful Muse | drive the | damned har | pies
> hence.

In the 1834 *Phi Beta Kappa Poem*, we find straight couplets, with the usual redundant syllable, or a "fourth pæonic" ($\times \times \times \diagup$), as in:

> A form which Nature cast | in the hero | ic mould

But in another line the poet attempts to avoid an extra syllable by a silly contraction of "th'alway." A final alexandrine, with a weak rime, is also used in this poem. A good example of iambic pentameter with couplet and alternate rime combined is in *The Rhodora* (1837):

> Rhodora! if the sages ask thee why
> This charm is wasted on the earth and sky,

Tell them, dear, that if eyes were made for seeing,
Then Beauty is its own excuse for being:
Why thou wert there, O rival of the rose!
I never thought to ask, I never knew:
But, in my simple ignorance, suppose
The self-same Power that brought me there brought you.

4. THE OCTOSYLLABIC COUPLET

It would perhaps be more accurate to speak of Emerson's four-stress rather than octosyllabic couplets, since the lines range freely from seven to nine syllables; yet in most cases eight does seem to be the basic pattern. One of the earliest is *Lines to Ellen* (1829):

Tell me, maiden, dost thou use
Thyself thro Nature to diffuse?
All the angles of the coast
Were tenanted by thy sweet ghost,

Over half the lines of this poem have eight syllables, beginning with an iambic foot; so we are justified in regarding the seven-syllable lines as "clipped," *i.e.*, iambic tetrameter with omission of the initial unstressed syllable, as in Milton's *L'Allegro* and *Il Penseroso*.

This poem also illustrates Emerson's carelessness with rimes, such as "flower" and "bore," "glowed" and "proud." It is often difficult to determine just how vowels in different combinations were pronounced in Emerson's day, but it seems highly improbable that "glowed" and "proud" rimed in 1829. In other poems we find rimes that are much more improbable, as "noon" and "Napoleon" in *Each and All*.

Each and All (1834?) is an excellent illustration of the freedom that Emerson early achieved in the four-stress couplet.   Here the pattern is also the eight-syllable line, as in:

> A gentle wife, but fairy none.

Yet surprisingly few lines in the poem are entirely regular. An extended passage is necessary to show the many variations:

> I thought the sparrow's note from heaven,
>
> Singing at dawn on the alder bough;
>
> I brought him home, in his nest, at even;
>
> He sings the song, but it cheers not now,
>
> For I did not bring home the river and sky; —
>
> He sang to my ear, — they sang to my eye.
>
> The delicate shells lay on the shore;
>
> The bubbles of the latest wave
>
> Fresh pearls to their enamel gave,
>
> And the bellowing of the savage sea
>
> Greeted their safe escape to me.
>
> I wiped away the weeds and foam,
>
> I fetched my sea-born treasures home;
>
> But the poor, unsightly, noisome things
>
> Had left their beauty on the shore
>
> With the sun and the sand and the wild uproar.

The regular-beat line occurs with barely sufficient frequency to keep the pattern from being utterly lost, the rhythm at other times playing around to duple-triple

time, occasionally galloping off into unmistakable anapestic movement, as in the last line above.

The first lines of *The Problem* (1839) illustrate a very
different rhythmical effect that Emerson frequently
achieves with the octosyllabic couplet:

> I like a church; I like a cowl;
>
> I love a prophet of the soul;
>
> And on my heart monastic aisles
>
> Fall like | sweet strains, | or pensive smiles:
>
> Yet not for all his faith can see
>
> Would I that cowlèd churchman be.

Here the emphatic cæsura (usually masculine), the short
breath-sweep, and the simple compressed diction, give a
steady jog that is more didactic than lyrical.

What we have called the "clipped" line often seems to
be composed of only two feet, a cretic ($/ \times /$) plus a
diiamb ($\times / \times /$), as in *Heroism*:

> Ruby wine | is drunk by knaves,
>
> Sugar spends | to fatten slaves,
>
> Rose and vine | -leaf deck buffoons;
>
> Thunder-clouds | are Jove's festoons,

This effect is of course aided by the use of end-stopped
lines and strong cæsuras. And again we notice how the
poet builds up his poem by piling image on top of image,
one to the line, the lines being held together by their
parallel thoughts. It is not surprising that this style
should sometimes demand elliptical statements. However,
"Sugar spends to fatten slaves" is syntactically awkward,
and unpardonably ambiguous; but it is rhythmical.

5. OTHER FOUR-STRESS VERSE

On the whole, Emerson's other four-stress lines have the same prosodic traits as the octosyllabic couplet, but there are a few differences worth pointing out. One is a smoother metrical flow and greater enjambment. The best example is, of course, the famous *Concord Hymn*, with its effective spondees, masculine rhythm, and longer breath-sweeps than are usually found in Emerson's four-stress verse:

> By the rude bridge that arched the flood,
>
> Their flag to April's breeze unfurled,
>
> Here once the embattled farmers stood,
>
> And fired the shot heard round the world.

Here the stanza form (*abab*) undoubtedly has a great deal to do with the syntactical arrangement of the thought, yet the transition from line to line is utterly unlike the majority of Emerson's poems. Each two lines has a simple thought, paralleled by another thought in the following two lines, giving us a real stanzaic unit, as opposed to Emerson's usual line- or thought-unit. Fortunately, this poem is superior to Whitman's *O Captain! My Captain!*, but the one is just as *un*characteristic of its author as the other.

Brahma, in precisely the same metrical form as *Concord Hymn*, is much more characteristic of Emerson's handling of the four-stress stanza:

> Far or forgot to me is near;
>
> Shadow and sunlight are the same;
>
> The vanished gods to me appear;
>
> And one to me are shame and fame.

May-Day and *Voluntaries* are good examples of a still more common method of treatment in Emerson's tetrameter. The rimes vary almost at random between couplets and alternate rime, alternate predominating. Parallelism is used freely, enjambment sparingly. And at any time the four-stress line may be shortened to three stresses, even two, or lengthened to five:

> Thy birds, thy songs, thy brooks, thy gales,
>
> Thy blooms, thy kinds,
>
> Thy echoes in the wilderness,
>
> Soothe pain, and age, and love's distress,
>
> Fire fain | ting will, | and build | hero | ic minds.

Part of *Voluntaries* has a predominantly 4 + 3 movement, though the pattern is four-stress:

> Yet on the nimble air benign
>
> Speed nimbler messages,
>
> That waft the breath of grace divine
>
> To hearts in sloth and ease.
>
> So nigh is grandeur to our dust,
>
> So near is God to man,
>
> When Duty whispers low, *Thou must,*
>
> The youth replies, *I can.*

Threnody also has some irregular lines, especially at the beginning, where it seems doubtful whether the pattern is four- or three-stress; yet the poem as a whole is definitely octosyllabic, with a combination of couplet and alternate rime in the manner of Emerson's "odes." The most irregular passage with respect to length of lines is the following:

And whither now, my truant wise and sweet,
O, whither tend thy feet?
I had the right, few days ago,
Thy steps to watch, thy place to know:
How have I forfeited the right?
Hast thou forgot me in a new delight?
I hearken for thy household cheer,
O eloquent child!
Whose voice, an equal messenger,
Conveyed thy meaning mild.

The trisyllabic foot is used sparingly:

The om | inous hole | he dug | in the sand,[19]

Only a few lines have over eight syllables, and many of the trimeters and tetrameters are "clipped," which leaves them with only seven syllables.

A more interesting irregularity is the occasional line with a trochaic substitution in the initial foot and a spondee in the second foot. Neither of these substitutions is unusual in itself, but we rarely find them used together in this combination. Some examples are:

Step the | meek fowls | where erst they ranged; . . .

Which the | four sea | sons do | not tend . . .

Nature's | sweet mar | vel undefiled, . . .

Brought the | old ord | er into doubt.

[19] The "–inous" of "ominous" may be elided — elision of "pure *n*."

The rimes are mainly masculine, yet the poem contains
a few light rimes, some feminine rimes, and an interesting
example of trisyllabic rime, the final monosyllable being
"redundant":

> Nature, who lost, cannot remake him;
> Fate let him fall, Fate can't retake him;

All the variations, both of rime and meter, are skilfully
distributed; so that at no time is the pattern doubtful
(with the possible exception of the opening lines). Nor
do the stresses ever so exactly coincide with the normal
pattern that the rhythms become monotonous. This poem
is one of Emerson's most successful achievements in balancing metrical freedom and uniformity.

Some of Emerson's short four-stress poems are as compressed and cryptic as Emily Dickinson's:

LETTERS

> Every day brings a ship,
>
> Every ship brings a word;
>
> Well for those who have no fear,
>
> Looking seaward, well assured
>
> That the word the vessel brings
>
> Is the word they wish to hear,

6. FOUR-PLUS-THREE MEASURE (AND VARIATIONS)

Emerson, as it should be obvious by now, never liked
to tie himself down to one set metrical form, and his desire
for rhythmical freedom seems to have grown steadily. He
never used the heroic couplet very much, and blank verse
intermittently and inconsistently. Four-stress verse was
always his favorite.

Therefore, it is not surprising that Emerson should

have written some dozen poems in ballad measure (*abab*,
4 + 3), since both the short lines and the influence of
the church hymn would have given the measure some
attractions for him; nor is it surprising that he did not
write more poems in this form, for it is too regular to
satisfy Emerson's unmistakable love for free cadences.
The most regular example is the first stanza of *The Bell*
(1823):

> I lóve thy músic, méllow béll,
> I lóve thine íron chíme,
> The lífe or déath, to heáven or héll,
> Which cálls the sóns of Tíme.

But not all of Emerson's poems that begin in this manner keep the pattern throughout, as, for instance, *Friend-
ship*, which is not arranged in stanzas and has variations
both in the recurrences of the rimes and the alternation
of four- and three-stress lines. *Boston Hymn* rimes both
abab and *abcb*, but is mainly three-stress. *Boston*, on the
other hand, is mainly four-stress.

In fact, three- and four-stress poems (containing a
random recurrence of either three- or four-stress lines)
are found in Emerson's *Works* more than any other
single verse form, being rivalled only by the four-stress
couplet. The total number of four-stress forms (with
variants) include about one-third of all the poems Emerson wrote.

Examples have already been given of the chief versification traits that we find in Emerson's tetrameters (with
trimeter variants), but one poem in this form, *The Humble-Bee*, affords some especially good illustrations of what
the critics refer to as Emerson's bad rimes:

> When the south wind, in May days,
> With a net of shining haze

Silvers the horizon wall,
And with softness touching all,
Tints the human countenance
With a color of romance,
And infusing subtle heats,
Turns the sod to violets,
Thou, in sunny solitudes,
Rover of the underwoods,
The green silence dost displace
With thy mellow, breezy bass.

"Heats" and "violets," "solitudes" and "–woods" are exceedingly far-fetched rimes, having similarity only of final consonant sounds ("–ts," "–ts"; "–des," "–ds"). Yet the poem is not necessarily injured by these "bad rimes," for exact rimes would probably be monotonous in this passage of short couplets. This excuse cannot always be made for Emerson's use of such rimes, but here they distinctly are not technical blemishes, and indicate that he may be more often justified in his so-called riming carelessness than is usually recognized.

Some of Emerson's uses of double-rime give us a form which is somewhere between three-stress and four-plus-three measures; *i.e.*, the double rimes are alternate, giving a four-stress line if we count a metrical stress on the second syllable of the double rime, as in *April:*

The April winds are magical
And thrill our tuneful frames;
The garden walks are passional
To bachelors and dames.
The hedge is gemmed with diamonds,
The air with Cupids full,
The cobweb clues of Rosamond
Guide lovers to the pool.

(In this poem, we also find "rock" riming with "provoke," "goblins" with "problems.")

7. THREE-STRESS VERSE

Very few of Emerson's poems regularly have only three stresses to the line, and none of these have metrical characteristics which we have not already noticed in other measures; but all of the three-stress verse is quite interesting, and deserves to be discussed, if for no other reason than to corroborate the generalizations of this chapter.

The freest in placing of accents, indefinite number of syllables to the line, and use of redundant final syllables is *The House:*

> Slow and warily to choose
> Rafters of immortal pine,
> Or cedar incorruptible,
> Worthy her design.
>
> She lays her beams in music
> In music every one,
> To the cadence of the whirling world
> Which dances round the sun —

Politics has fairly regularly five syllables to the line, yet we notice that even in this restricted meter Emerson can produce a surprising number of different cadences, as in the following passage, where each line has a new cadence:

> Gold and iron are good [20]
> To buy iron and gold;

[20] "Iron" is practically always a monosyllable.

All earth's fleece and food
For their like are sold.

Power affords an excellent illustration of a constant shifting of a trisyllabic foot (or "redundant syllable") in an iambic trimeter:

His tongue was framed to music,

And his hand was armed with skill;

His face was the mould of beauty,

And his heart the throne of will.

In *Quatrains* the thought is pressed into epigrammatic form:

ORATOR

He who has no hands
Perforce must use his tongue;
Foxes are so cunning
Because they are not strong.

POET

To clothe the fiery thought
In simple words succeeds,
For still the craft of genius is
To mask a king in weeds.

The World-Soul has a much more elaborate and consistent construction than most of Emerson's poems. Yet it is significant that the eight-line stanza has only two rimes, four of the eight lines being without rime. The scheme is *abcbdefe:*

Cities of proud hotels,

Houses of rich and great,

Vice nestles in your chambers,

Beneath your roofs of slate.

It cannot conquer folly, —

Time-and-space-conquering steam, —

And the light-outspeeding telegraph

Bears nothing on its beam.

Again we notice a constant shifting of stresses and the use of parallelism, that is, appositive-parallel construction. *E.g.*, "Cities of proud hotels, Houses of rich and great."
Still more parallelism, however, is found in the first stanza, where it is combined with reiteration, which controls the rhythm:

Thanks to the morning light,

Thanks to the foaming sea,

To the uplands of New Hampshire,

To the green-haired forest free;

Thanks to each man of courage,

To the maids of holy mind,

To the boy with his games undaunted

Who never looks behind.

8. THE ODE

One of Emerson's so-called "odes," the *Ode* "Sung in the Town Hall, Concord, July 4, 1857," is no ode at all but merely a patriotic poem in the four-plus-three ballad measure; yet *Ode, Inscribed to W. H. Channing* and *Ode to Beauty* are in a metrical form which was called "ode" in Emerson's day, *i.e.*, a poem of irregular lines without any particular stanzaic pattern — a form which Abraham Cowley introduced into English poetry in the seventeenth century, mistakenly thinking it to be "Pindaric."
The Channing *Ode* is arranged in paragraphs (usually

composed of one sentence) of different lengths. Both alternate and couplet rimes are used, with a random arrangement. The meter is predominantly iambic, with from two to five stresses to the line, but ordinarily either two or four. There is little enjambment, though in many lines thought or metaphor extends over two lines. On the whole, Emerson's odes display the same prosodic characteristics that we have observed in his other three- and four-stress verse. The variations of lines of different lengths can only be illustrated by long passages, but two catalog passages may be quoted here, the first from the Channing *Ode:*

> 'Tis fit the forest fall,
> The steep be graded,
> The mountain tunnelled,
> The sand shaded,
> The orchard planted,
> The glebe tilled,
> The prairie granted,
> The steamer built.

And the second from *Ode to Beauty:*

> The frailest leaf, the mossy bark,
> The acorn's cup, the raindrop's arc,
> The swinging spider's silver line,
> The ruby of the drop of wine,
> The shining pebble of the pond,
> Thou inscribest with a bond,
> In thy momentary play,
> Would bankrupt nature to repay.

9. IRREGULAR SHORT LINES

Other irregular poems of Emerson's may have been intended for odes, as, for example, *In Memoriam* (an elegy for the poet's brother Edward); and the irregular odes of other poets may have influenced Emerson in his use of different-length lines in about two dozen more

poems. But he used irregular measure throughout most
of his poetic career; *cf. A Mountain Grave* (1831), *Monad-
noc* (1845), *Merlin* (1846), and *Terminus* (1866?). This
form appears to have been most popular with the poet
during the 1840 decade, which is probably the period of
his greatest poetic achievements.

Most of these poems have a combination of couplet
and alternate rimes, but *The Sphinx*, famous for its
obscurity, rimes *abcbdefe* or *abcbdede*. The lines are mainly
two- and three-stress, as in the first stanza:

> The Sphinx is drowsy,
>> Her wings are furled:
> Her ear is heavy,
>> She broods on the world.
> "Who'll tell me my secret,
>> The ages have kept? —
> I awaited the seer
>> While they slumbered and slept: —

Yet the majority of the poems in this group have much
more irregular lines, such as *Give All to Love* with its two,
three, and four stresses; *Destiny*, with its variable short
lines and random couplets; or *Woodnotes*, with its sections
of trimeter, tetrameter, and heroic couplets (the heroic
couplet section, however, unbroken by shorter lines).

The technique, as usual, is the pyramiding of images.
And the diction, though terse, is usually free and easy.
Sometimes, though, this style results in unnatural inver-
sions, as in the first stanza of *Saadi:*

> Trees in groves,
> Kine in droves,
> In ocean sport the scaly herds,
> Wedge-like cleave the air the birds,

> To northern lakes fly wind-borne ducks,
> Browse the mountain sheep in flocks,
> Men consort in camp and town,
> But the poet dwells alone.

"Scaly herds" is typically eighteenth century, and the inversion "Wedge-like cleave the air the birds" is obviously used for the sole reason of making "birds" rime with "herds." Nevertheless, the imagery, arranged in climactic order, is effective.

Emerson's rimes in passages of this kind, however, are often a hindrance rather than a help. The dimeter couplets have too much rime, and at other times alternate rime appears to establish awkward connections between dissimilar lines. But Emerson's many inaccurate rimes are an indication that he was either trying to overcome these difficulties or that he did not regard rime as one of the greatest essentials in his versification. And it is notable that occasionally these irregular passages contain unrimed lines, or sometimes several blanks, as in the beginning of *Experience:*

> The lords of life, the lords of life, —
> I saw them pass
> In their own guise,
> Like and unlike,
> Portly and grim, —
> Use and Surprise,
> Surface and Dream,
> Succession swift and spectral Wrong,

10. EMERSON AND FREE VERSE

This brings us to the interesting question of just how near Emerson came to "free verse." We have already observed that his prosody points logically toward some sort of "free" versification. Moreover, his own practice of composing by accumulated metaphors and images, of varying the accentuation until it may more accurately be called "cadenced" (Miss Amy Lowell's beloved term) than "metered," and of general carelessness or indifference with respect to rime, all go a long way toward the achievement of his prosodic ideals. It is not surprising, therefore, to find that many of Emerson's first drafts of his poems are actually what we today call "free verse." The 1845 journal version of *Merlin* (1846), for example, not only illustrates but even expresses a free verse theory:

> I go discontented thro' the world
> Because I cannot strike
> The harp to please my tyrannous ear:
> Gentle touches are not wanted,
> These the yielding gods had granted.
> It shall not tinkle a guitar,
> But strokes of fate
> Chiming with the ample winds,
> With the pulse of human blood,
> With the voice of mighty men,
> With the din of city arts,
> With the cannonade of war,
> With the footsteps of the brave
> And the sayings of the wise,
> Chiming with the forest's tone
> When they buffet boughs in the windy wood,
> Chiming with the gasp and moan
> Of the ice-imprisoned flood.
> I will not read a pretty tale
> To pretty people in a nice saloon
> Borrowed from their expectation,
> But I will sing aloud and free
> From the heart of the world.

A very few of these lines may have been intended to rime, such as "wood" and "flood," or Emerson might even have regarded "saloon" and "expectation" as rimes! But rime most emphatically is not part of the scheme. It may be argued that this is merely a notebook fragment, never intended for a poem in this form, since it was reworked into a more conventional form before it was printed; yet even so, it is an interesting unpolished gem. And if many of Emerson's poems remind us of free verse, it is important to remember how some of them were first written down.

The first rhapsody of *May-Day* contains these lines:

> We will go to the relenting mountains,
> And listen to the uproar of joy,
> And see the sparkle of the delivered rivers,
> And mark the rivers of sap
> Mounting in the pipes of the trees,
> And see the colors of love in birds,
> And in frogs and lizards,
> And in human cheeks,
> In the song of birds
> And songs of men.

An old version of *Solution* is freer still:

> I am the Muse,
> Memory's daughter,
> I stood by Jove at the first —
> Take me out, and no world had been,
> Or chaos bare and bleak.
>
> .   .   .   .   .   .
>
> Long I wrought
> To ripen and refine
> The stagnant, craggy lump
> To a brain
> And shoot it through
> With electric wit . . .[21]

In some of these fragments, of course, the line arrangement is purely arbitrary (even as with much modern free verse), it often being possible to combine lines without in any way disturbing the rhythm or effectiveness of the imagery. But other examples do seem to demand the ar-

---

[21] There is a similarity between this rhythm (and even to some extent the thought of the poem) and the blank verse of Byron's *Darkness* (w. 1816).

rangement which Emerson first gave them, as in the first
draft of *Spiritual Laws:*

> Heaven is alive;
> Self-built and quarrying itself,
> Upbuilds eternal towers;
> Self-commanded works
> In vital cirque
> By dint of being all;
> Its loss is transmutation

The final version stands:

> The living Heaven thy prayers respect,
> House at once and architect,
> Quarrying man's rejected hours,
> Builds therewith eternal towers;
> Sole and self-commanded works,

Whichever version we may prefer, it is fairly obvious
that the first comes nearer to Emerson's own theory, though
there is nothing in this theory that demands the retention
of the spontaneous poem rather than a reworked version.

Yet the important thing is that these fragments show
unmistakably Emerson's method of poetic composition;
and the technique places greater importance on images,
cadenced phrases, and rhetoric than on rimes and meters.
Thus does his practice carry out his prosodic theory,
thereby laying a foundation for the versification of Walt
Whitman and the later "free verse" movement.

II. THE TRANSCENDENTAL POETS

Emerson himself did not take an active part in the
"movement" of "transcendentalism," but he was intimately associated with the leaders of the movement, and
his own poetry remains the best expression of the transcendental doctrine. It is appropriate, therefore, to consider at this place those minor poets who are known as
transcendentalists.

We may date the beginning of transcendentalism from about 1836; and by the summer of 1839 the movement had reached the peak of its development, though it lingered on for many years. The early forties were perhaps the most characteristic years. The philosophical sources of transcendentalism have been studied by many investigators, but too little attention has been given to the prosodic origins of the transcendental poetry. It is certain that Hindu, Persian, and other Oriental sources exerted some influence,[22] but it is likely that these sources have been over-emphasized. Professor Gohdes reminds us that East and West always meet where mysticism is concerned [23] — and whatever else the transcendentalists were or were not, they certainly were mystics.

Names usually associated with transcendentalism are Emerson, Alcott, Parker, Channing, and Margaret Fuller. But Cooke in his Anthology of *The Poets of Transcendentalism* includes the work of thirty-five other poets.[24] If we are to include the names of all poets who were deeply influenced by, or wrote like, the transcendentalists, however, we would have to take in Whitman, Melville (*i.e.*, as a poet), Emily Dickinson, and many others. Yet this list of thirty-five gives us some idea of the tremendous depth and breadth of the transcendental influence upon the poets and poetry of the period.

Most of the transcendentalists delighted in paradox, but none of their paradoxes are more curious than some of the problems which their work presents today to the student of poetry and prosody. The transcendentalists

[22] *Cf.* Walter L. Leighton, *French Philosophers and New England Transcendentalism* (University of Virginia, 1908), pp. 7–8. *Cf.* also F. I. Carpenter, *Emerson and Asia*, Harvard University Press, 1930; and Arthur Christy, *The Orient in American Transcendentalism*, Columbia University Press, 1932.

[23] Clarence L. F. Gohdes, *The Periodicals of Transcendentalism* (Duke University Press, 1931), p. 4.

[24] George Willis Cooke, *The Poets of Transcendentalism* (Boston: Houghton, Mifflin Company, 1903). See table of contents.

were philosophers, yet they are important today not for
their philosophy so much as the poetry which they wrote
in the attempt to convey their philosophy. And as for
poetic technique, if they held any special beliefs on the
subject at all, they were merely that technique was relatively unimportant. Yet it is this very indifference to
technique — or the shifting of the responsibility to the
realms of the Over Soul and similar poetic genii — which
is especially important in the history of American prosody;
for without these transcendental poets there would almost
certainly never have been a Walt Whitman, an Emily
Dickinson, and very probably not the twentieth-century
American *vers librists*.

Yet, "Poetry was to all [the transcendentalists]," says
Cooke, "the occasional rather than the chief medium of
expression. With the exception of Lowell, they were not
poets by profession, and even with him prose was used
oftener than verse. Although Emerson early declared
that his calling was that of a poet, yet he gave to the
lecture and the essay the preference. With Thoreau,
Margaret Fuller, Higginson, and Wasson, as well as others,
poetry was occasional or incidental. To a large number
poetry was an accident, and they wrote one or two or a
half-dozen poems only. There was something in transcendentalism that made them poets in youth or at rare
moments; but they were grave theologians or philosophers
for the rest of their lives." [25]

Thus there came into American versification through
the transcendental poets a new amateurish spirit. But
the main reason for this was not a deliberate neglect of
form but a greater concern with thought-content. The
poetry of the transcendentalists "contains a gospel, and
not an appeal to emotion and imagination. . . . These
Poets are more concerned as to what to say than as to how
to say it." [26] Therefore, "The form is often rugged, the
verse is halting and defective. Their metres stumble,

[25] Cooke, *op. cit.*, pp. 24–25.   [26] *Ibid.*, p. 23.

and their rhymes are not correct. They are too meta-
physical, subtle, and complicated in their thought to sing
themselves clearly and strongly out into beautiful
words. . . ." [27]

And of course the emphasis on individuality and the
belief that the poet's message is divinely inspired — that,
in a more literal sense than Sidney ever intended, the
poet had merely to look into his own heart and write —
would minimize deliberate artistry and place a new and
special dignity on personal idiosyncrasies. It is right here
that we have the genesis of the later prosodic "revolt."

Thoreau's *Conscience* is typical of much of the versification of the early transcendental poets. The form may be
called roughly that of the pseudo-Pindaric (or Cowley?)
"ode." The lines are iambic, but the number of syllables
varies from four to seven. Short lines predominate, however (the chief difference between these odes and Cowley's, the lines of the latter being as a rule longer), with
couplet and alternate rimes. The following extract is
fairly characteristic:

> I love a soul not all of wood,
> Predestinated to be good,
> But true to the backbone
> Unto itself alone,
> And false to none;

Here the phrase comes nearer being the verse-unit than
any preconceived metrical pattern. Another important
characteristic is the terseness and compactness of the
expression, a feature which often prevents a smooth
rhythmical flow but at the same time gives an epigrammatic effectiveness. Even the use of short lines is typical
of most of the transcendental verse. A few poets continued to use pentameter, but the octosyllabic base and
the loose "ode" predominate in the whole bulk of transcendental poetry. A fairly representative octosyllabic

[27] Cooke, *op. cit.*, p. 24.

quatrain is the following from Christopher F. Cranch's *Gnosis:*

> We are spirits clad in veils;
> Man by man was never seen;
> All our deep communing fails
> To remove the shadowy screen.

Many reasons might be given to explain the transcendental preference for short lines and brevity of the whole poem, but some of the most obvious reasons are: amateurs seldom attempt long, sustained poems; poetry which depends largely upon the inspirational mood (approaching the mystic trance) usually results in fragmentary achievements (*cf. Kubla Khan*); and short-line measures are more readily adapted for ideas which are themselves fragmentary, incomplete, mere echoes from the sublimal Over Soul, "Inner Self," or whatever the mystic terminology may be.

SELECTED BIBLIOGRAPHY

Ralph Waldo Emerson

Text

Emerson, Ralph Waldo, *Poems*, ed. by Edward W. Emerson. Boston: Houghton Mifflin Company, 1904.
[The editor's notes contain dates of composition, notebook fragments of some of the poems, and other valuable information.]

——, *Journals*, ed. by E. W. Emerson. Boston: Houghton Mifflin Company, 1909. 10 vols.

——, *Ralph Waldo Emerson*, ed. by Frederick Carpenter. (American Writers Series.) New York: American Book Company, 1934.
[Selections, with a critical Introduction.]

Criticism

Gorley, Jean, "Emerson's Theory of Poetry," *Poetry Review* (August, 1931), pp. 263–273.

Kreymborg, Alfred, "The Intoxicated Emerson," *Our Singing Strength.* New York: Coward-McCann, 1929. Chapter VII.

Sutcliffe, Emerson Grant, "Emerson's Theories of Literary Expression," *University of Illinois Studies in Language and Literature* (1923), VIII, No. 1, 9–143.

——, "Whitman, Emerson and New Poetry," *New Republic* (1919), XIX, 114–116.

Thompson, Frank T., "Emerson's Theory and Practices of Poetry," *Publications of the Modern Language Association* (1928), XLIII, 1170–1184.

Transcendentalism

Editions, Etc.

Alcott, Amos Bronson, *New Connecticut.* An Autobiographical Poem. Boston, 1887.

——, *Sonnets and Canzonets.* Boston, 1882.

Channing, William Ellery, *The Works of . . .,* 20th complete ed., with an introduction. Boston, 1871. (6 vols in 3.)

Dial, The. Vols. 1–4. 1840–1844. Editors: Margaret Fuller, R. W. Emerson, George Ripley.

Fuller (Ossoli), Sarah Margaret, *Works,* ed. by Arthur B. Fuller. Boston, 1881. 2 vols.

Parker, Theodore, *Transcendentalism;* a Lecture. Boston, 1876.

——, *The Collected Works of . . .,* ed. by Frances Power Cobbe. London, 1863–1871. 14 vols.

The Poets of Transcendentalism. An Anthology, ed. with an introduction and notes by George Willis Cooke. Boston: Houghton Mifflin Company, 1903.

Criticism

Frothingham, O. B., *Transcendentalism in New England, a History.* New York, 1876.

Goddard, Harold Clarke, *Studies in New England Transcendentalism.* Columbia University Press, 1908.

Gohdes, Clarence L. F., *The Periodicals of American Transcendentalism.* Duke University Press, 1931.

Leighton, Walter L., *French Philosophers and New England Transcendentalism.* Charlottesville, Virginia, 1908.

CHAPTER V

John Greenleaf Whittier

I. INTRODUCTION

THOUGH Whittier was born only four years after Emerson and began writing about the same time Emerson did, the versification of the two poets is from fifty years to a century apart. Indeed, Whittier's technique has more in common with that of the Colonial poets than even Freneau's. It is not so easy, however, to place it with respect to the chronological development of English poetry, since it certainly possesses none of the strait-laced, polished perfection of typically eighteenth-century English versification, nor the naturalness and freedom which we find in the 1798 *Lyrical Ballads*, though in other respects Wordsworth and Whittier do have much in common. But it is impossible to ignore Whittier's metrical practices or to dismiss his poetry as no longer important. The astounding popularity, for example, of *Snow-Bound* (on which, it is said, the poet made a profit of $10,000) shows how representative of its age Whittier's poetry was.

The circumstances under which Whittier wrote and the particular poems with which he first achieved recognition are highly significant in understanding his versification. His first published poem, *The Exile's Departure*, was printed in a small newspaper, the Newburyport *Free Press*, which also published other juvenile poems of Whittier's. This was only the beginning of the young poet's connection with newspapers, for he learned his art, such as it was, by contributing verse to what we today call "country newspapers." It is not surprising, therefore, that he should have become a journalistic poet.

We must not forget that Whittier's education was extremely meager, and part of his metrical limitations are
no doubt the result of insufficient education. Miss Pray,
whose thorough study of Whittier's apprenticeship as a
poet makes her opinions authoritative, says, "In regard
to young Whittier's early literary models we know that
his main source for work of contemporary writers was
the weekly newspaper. This contained scattered examples of Scott, Moore, Hemans, Byron, Willis, 'L. E. L.,'
Sigourney, Brainard, Percival, and others of less importance . . . Whittier had read at least some of 'Ossian'
at an early age . . . when about fourteen or fifteen, he
bought a copy of Shakespeare when on a trip to Boston,
. . . Burns and Dinsmore were also early poetic acquaint-
ances. These, with the Bible, were probably about all
the poetic inspiration he received until his three terms at
Haverhill Academy broadened his acquaintance with
literature." [1]

At Haverhill Whittier no doubt studied the English
"classics," but he began his metrical experiments at an
early age, and it is safe to say that his poetic style had
already begun to crystallize before his knowledge of literature was wide enough for extensive influence. The
poetry of Burns, the Bible, and the few contemporary
poets mentioned by Miss Pray must not be minimized as
sources of Whittier's versification, yet the journalistic
influence was surely very great, both in bringing the young
poet into contact with poems printed in newspapers and
in providing a means of presenting his own poems to the
public. Of course Whittier's own native abilities directed
to a large extent his choice of rhythms, measures, and
stanzas, but the forms which the Quaker poet used all of
his life were those which we might expect as a result of his
contact with newspaper verse: namely, ballad measure,
octosyllabics, and pentameter — in other words, the sim-

[1] Frances Mary Pray, *A Study of Whittier's Apprenticeship as a
Poet* (Ph.D. thesis at Pennsylvania State College, 1930), pp. 107–108.

plest and most conventional forms. About a third of all of Whittier's poems are four-stress, about a fourth are ballad meter, and somewhat over a tenth are iambic pentameter.[2]

Whether the Quaker poet adopted the style and the technique of the journalist in order to be heard, or whether he was unconsciously influenced by the newspapers to which he contributed in early life, it is difficult to say precisely, and relatively unimportant, though both explanations are probably true.

But it is of considerable importance to the present discussion that we have no evidence that at any time Whittier groped for a technique to express the poetry he felt and thought. "It is doubtful," said the late Professor Cairns, "that he ever fully appreciated the value of form in poetry."[3] He lived until 1892, writing almost to the very end, but Emerson, Poe, Whitman, Tennyson (who was born a year later and died the same year as Whittier), and other poets of his lifetime had hardly the slightest evident influence on his poetic technique.

Though Whittier did write some literary criticism, there is scarcely a word on prosody. About as near as he ever came to expressing a theory on verse technique is the remark he made to Lucy Hooper that a long poem "unless consecrated to the sacred interests of religion and humanity would be a criminal waste of life."[4] Yet this really does not even imply a theory of prosody, though it may indicate preferences. About the *Psalm of Life*, which he had just read in the *Knickerbocker*, he says: "It is seldom that we find an article of poetry so full of excellent philosophy and *common sense* as the following. We

[2] This estimate does not include the juvenile poems printed by Miss Pray, *op. cit.*, but the fractions would probably be about the same even if these poems were counted.

[3] William B. Cairns, *History of American Literature* (New York, 1912), p. 263.

[4] Bliss Perry, *Whittier, A Sketch of His Life* (Boston, 1897), p. 12.

know not who the author may be, but he or she is no common man or woman. These nine simple verses are worth more than all the dreams of Shelley, and Keats, and Wordsworth. They are alive and vigorous with the spirit of the day in which we live — the moral steam enginery of an age of action." [5]

This emphasis on "the spirit of the day in which we live" is an expression of that typical American idealism of the times, which we find in Emerson's *American Scholar* (and in the national aspect of his theory of poetry), as well as in Walt Whitman's whole poetic theory; but the "moral steam" is typical of no one, not even Longfellow, so much as Whittier himself. And it indicates, if not an antagonism, at least an obtuseness toward artistic form and technique. Emerson can theorize about natural ruggedness and Walt Whitman can "chant his barbaric yawp over the roofs of the world," but Whittier can write as "rugged" or as "barbaric" as either and apparently never give the question much thought one way or the other, notwithstanding the fact that he occasionally remembers to justify himself by expressing a preference for the heart rather than the head:

> To paint, forgetful of the tricks of art,
>   With pencil dipped alone in colors of the heart.
>   *In Peace*

Of course Whittier did write to the editor of *The Atlantic Monthly* regarding *Snow-Bound:* "I hope I have corrected a little of the bad grammar and rhythmical blunders which have so long annoyed Harvard graduates." Some of the grammatical changes were most urgently necessary, but the final versification of the poem is not greatly different from many other poems which do not seem to have been revised.

Whittier's indifference to prosody, however, does not make his versification uninteresting to examine; and

[5] Perry, *op. cit.*, p. 13.

though we have emphasized his reversion to older forms and techniques rather than the progressiveness of his metrical practices, there are, nevertheless, some aspects of his style and diction which point to the future rather than the past. Kreymborg, for instance, finds Whittier's conversational tones of Yankee speech "anticipating the poetic methods of Robert Frost." [6] And if this is true, then certainly Whittier has an important place in the historical development of American versification.

2. OCTOSYLLABICS

The octosyllabic four-stress line was always Whittier's favorite measure. He began using it early (since *The Spirit of the North, Judith at the Tent of Holofernes,* and *Metacomb* were all written in 1829); and hardly a year passed between 1829 and 1892 (*cf. An Outdoor Reception,* 1892) that he did not write several poems in this form.

A chronological study of these octosyllabic poems reveals very few developments in versification, and even the few minor variations may be the result of different subject-matter rather than any real change in technique. The first two poems, however, present two metrical traits which are found more rarely in Whittier's later octosyllabics.

The first stanza of *The Spirit of the North* is practically three-stress:

> Spirit of the frozen North,
>
> Where the wave is chained and still,
>
> And the savage bear looks forth
>
> Nightly from his caverned hill!
>
> Down from thy eternal throne,
>
> From thy land of cloud and storm,

6 Alfred Kreymborg, *op. cit.,* p. 89.

Where the meeting icebergs groan,
Sweepeth on thy wrathful form.

A "metrical stress" can, it is true, be forced in every line, but this makes an artificial reading. There are enough four-stress lines, however, to indicate the pattern, which is "clipped" (initial unstressed syllable omitted) iambic tetrameter, as in

Lord of sunless depths and cold!

A certain amount of parallelism is also inevitable in couplets, especially octosyllabic ones, yet Whittier probably used parallelism much more than the average couplet writer. One stanza in this poem is unusual in its initial parallel verbs (present and past participles) and final parallel nouns (a device which is exceedingly important in Whitman's verse).

Throned amid the ancient *hills,*
Piled with undecaying *snow,*
Flashing with the path of *rills,*
Frozen in their first glad *flow;*
Thou hast seen the gloomy *north,*
Gleaming with unearthly *light,*
Spreading its pale banners forth,
Checkered with the stars of *night.*

Technically (*i.e.*, following the punctuation) some enjambment is found in practically all of Whittier's poems, but actually (*i.e.*, in natural reading) it is very rare in his octosyllabics. Indeed, one stanza of *Judith at the Tent of Holofernes* contains more enjambment than is characteristic of the poet's later style:

Sunlight on the mountains streameth
Like an air-borne wave of gold!
And Bethulia's armor gleameth
Round Judea's banner-fold.

> Down they go, the mailëd warriors,
>   As the upper torrents sally
> Headlong from their mountain barriers
>   Down upon the sleeping valley.

Whittier's four-stress verse is mainly in couplets and alternate rime, but the thought-unit is ordinarily two lines, even in the alternate rime, as in *Memories:*

> How thrill once more the lengthening chain
>   Of memory, at the thought of thee!
> Old hopes which long in dust have lain,
> Old dreams, come thronging back again,
>   And boyhood lives again in me;
> I feel its glow upon my cheek,
>   Its fulness of the heart is mine,
> As when I leaned to hear thee speak,
>   Or raised my doubtful eye to thine.

Naturally, we expect such an arrangement in the couplets, especially where they are paragraphed separately, as in *Maud Muller:*

> Maud Muller on a summer's day
> Raked the meadow sweet with hay.
>
> Beneath her torn hat glowed the wealth
> Of simple beauty and rustic health . . .
>
> "Thanks!" said the Judge; "a sweeter draught
> From a fairer hand was never quaffed."
>
> He spoke of the grass and flowers and trees,
> Of the singing birds and humming bees;

And *Barbara Frietchie, The Sisters,* and other poems are in similar couplets. Refrains and repetends were seldom used by Whittier in any meters, yet the parallelism of these couplets sometimes results in a reiteration of words and phrases, as in *Barbara Frietchie:*

> Forty flags with their silver stars,
> Forty flags with their crimson bars,

The four-stress triplet is, of course, analogous to the couplets of *Maud Muller*, as, for example, in *The Palm-Tree:*

> Branches of palm are its spars and rails,
> Fibres of palm are its woven sails,
> And the rope is of palm that idly trails!

Skipper Ireson's Ride is interesting as being one of Whittier's few poems to have a refrain. Each eleven-line couplet-stanza ends either with:

> Old Floyd Ireson, for his hard heart,
> Tarred and feathered and carried in a cart
> By the women of Marblehead!

Or the dialect version:

> "Here's Flud Oirson, fur his horrd horrt,
> Torr'd an' futherr'd an' corr'd in a corrt
> By the women o' Morble'ead!"

But more important is a rhythmical peculiarity which we find in this poem, in *The Barefoot Boy*, in *Snow-Bound*, and in other octosyllabic couplets of Whittier's mature years. The verse is divided by an emphatic cæsura and a diction which pairs off the line into a jerky 2 + 2 movement:

> Body of turkey, head of owl,
> Wings a-droop like a rained-on fowl,
> Feathered and ruffled in every part,
> Skipper Ireson stood in the cart.
> Scores of women, old and young,
> Strong of muscle, and glib of tongue,
> Pushed and pulled up the rocky lane,
> Shouting and singing the shrill refrain:

The Barefoot Boy has less of this rhythm, though it is always felt as the underlying pattern, and many of the lines have exactly the same cadence:

> Blessings on thee, little man,
> Barefoot boy, with cheek of tan!

The methods of producing this two-stress movement
are numerous, but two in particular deserve to be mentioned. One is by means of an alliterative pair or repeated
word, as in *The Barefoot Boy:*

> Hand in hand with her he walks,
>
> Face to face with her he talks,
>
> Part and parcel of her joy —
>
> Blessings on the barefoot boy!

It is also important to notice that in such passages the
diction practically forces a secondary stress on the weak
syllable that we would ordinarily mark (if at all) with a
metrical stress.

The other important method of producing this rhythm
is by means of the adjective-plus-noun construction, often
composing the last half of the line:

> Maud Muller on a *summer's day* . . .

> "My father should wear a *broadcloth coat;*
> My brother should sail a *painted boat.*
>
> .   .   .   .
>
> Oh for boyhood's *painless play,*
> Sleep that wakes in *laughing day,*
> Health that mocks the *doctor's rules* . . .
> Blessings on the *barefoot boy!*

Inversions both for the sake of rime and to maintain
this two-footed rhythm, with its tendency to syncopate
and to singsong, are characteristic of Whittier's technique. Most of the poet's 158 four-stress poems contain
examples, but the following lines from *Snow-Bound* illustrate the general style:

> The cock his lusty greetings *said,*
> And *forth* his speckled harem *led;*
> The oxen lashed their tails, and hooked,
> Their mild reproach of hunger *looked;*

The hornëd patriarch of the sheep,
Like Egypt's Amun roused from sleep,
Shook his sage head with gesture mute,
And emphasized with stamp of foot.

. . . .

A careless boy that night *he seemed;*
But at his desk he had the look
And air of one who *wisely* schemed,
    And hostage from the future *took*
    In trainëd thought and lore of book.

. . . .

My uncle ceased his pipe *to smoke,*
Knocked from its bowl the refuse *gray,*
And laid it tenderly *away;*
Then roused himself to *safely* cover
The dull red brands with ashes *over.*

The homely description, rustic sentiment, and home-spun thought no doubt made *Snow-Bound* popular in its day, and it is perhaps a great *American* poem for precisely these qualities; yet its monotonous rhythm and equally monotonous rime also had something to do with its contemporary fame. The monotony of the couplet rimes is broken occasionally by the substitution of alternate rime for four lines, but this one variation helps very little.

Another variation from the strict iambic tetrameter pattern, however, is found in a fairly large number of Whittier's four-stress poems. It is the substitution of an anapestic foot, though this substitution often becomes a part of the rhythmical pattern, so that it is no longer a variation. In *The Wreck of Rivermouth* the pattern is iambic, with the substitution of one anapest, usually in the second or third foot:

Rív | ermoùth Rócks | are fáir | to sée,
By dáwn or súnset shóne acróss,

When the ebb | of the sea | has left them free
To dry their frin | ges of gold | -green moss:
For there the riv | er comes wind | ing down,
From salt sea-mead | ows and up | lands brown,
And waves | on the out | er rocks afoam
Shout to its waters, "Welcome home!"

But the pattern may contain two anapests, as in *John Underhill:*

He shook | from his feet | as he rode | away
The dust of Massachusetts Bay. . . .
Or thought | how he rode | with his lan | ces free
By the Low | er Rhine | and the Zuyder-Zee,
Till his wood | -path grew | to a trod | den road,
And Hilton Point | in the dis | tance showed.

The majority of lines in *John Underhill,* however, contain only one anapest. Two to a line are found more often in *The King's Missive.*

At times there seem to be analogies between Whittier's metrics and those of the popular English nursery-rimes. For instance, many lines of *Snow-Bound* have "Jack and Jill went up the hill" cadences, and some of the iambic-anapestic rhythms may perhaps be compared to "Ride a cock-horse to Banbury Cross." Certainly the nursery-rime analogy should not be over-emphasized, yet it occasionally helps us to explain not only what Whittier did metrically but also why he did it, and probably why his rhythms have appealed to the folk-mind. For Whittier is just as truly the folk-poet of New England as James Whitcomb Riley is the "Hoosier poet."

3. FOUR-PLUS-THREE MEASURE (BALLAD METER)

"We have no American ballad-writer — that is writer
of ballads founded on our native history and tradition —
who can be compared with [Whittier], either in the range
or skillful treatment of his materials," said Bayard Taylor.[7] Nearly all critics acknowledge Whittier's supremacy
as a ballad writer, and it is probably true that his ballad
meters are superior to his other rhythms.

But "ballad" is often interpreted very broadly. W. S.
Kennedy, for instance, cites *The Witch's Daughter*, *Telling
the Bees*, and *The Tent on the Beach* as "faultless ballads."
And *Snow-Bound*, he says, is closely allied to the ballad.[8]
Whereas, in reality, *The Witch's Daughter* is in four-stress
triplets; *Telling the Bees* is in a four-two-four-four stanza
(only similar to ballad meter); and *The Tent on the Beach*
is in an eight-line stanza with four-, five-, and six-stress
lines.

When we speak of a ballad today we mean either a folk
ballad, of unknown authorship, or a literary imitation of
the folk ballad. Some genuine ballads are *Lord Randall*,
Bonny Barbara Allan, *The Wife of Usher's Well*, *Sir Pat-
rick Spens*, and the whole cycle of Robin Hood ballads.
Some literary ballads are Wordsworth's *Lucy Gray*,
Scott's *Jock of Hazeldean*, Longfellow's *The Wreck of the
Hesperus*, Hood's *Faithless Nelly Gray*, and Holmes's
mock-ballad *The Specter Pig*.

The ballad tells a story (usually tragic, sentimental,
or humorous) naïvely and objectively, *i.e.*, a mere statement of bare facts, with ordinarily an undercurrent of
pathos. Metrically, the ballad is usually composed of
long lines of seven stresses, conventionally printed as two
lines of four and three stresses each, riming *abcb*. The
stanzas are composed of four or six verses — sometimes

---

[7] Quoted by J. Scott Clark in *A Study of English and American
Poets* (New York, 1909), p. 745.

[8] *Ibid.*

eight — though this is simply a double quatrain. Repetitions, refrains, and repetends are not essential to the ballad, yet they are found in the majority of folk poems. The genuine ballad is, of course, always intended to be sung, and most poems in this measure may be set to music. Many of Whittier's poems are in the genuine ballad tradition, both as to thought and form, though no poem of his is as faithful an imitation of the folk ballad as Longfellow's *Wreck of the Hesperus.* But *The Dead Ship of Harpswell* indicates the form:

> And men shall sigh, and women weep,
> Whose dear ones pale and pine,
> And sadly over sunset seas
> Await the ghostly sign.
> They know not that its sails are filled
> By pity's tender breath,
> Nor see the Angel at the helm
> Who steers the Ship of Death!

All 4 + 3 measures, however, with rimes *abab*, etc., are frequently classed as ballad meter, in spite of the fact that they are not strictly ballads. This verse form ranks second in frequency among Whittier's poems, but it is a measure which he used with great ease and success. One example is *Burns on Receiving a Sprig of Heather in Blossom,* which begins:

> No more these simple flowers belong
> To Scottish maid and lover;
> Sown in the common soil of song,
> They bloom the wide world over.

The simplicity and regularity of this form renders detailed analysis unnecessary, yet we may observe in passing that this very simplicity and regularity make metrical stresses seem natural secondary speech accents, thus indicating that the lines are nearer to song than ordinary poetry. The following extracts from *My Playmate* illustrate the extremely simple rhythms and unaffected melodies characteristic of many of Whittier's poems in this measure:

> The pines were dark on Ramoth hill,
> Their song was soft and low;
> The blossoms in the sweet May wind
> Were falling like the snow.
>
> The blossoms drifted at our feet,
> The orchard birds sang clear;
> The sweetest and the saddest day
> It seemed of all the year.
>
> .   .   .   .
>
> She kissed the lips of kith and kin,
> She laid her hand in mine:
> What more could ask the bashful boy
> Who fed her father's kine?

The contrast of these conventional poetic constructions and smooth rhythms with the strained inversions and jerky beats of Whittier's four-stress couplets is surprising. Of course we do find an occasional inversion here, such as "What more could ask the bashful boy," but it is much less awkward than "My uncle ceased his pipe to smoke." Not all of Whittier's ballad-measure poems, however, are lyrics such as *My Playmate*. The Quaker poet could fight as well as sing to this tune, as for example, in *Lines on the Portrait of a Celebrated Publisher*.

In addition to the ballad measure, Whittier also used four- and three-stress lines in various combinations. Some of the most common are aba_4b_3, in about twenty-five poems, including *The New Year, Flowers in Winter*, and *Between the Gates*; abc_4b_3 in *What the Voice Said*; and aa_4bb_3 in *The Maids of Attitash*.

4. SEVEN-STRESS VERSE

The seven-stress line, as has already been indicated, is merely ballad meter arranged in its natural rhythmical units. Metrically, there is no difference whatever, for the few variations from the norm are the same ones that we find in Whittier's 4 + 3 measure, *viz.*, an inverted foot (usually the initial one); a metrical stress, meaning here that the line has only six natural speech accents; and the occasional spondee, or more commonly a primary-secondary-primary accentuation, like "cold north light." The well-known *Massachusetts to Virginia* is characteristic of Whittier's seven-stress measure:

We hear thy threats, Virginia! thy stormy words and high

Swell harshly on the Southern winds which melt along our sky;

Yet, not one brown, hard hand forgoes its honest labor here,

No hewer of our mountain oaks suspends his axe in fear.

Wild are the waves which lash the reefs along St. George's bank;

Cold on the shores of Labrador the fog lies white and dank;

Through storm, and wave, and blinding mist, stout are the
    hearts which man

The fish | ing-smacks | of Mar | blehead, | the sea | boats of |
    Cape Ann.

The cold | north light | and win | try sun | glare on | their ic | y
    forms,

Bent grim | ly o'er | their strain | ing lines | or wrest | ling with |
    the storms;

Free as the winds they drive before, rough as the waves they
    roam,
They laugh to scorn the slaver's threat against their rocky home.

None of Whittier's four-stress couplets can compare in
vigor and flowing rhythms with these stanzas. And several of the lines have cadences which remind us of Mase-
field's *Sea-Fever:*

And all I ask is a tall ship and a star to steer her by,

Some of Whittier's seven-stress poems have one or two
trisyllabic feet, as in *The Vaudois Teacher:*

The cloud went off | from the pil | grim's brow, | as a small | and
    meagre book,
Unchased with gold or gem of cost, | from his fold | ing robe he
    took!
"Here, lady fair, | is the pearl | of price, | may it prove | as such
    to thee!
Nay, keep thy gold — I ask it not, | for the word | of God is
    free!"

But this variation can easily slide over into an eight-stress
(or a 4 + 4) movement, as it often does in *The Garrison
of Cape Ann:*

Thrice around the block-house marching, met, unharmed, its
    volleyed flame;
Then, with mocking laugh and gesture, sunk in earth or lost
    in air,

5. FIVE-PLUS-THREE MEASURE

Closely allied to the seven- (and eight-) stress line is the 5 + 3 form, as in *The Christian Tourists* and *The Hive at Gettysburg* (*ababcdcd*), or *The New Exodus* (*abab*):

And, líke the Cóptic mónks by Móusa's wélls,

We dréam of wónders pást,

Vágue as the táles the wándering Árab télls,

Each drówsier thàn the lást.

The stanzas in this measure range from four lines, as above, to twelve (*cf. Freedom in Brazil*). Other combinations are $a_3bb_5a_3$ (*cf. A Legacy* and *The Christian Slave*), aba_5b_3 (*cf. At Last*), and $aa_5b_3cc_5b_3$ (*cf. The Christmas of 1888*).

6. IAMBIC PENTAMETER

Few of Whittier's iambic pentameters are today printed in anthologies, for none of them have become household poems, as have *The Barefoot Boy* and *Snow-Bound*. It is puzzling that this should have been Whittier's third most used form, and that he never learned to handle it more skilfully and effectively.

He wrote about a dozen blank verse poems,[9] including *The Deity* (1825) and *The Bay of Seven Islands* (*i.e.*, "Introduction," 1882); over eighty pentameter lines with alternate rime, or a combination of alternate and couplet; and over twenty poems in heroic couplets. The blank verse is perhaps the least successful, mainly because of irregular and awkward rhythm. The accents often have a tendency to bunch, so that the rhythm is either off-balance or else balanced by two stresses to each half line, making the cadences inappropriate for blank verse. *The*

---

[9] Not including the uncollected juvenile poems printed by Pray, *op. cit.*

Fair Quakeress is a good example of Whittier's early blank verse style:

> She was a fair young girl, yet on her brow
> No pale pearl shone, a blemish on the pure
> And snowy lustre of its living light,
> No radiant gem shone beautifully through
> The shadowing of her tresses, as a star
> Through the dark sky of midnight; and no wreath
> Of coral circled on her queenly neck,
> In mockery of the glowing cheek and lip,
> Whose hue the fairy guardian of the flowers
> Might never rival when her delicate touch
> Tinges the rose of springtime.

The main fault with such versification is simply that it does not have the superb pulsations, the ebb and flow, or the marvelous sweeps of really effective blank verse. It is not line-moulded, or couplet-moulded, but it lacks melodious cadences. Some later examples contain more of the 2 + 2 effect, as in *Nauhaught, the Deacon.*

> Mellowed and mingled with the whispering leaves,
>
> As, through the tangle of the low, thick woods,
>
> He searched his traps. . . .

Even where the accents are more regular, the cæsura is so emphatic that we almost expect a rime at the end of each half line:

> Even as he spake | he heard at his bare feet
>
> A low, metallic clink, | and, looking down,
>
> He saw a dainty purse | with disks of gold
>
> Crowding its silken net.

Whittier's rimed iambic pentameter often has the same jerky movement as his blank verse, but the rime would necessarily interfere with the breath-sweeps that we expect in blank verse, so that the rimed verse gives the impression of being superior, as in the prelude to *The Pennsylvania Pilgrim*, which Whittier felt sure was his best poem:

I sing the Pilgrim of a softer clime

And milder speech than those brave men's who brought

To the ice and iron of our winter time

A will as firm, a creed as stern, and wrought

With one mailed hand, and with the other fought.

The heroic couplets have practically the same versification as the alternately rimed pentameter. And even where the rhythm is comparatively regular, we find the same half-line units, as in *Miriam:*

The years are many since, in youth and hope,
Under the Charter Oak, our horoscope
We drew thick-studded with all favoring stars.
Now, with gray beards, and faces seamed with scars
From life's hard battle, meeting once again,
We smile, half sadly, over dreams so vain;

The similarity between these half-line divisions and the two-stress movement of the four-stress couplets of *Snow-Bound* reveals a deep-seated practice in Whittier's verse technique.

7. THE ANAPEST

We find Whittier using the anapest in various manners: as a substitution in iambic meter (already discussed); in couplets (*cf. The Cities of the Plain, The Hunters of Men, Ritner*, etc.); in alternate rime (*cf. The Exile's Departure*); and in other combinations. About twenty-five poems are characteristically anapestic. *April* is representative:

'Tis the noon | of the spring | -time, yet nev | er a bird

In the wind | -shaken elm | or the ma | ple is heard;

For green | meadow-grass | es wide lev | els of snow,

And blow | ing of drifts | where the cro | cus should blow; . . .

The wail | and the shriek | of the bit | ter north-east,

Raw and chill, | as if win | nowed through i | ces and snow,

St. John is two- and three-stress anapestics:

"To the winds | give our banner!

Bear home | ward again!"

Cried the Lord | of Acadia,

Cried Charles | of Es | tienne!

From the prow | of his shallop

He gazed, | as the sun,

From its bed | in the ocean,

Streamed up | the St. John.

Telling the Bees has fewer anapestic feet than *April* or *St. John*, but the rhythm has a trisyllabic movement:

Here | is the place; | right ov | er the hill

Runs the path I took;

You can see | the gap | in the old | wall still,

And the step | ping-stones | in the shal | low brook.

8. STANZAS

In discussing his various measures some of Whittier's stanzas have been mentioned, yet his more complicated forms need to be listed. He did not, as we have observed, emphasize this side of his technique. The couplet and alternate rime were his natural forms. Refrains and repetends he used only occasionally, probably because he laid no special emphasis upon melody, upon mere sound as a poetic ingredient desirable in itself. Poe and Whittier are in this respect at opposite poles.

Nor was Whittier skilful in using the stanza either as a unit of thought or as a rhythmical unit. His thought is diffuse and would overflow any such limitations as a mere stanza; and his rhythms are confined to phrases and half-lines, as we have already seen. Therefore, his *abab* stanzas would of course rank first in frequency. These we have already studied in the section on the $4 + 3$ measure, and the *abba* $5 + 3$ verse.

The only other stanza that suited Whittier's technique is the tail-rime arrangement. The following list includes the most interesting forms: $aaa_4b_2a_4b_2$, *The Drunkard and His Bottle;* $abaa_4b_6$, *Proem;* $aa_3b_2ccc_3b_2$, *To a Friend;* $abaa_4b_3cc_5$, *The Female Martyr;* aba_5b_2, *A Summons;* $a_5b_2cc_5b_3$, *Chalkley Hall;* $aa_5b_2cc_5b_2$, *The Reward;* $a_4b_3aa_4b_3$, *The Brewing of Soma;* $aa_4b_3cc_4b_3$, *To —: Lines Written After a Summer Day's Excursion* and *An Easter Flower Gift;* $a_4b_2aa_4b_6$, *Hampton Beach.* The repetition of the *b*-rime helps to hold the stanza together and give the last line a certain finality which suggests that a unit of thought has been completed. And it is true that Whittier's tail-rime stanzas are less diffuse than his couplets and other rime-schemes. Even in his couplet and ballad stanzas, however, he practically never runs over a sentence into the next stanza. But this does not necessarily mean that the thought is not run over, though it does prevent the spreading of imagery and metaphors from one stanzaic group to another.

9. GENERAL SUMMARY AND CONCLUSIONS

Whittier's rhythms are almost never spontaneously lyrical, overflowing the bounds of rules because the poet feels more emotion than he can express by "the tricks of art." His prodigious output and his journalistic style suggest that he composed easily, but his rhythms impress us as being simple and his cadences few and awkward because his own poetic abilities were meager. This deduction is borne out by the poet's inability to write good iambic pentameter, the failure being greatest in blank verse. The octosyllabic line and the simple ballad measure are the only metrical forms that Whittier could use with anything like repeated success. Even within these restricted rhythms, the phrase and the half-line appear to have been his rhythmical units. Whether or not he really composed by half-lines is immaterial; the final effect is what we might expect if he had. It is obvious, therefore, why he never wrote a sonnet, or any poem in a form that demanded perfect control over technique.

Most critics deride Whittier for his inferior rimes, a subject to which too much importance is usually attached. If bad rimes do not prevent John Milton's poetry from attaining immortal grandeur, then, we might say, they are not worth discussing. But Milton's versification is so superb in almost every other respect that it is an impertinence to criticize his rimes. Whittier's prosodic violin has too few strings anyway, and his bad rimes certainly do not help, even if they do not hinder a great deal. However, they are probably fewer than most of his adverse critics realize.

Some of the offending rimes are simply due to dialect pronunciation, as in "foot" — "root," possibly in "wrongs" — "tongues" and "mows" — "cows," and certainly in that famous couplet from *Maud Muller:*

> For of all sad words of tongue or pen,
> The saddest are these: "It might have been!"

In *St. John,* "Estienne" is three times rimed with "again" and once with "seen." Either way may be questionable, but certainly both are not right.

A more serious fault is bad grammar. In *Knight of St. John,* we find, "Closed o'er my steed and I." Despite

Whittier's assurance to the editor of *The Atlantic Monthly* that he had corrected *Snow-Bound* to please Harvard graduates, there is an awkward shift of tense in the second paragraph. And the past tense is used in every other clause in the passage except in one line: "The cattle *shake* their walnut bows."

This same poem contains other awkward and puzzling passages, such as:

> The bridle-post an old man sat
> With loose-flung coat and high cocked hat;

wherein the adverb *like* was apparently omitted to preserve the count of eight syllables. Again we find in the same poem:

> Our uncle, innocent of books,
> Was rich in lore of fields and brooks,
> The ancient teachers never dumb
> Of Nature's unhoused lyceum.

But while we know that "ancient teachers" must be in apposition to "fields and brooks" and not "uncle," the passage is none the less awkward. (We can shrug our shoulders over "dumb" — "lyceum.")

A characteristic of Whittier's style which has not so far been mentioned is his wealth of biblical allusions and paraphrases. Allusions are not ordinarily a trait of versification, yet Whittier's poems contain so many that they color his style, and raise an interesting question regarding his rhythms. Why, since Whittier was so steeped in biblical phraseology, was he not influenced by the cadences of the King James Version? We find them in Walt Whitman, who used much fewer allusions, but not in Whittier's strained inversions and monotonous octosyllabic couplets. The answer is obvious: Whittier did not have the ear to catch the marvelous music of the biblical cadences. He was a reporter of rustic life, a newspaper versifier, and a ballad singer of some ability. But despite his heavy-

fingered rhythms, Whittier's poetic diction is idiomatic,
with a Yankee resonance that may well remind Kreymborg of our contemporary Yankee, Frost. *Snow-Bound*
even contains three images prophetic of Emily Dickinson,
far-fetched as that comparison may seem!

> The shrieking of the mindless wind,
> The moaning tree-boughs swaying blind,
> And on the glass the unmeaning beat
> Of ghostly finger-tips of sleet.

10. MINOR POETS OF THE CIVIL WAR

By the middle of the nineteenth century the chronology of American versification becomes exceedingly complicated. The major poets Whittier, Holmes, Longfellow,
Whitman, Lowell, and Lanier were all writing poetry at
the same time. The classification is further complicated
by the fact that there were groups of minor poets writing
at Cambridge, in New York, in the South, in the West,
etc. Most literary histories attempt to solve the chronological difficulties by geographical divisions, but such a
classification is obviously unsatisfactory for a history of
prosodic theories and verse technique.

Some arbitrary schematization, however, is necessary.
And one of the least objectionable schemes seems to be
to group the versification of the minor poets by types and
general tendencies. Thus the end of the Whittier chapter
is an appropriate place for a brief treatment of the versification of the Civil War poems, for Whittier was perhaps
the greatest of the abolitionist poets, and the ballad is
the most typical metrical form used by Whittier and the
minor Civil War poets.

Of all the minor Civil War poets Edmund Clarence
Stedman's versification is most interesting for its range
and variety. *Wanted — a Man* is four-stress, in a rhythm
similar to that of *Christabel*, in fact, the Coleridge influence upon Stedman was very strong. Free use of

trisyllabic substitution is also found in *Treason's Last Device*. In both of these poems initial truncation gives many of the lines a lyrical buoyancy, and *Sumter* is fairly definitely trochaic. *How Old Brown Took Harper's Ferry*, riming $abab_8C_2C_3c_8$, is also trochaic. The long lines break up into a 4 plus 4 movement that reminds us of Hiawatha:

> Then his beard became more grizzled,
>   and his wild blue eye grew wilder,
> And more sharply curved his hawk's-nose,
>   snuffing battle from afar;

Alice of Monmouth contains practically every meter that was in use at the time, including octosyllabic couplets, seven-stress quatrains, three-stress quatrains with initial trochees, the irregular ode arrangement, pentameter, heroic couplets, and two very unusual experiments, *viz.:* three-stress unrimed verse, with an iambic base (in section V), and unrimed alexandrines (in section XIX). The alexandrines are reminiscent of Bryant's; some of the ode sections suggest comparisons with Whitman's war poems, such as *Beat! Beat! Drums!* and Stedman's whole verse technique is closely related to Lowell's versification.

All of Herman Melville's "Battle-Pieces" are interesting, but the trochaic *Apathy and Enthusiasm* has fluency, melody, and easy flowing enjambment hard to find in most of the Civil War poetry. Perhaps the most lyrical poem, however, is George Henry Boker's *Dirge for a Soldier*, in the same rhythm as Scott's *Soldier, Rest!* of *The Lady of the Lake* (Canto I):

> Close his eyes; his work is done!
>   What to him is friend or foeman,
> Rise of moon, or set of sun,
>   Hand of man, or kiss of woman?
>   Lay him low, lay him low,
>   In the clover or the snow!
>   What cares he? he cannot know:
>   Lay him low!

This is essentially a singing rhythm, and in this respect is characteristic of much of the Civil War verse.

The ballad was the favorite measure of this group of minor poets. Some examples are Boker's *On Board the Cumberland*, Francis Orray Ticknor's *The Sword of the Sea*, Ethel Lynn Beers's anapestic *The Picket-Guard*, Henry Timrod's *Charleston*, and combinations of the ballad measure, such as Henry Howard Brownell's *The River Fight* and Abram Joseph Ryan's *The Sword of Robert Lee*.

The significant songs of the period are: Annie Chambers Ketchum's *The Bonnie Blue Flag*, Albert H. Pike's *Dixie*, James Ryder Randall's *Maryland! My Maryland!*, Julia Ward Howe's *Battle Hymn of the Republic*, George Frederick Root's *The Battle Cry of Freedom*, *Tramp, Tramp, the Boys are Marching*, *Just Before the Battle, Mother*, and Charles Sprague Hall's *John Brown's Body*.

It is doubtful whether these Civil War poems had any appreciable effect upon the historical development of American versification, but the emotionalism of the times did inspire many people to try writing verse. Some of the most popular poets of the day, such as Brownell, wrote awkward lines which are scarcely remembered today, but undoubtedly the songs and ballads of the period had some influence upon the later lyrics of Holmes, Longfellow, Lowell, Lanier, and others.

SELECTED BIBLIOGRAPHY

John Greenleaf Whittier

Text

Whittier, John Greenleaf, *The Complete Poetical Works*, etc., ed. by H. E. Scudder. (Cambridge edition.) Boston: Houghton Mifflin Company, 1894.

Criticism

Howe, Will D., "Whittier," *American Writers on American Literature*, ed. by John Macy. New York: Horace Liveright, 1931. Chapter X, 125–134.

Kreymborg, Alfred, "A Rustic Quaker Goes to War," *Our Singing Strength*. New York: Coward-McCann, 1929. Pp. 84–96.

Pray, Frances Mary, *A Study of Whittier's Apprenticeship as a Poet, 1825–1835*. Ph.D. thesis at Pennsylvania State College, 1930. Privately printed.
[Includes a critical interpretation of Whittier's apprenticeship and a reprinting of all Whittier's available uncollected juvenile poetry.]

MINOR POETS

Howe, Will D., "Poets of the Civil War I: The North," *Cambridge History of American Literature*. New York: G. P. Putnam's Sons, 1918. II, 275–287.

Mims, Edwin, "Poets of the Civil War II: The South," *Cambridge History of American Literature*. New York: G. P. Putnam's Sons, 1918. II, 288–312.

CHAPTER VI

Henry Wadsworth Longfellow

I. INTRODUCTION

No American poet has been so widely acquainted with the versification of the major poets of the world as Longfellow. His translations alone include twelve languages.[1] Yet unlike Poe, Lanier, and some of the more recent poets, he had no special prosodic theory of his own; not even so much as Bryant, though Longfellow published several books and articles on the language and poetry of both Romance and Germanic tongues. This is not to say, of course, that his metrical practice does not rest on definite principles, some of which he introduced into American (and English) versification; but Longfellow was not a theorizer and analyzer of prosody, or of any other subject, except possibly æsthetics. He was, instead, an adapter and appreciator.

This limitation (if such it be) the poet himself realized. In "Table Talk" he says, "I have many opinions in Art and Literature which constantly recur to me in the tender guise of a sentiment." Sentiment exactly describes the opinions which he does express in his *Journal*, and indicates a lifelong preference for emotional over rational thinking. "A clever dialectician," he continues, "can prove to me that I am wrong. I cannot answer him. I let the waves of argument roll on; but all the lilies rise again, and are beautiful as before." [2]

[1] They are: French, Italian, Spanish, Portuguese, Latin, Greek, German, Danish, Finnish, Swedish, Anglo-Saxon, and Old French.

[2] *The Poetical Works of Henry Wadsworth Longfellow* (Cambridge, Mass., 1886), III, 412. Longfellow's *Works* are hereafter referred to only by volume and page.

Longfellow very shrewdly puts his finger on a psychological fact which deludes many (perhaps most) poets who attempt to theorize on poetic technique. In his *Journal*, for May 18, 1880, he records, "Our opinions are biased by our limitations. Poets who cannot write long poems think that no long poems should be written." [3] There is here, no doubt, an allusion to Poe, who had so exasperated Longfellow thirty-five years before with his false charges of plagiarism. Like a parable, however, the remark contains a more general and important truth. Indeed, Longfellow's observation is triple as well as double-edged, for this opinion regarding criticism is indicative of his own limitation.

Analytical criticism always seemed to him mere fault-finding, an attitude which is probably to some extent the result of the unsympathetic criticism (especially Poe's) which the publication of some of his poems aroused, but also a result of his natural traits of character. Longfellow's linguistic success is sufficient proof that he had a mind for details, yet critical analysis of technique was simply uncongenial to him. We hear the poet's opinions through Michael Angelo:

> This is no longer
> The golden age of art. Men have become
> Iconoclasts and critics. They delight not
> In what an artist does, but set themselves
> To censure what they do not comprehend.[4]

"Iconoclasts and critics" are blood-brothers according to Longfellow's way of thinking. "Many critics," he writes in his *Journal*, "are like woodpeckers, who, instead of enjoying the fruit and shadow of a tree, hop incessantly around the trunk, pecking holes in the bark to discover some little worm or other." [5]

While he had no theory of prosody, Longfellow did have a general theory of art (or perhaps it would be more

[3] XIV, 308   [4] VI, 139.   [5] XIV, 403.

accurate to say several theories), but his ideas on this
subject were progressive rather than static and have so
many divagations and debatable aspects that it would be
unwise to attempt an outline in the limited space of this
introduction. It is necessary, however, for us to note some general
phases of Longfellow's theories bearing upon poetic expression. The following extracts from his *Journal* may
serve our purpose, though they do not indicate the genetic
development of the poet's beliefs and attitudes in criticism.

No poet paints critically from nature; but the ideal world
of poetry is not only peopled with its own children, but is
shadowed and beautified with its own woods and waters. The
most striking features of different landscapes are taken and the
outline filled up by the imagination.[6]

It is this *religious* feeling, — this changing of the finite for
the infinite, this constant grasping after the invisible things of
another and higher world, — which marks the spirit of modern
literature . . . to the modern poet the world beyond the grave
presents itself with all the force of reality, and yet with all the
mystery of a dream.[7]

Nov. 14 [1845]. Felt more than ever to-day the difference
between my ideal home-world of Poetry, and the outer, actual,
tangible Prose world. When I go out of the precincts of my
study, down the village street to college, how the scaffoldings
about the Palace of Song come rattling and scattering down![8]

Vittoria, in *Michael Angelo,* says that:

> Art is the gift of God, and must be used
> Unto His glory. That in art is highest
> Which aims at this.[9]

And Michael Angelo defines art as:

> All that embellishes and sweetens life,
> And lifts it from the level of low cares
> Into the purer atmosphere of beauty;
> The faith in the Ideal . . .[10]

---

[6] XII, 45   [7] *Ibid.*, p. 186.   [8] XIII, 25.
[9] VI, 143.   [10] *Ibid.*, p. 144.

On another occasion, Longfellow quotes Cowley with approval: "The soul must be filled with bright and delightful ideas when it undertakes to communicate delight to others, which is the main end of poetry." [11]

To recapitulate, then, the chief end of poetry is to give delight, to build an ideal world of "escape" from a realistic world, and, finally, to honor God. This end is harmonious, in that lifting life "Into the purer atmosphere of . . . faith in the Ideal" would be, according to Longfellow's philosophy,[12] a faith in God. But the important thing for us is that the poet's highest aim is to build a "Palace of Song." The "Ivory Tower," the "escape" theory of the function of art, is nowhere more explicitly acknowledged than in Michael Angelo's definition. Whether or not Longfellow ever outgrew this theory is debatable, yet it is unmistakably an aid in understanding his prosodic attitudes, for no individualistic versification such as Emerson's, Whitman's, or Emily Dickinson's can answer Longfellow's purposes.

Strangely enough, despite Longfellow's every reason for disliking Poe, this theory is surprisingly like Poe's, even to its agreement that a poem should be short: "A story or a poem should be neither too short nor too long. . . . Real estate on Mount Parnassus should be sold by the foot, not by the acre." [13]   Judging by his practice, he did not believe that thirty lines is the proper length for a poem; but the important thing is that this statement, like Poe's, reveals a predilection for "mood," "atmosphere," and idealistic effect.

Still more important is the fact that the "Palace of Song" theory was not original with Longfellow. Poe divorced it from morality; Tennyson, perhaps the best European counterpart of Longfellow, wedded it to moral-

---

[11] XIII, 87.
[12] Longfellow's philosophy has never been sufficiently analyzed in a published study.
[13] XIV, 411, 412.

ity. It is the *Zeitgeist*, of which American Transcendentalism is one expression. But it was the European virus
that Longfellow caught. Professor Howard Mumford
Jones has pointed out the relation of Longfellow's language and thought to the "seraphic, sentimental, and
diffuse" poetry of Europe at the time when Longfellow
was abroad: "Words like Soul, the Divine, Man, Mind,
Progress, Humanity were on the lips of the learned and
artistic. One group of French writers was calling for a
return to the medieval papacy; another was hymning the
throne and the altar; a third was poetizing Christianity.
The Schlegels were become Catholic and mystical; form-
lessness was, with the German romantics, exalted into an
ideal; *Sehnsucht* and self-development were powerful
words. What Longfellow brought back with him was
this amorphous idealism, this vague belief in progress as
a world-law (he studied Herder), this inclination to solve
the poetical problem in terms of emotional moralizing as
the Germans solved it." [14]

We cannot expect Longfellow to "solve the poetical
problem" by a revolutionary versification. He will take
the conventional forms which he finds ready at hand, and
he will attempt to express his "emotional moralizings" as
lucidly, pleasantly, and musically as possible. We may
expect the versification of the Germans, the Scandina-
vians, and the Italians (among whom the young professor
spent much time studying) to influence his own technique.
But these foreign manners of poetic expression he will
assimilate without any detailed analyses or theorizings to
justify himself. The resulting versification must, of necessity, be eclectic; not a technique as "different" as Whitman's, or even Emerson's, and yet not altogether like the
old.

[14] *American Writers on American Literature* (New York, 1931),
Chapter IX, "Longfellow," by Howard Mumford Jones, pp. 115–116.

2. FOUR-STRESS IAMBIC VERSE

The measures which Longfellow used in his juvenile poetry were principally four-stress iambic, blank verse, heroic couplet, and ballad measure; in other words, the most conventional of all verse forms. These same measures are also found in great abundance in his mature verse, but they are more characteristic of his earlier period.

Some of Longfellow's most popular poems are in the four-stress iambic lines, such as *Excelsior* and *The Arrow and the Song*, written in 1841 and 1845 respectively. However, our discussion should begin with some of the earlier poems. *Woods in Winter* (1824–1825) is severely simple and regular, in *abab* stanzas:

> When winter winds are piercing chill,

Some lines, it is true, contain an initial spondee:

> Chill airs | and wintry winds! my ear

Yet the poem as a whole is very regular, with each two lines forming a thought-unit. *It Is Not Always May* is in exactly the same form, and is reminiscent of Herrick, both in versification and thought:

> Enjoy the Spring of Love and Youth,
> To some good angel leave the rest;
> For Time will teach thee soon the truth,
> There are no birds in last year's nest!

The Rainy Day (published in *Ballads and Other Poems*, 1841) is interesting for its resemblance in melody and mood to Poe's *The Raven* (1845). But there is probably no question of influence, especially since Poe's syncopated rhythms are trochaic, though both poems have double rime, alliteration, repetitions, and tone-colorings which are unmistakably similar.

> The day is cold, and dark, and dreary;
> It rains, and the wind is never weary;
> The vine still clings to the mouldering wall,
> But at every gust the dead leaves fall,
> And the day is dark and dreary.

The last line is a refrain. The first line is also repeated in the second stanza with the change of "day" to "life," and the second line is repeated verbatim. The second stanza, furthermore, echoes with a spiritual connotation the whole of the physical imagery of the first stanza, a technique which always appealed to Longfellow (*cf. The Arrow and the Song*).

Excelsior, except for its couplet rimes and single-word refrain, is quite similar in rhythm to the early *Woods in Winter*. "Anabatic" this monotonous tread has been called. *The Goblet of Life* is different mainly in its rime-scheme, $aaaa_4B_3$. And *The Fire of Drift-Wood* is so regular that it has a tendency to singsong:

> We spake of many a vanished scene,
> Of what we once had thought and said,
> Of what had been, and might have been,
> And who was changed, and who was dead;

Though the accentuation is practically the same, *Vittoria Colonna* has more variable breath-sweeps. One stanza, for example, has enjambment of every line except the last, the whole being read at one sweep:

> For death, that breaks the marriage band
> In others, only closer pressed
> The wedding-ring upon her hand
> And closer locked and barred her breast.

In the seventh stanza, parallelism modifies the cadence:

> The shadows of the chestnut trees,
> The odor of the orange blooms,
> The song of birds, and, more than these,
> The silence of deserted rooms;

Despite the fact that these poems are four-stress, they have much in common with the ballad. So also does "King Olaf's War-Horns," in *The Saga of King Olaf*, but here the ballad qualities are confined mainly to the subject-matter, the manner in which the conversation is used, and to some of the phraseology. The versification is totally unlike Longfellow's earlier lines.

The initial foot is characteristically trochaic, though it may be "clipped" iambic (*i.e.*, with the initial unstressed syllable omitted) where the line has only seven syllables. The stanza ends with two two-stress iambic, anapestic, or choriambic ($\diagup \times \times \diagup$) lines. We also find almost as much parallelism as in *Hiawatha*. *E.g.*, the first stanza:

> "Strike | the sails!" | King Ó | laf said;
> "Never | shall men | of mine | take flight;
> Never | away | from bat | tle I fled,
> Never away from my foes!
>   Let God dispose
> Of my life | in the fight!"

Sometimes the line has an initial iamb followed by an anapest:

> The blare | of the horns | began to ring,

Or the nine syllables may compose three anapests:

> In the midst, | but in front | of the rest.

Section XIX ends with two choriambs:

> Pledges to thee,
> Ólaf the King!

The octosyllabic couplets (varied by occasional alternate rime) of the preludes to *Tales of a Wayside Inn* are almost as different metrically from the four-stress lines of

The Saga of King Olaf (1862) as the *Saga* is from the early
Woods in Winter. The meter is fairly regular, but we
often find a metrical stress in the third foot; and parallelism is used extensively, as in the first "Prelude":

> And when he played, the atmosphere
>
> Was filled with magic, and the ear
>
> Caught echoes of that Harp of Gold,
>
> Whose music had so weird a sound,
>
> The hunted stag forgot to bound,
>
> The leaping rivulet backward rolled,
>
> The birds came down from bush and tree,
>
> The dead came from beneath the sea,
>
> The maiden to the harper's knee!

Here the parallelism and reiteration are probably a
development from the *Hiawatha* rhythm, which Longfellow had perfected about eight years earlier. There is
perhaps still more *Hiawatha* influence, however, in the
"clipped" seven-syllable couplets of *The Legend Beautiful.*

> In his chamber all alone,
>
> Kneeling on the floor of stone,
>
> Prayed the monk in deep contrition
>
> For his sins of indecision, . . .
> Not as crucified and slain,
> Not in agonies of pain,
> Not with bleeding hands and feet,
> Did the Monk his Master see;
> But as in the village street,
> In the house or harvest-field,
> Halt and lame and blind He healed,
> When He walked in Galilee.

3. EIGHT-STRESS VERSE

The Belfry of Bruges is a good illustration of the fact
that an eight-stress line is metrically very close to four-
stress verse. In the original volume of this title-poem,
The Belfry of Bruges was preceded by *Carillon* in four-
stress couplet and alternate rime, as in the first stanza:

> In the ancient town of Bruges,
>
> In the quaint old Flemish city,
>
> As the evening shades descended,
>
> Low and loud and sweetly blended,
>
> Low at times and loud at times,

The first two couplets of *The Belfry of Bruges:*

In the market-place of Bruges stands the belfry old and brown;
Thrice consumed and thrice rebuilded, still it watches o'er the
town.

As the summer morn was breaking, on that lofty tower I stood,
And the world threw off the darkness, like the weeds of widow-
hood.

Nuremberg, originally published in this volume, is in the
same meter:

Quaint old town of toil and traffic, quaint old town of art and
song,

It is not a very important point, but here the question
naturally arises as to whether this is trochaic or iambic
rhythm. Where the line ends with a double rime, like
"blended" — "descended," the scansion is undoubtedly

trochaic; and about half the rimes of *Carillon* are double.
Yet there are no double rimes in either *The Belfry of
Bruges* or *Nuremberg*, so that the pattern is technically
"clipped" octameter, or catalectic trochaic (*i.e.*, with the
final unaccented syllable missing). Those metrists who
like to scan with "rests" and "rest beats," by counting a
decided pause at either the cæsura or the line-end as the
equivalent of an accented or unaccented syllable, would
make either the fourth foot a dactyl or the fifth an iamb.

Quaint old town of toil and traffic, (×) quaint old town of art
and song. (×)

It must be confessed, however, that these lines do have
practically the same lilt as *Hiawatha*, which is unmistakably trochaic. Here it is perhaps safer merely to label
the rhythm as four-stress or 4 + 4, without attempting
to name the meter.

A more important observation is that Longfellow's
eight-stress line, like Poe's (in *The Raven*), tends to syncopate:

Quaint old town of toil and traffic, quaint old town of art and
song,

To some extent, this is also true of the four-stress lines:

In the ancient town of Bruges,

In the quaint old Flemish city,

But the reader is more likely to syncopate the longer line.
And this is the chief difference between these two measures.

4. BALLAD MEASURE

The Wreck of the Hesperus (1839) is Longfellow's closest
imitation of the folk ballad, both as to form and subject-
matter. The genuine folk ballad is in 4 + 3 measure,

riming *abcb*, and has a two-line thought movement, an evidence that its natural rhythmical unit is seven stresses.[15]

In this ballad, Longfellow also uses pleonasm, tag-phrases from the folk poems, inversions, alliterative pairs, and typical ballad dialogue. All of these are illustrated in the following extract:

It was the schooner Hesperus,
  That sailed the wintry sea;
And the skipper had taken his little daughter,[16]
  To bear him company.

. . . .

Then up and spake an old Sailor,[16]
  Had sailed to the Spanish Main,
"I pray thee, put into yonder port,
  For I fear a hurricane.

"Last night, the moon had a golden ring,
  And to-night no moon we see!"
The skipper, he blew a whiff from his pipe,
  And a scornful laugh laughed he.

. . . .

"Come hither! come hither! my little daughter,
  And do not tremble so;
For I can weather the roughest gale
  That ever wind did blow."

. . . .

"O father! I hear the church-bells ring,
  Oh say, what may it be?"
"'Tis a fog-bell on a rock-bound coast!"
  And he steered for the open sea.

[15] Some scholars believe that the ballad measure developed from the old "Romance verse" (with eight stresses, the pause at the end of the second line counting for the eighth stress in ballad measure). *Cf.* Johannes C. Andersen, *The Laws of Verse* (Cambridge University Press, 1928), p. 60.

[16] "Daughter" and "Sailor" are, of course, attempts at archaism, though the distorted pronunciation also helps to maintain the regular

Similes, too, are especially characteristic of the style:

> Blue were her eyes *as* the fairy-flax,
> Her cheeks *like* the dawn of day,
> And her bosom white *as* the hawthorn buds,
> That ope in the month of May.

Some critics have objected to so many similes, calling them monotonous, yet the whole poem is monotonous if judged by any standards except those of the folk ballad, which the poet was obviously and deliberately imitating.

Though the rhythm of this ballad is predominantly iambic, the main requirement of the pattern (as in the folk ballads) is that the line have either four or three primary accents (depending upon its position in the stanza). Of course an accent may be forced, as in the intended pronunciation of "hurricane." But the number of unaccented syllables is not fixed. Anapestic feet are common, as in:

And he steered | for the op | en sea.

Or we may find the wholly anapestic line:

And the skip | per had tak | en his lit | tle daughter,

Yet the rhythm and tempo of the line are not disturbed by these trisyllabic feet, since the two unaccented syllables are usually light enough to be pronounced rapidly. And, after all, the ballad is a singing rhythm; it has a tune which forces itself upon the reader willy-nilly.

The Beleaguered City is a more sophisticated ballad, in the same rhythm but without most of the popular ballad tags and mannerisms. *Victor Galbraith* is more like a folk poem in its reiteration and refrains, yet is a "literary" poem:

---

beat of the singsong rhythm. Here we use the "metrical stress" reversed, thus, "ᶜ," because the poet apparently intended to force the primary stress on the final syllable.

He looked at the earth, he looked at the sky,
He looked at the files of musketry,
    Victor Galbraith!

The rime-scheme, moreover, is $aa_4B_2aa_4bB_4$, so that it is not strictly ballad in form.

The Village Blacksmith is in the conventional ballad measure, but it is not an imitation of the folk ballad traditions.

Week in, week out, from morn till night,
    You can hear his bellows blow;
You can hear him swing his heavy sledge,
    With measured beat and slow,
Like a sexton ringing the village bell,
    When the evening sun is low.

Its severe simplicity of diction and regularity of rhythm is likely to make us underestimate the technical achievements of this well-known poem. There are only two inversions in the whole piece: "a mighty man is he" and "Onward through life he goes." The natural speech and syntax of *The Village Blacksmith* was practically unique in American versification in 1839.

The lyric, *My Lost Youth*, is related to the ballad measure, though the rime-scheme is $a_4b_3aa_4bcDD_3E_4$. The refrain is especially interesting, the first line containing a bacchic ($\times$ / /) plus a minor ionic ($\times \times$ / /); the second line beginning with an anapest and ending with a spondee:

"A boy's will | is the wind's will,
And the thoughts | of youth | are long, | long thoughts."

The possessives, however, demand a certain degree of pause (the length depending upon the reader's interpretation), and the first line can be scanned with metrical "silences":

A bóy's (×) will ís the wínd's (×) wíll,

Other related stanzaic forms are *Endymion*, aa_4bb_3; the 5 + 3 measure of *Hymn to the Night*, *The Warden of the Cinque Ports*, *Hawthorne*, etc.

5. THREE-STRESS VERSE

Of the three-stress verse, *The Day is Done* (*abcb*) is nearest the ballad form, *The Witnesses* (*abab*) coming second. *The Skeleton in Armor* is better known, but its triplet rimes and initial trochees place it far apart from ballad rhythms. Practically all the rimes are masculine, though here and there a feminine rime gives a final trochaic foot:

Bléw the fóam líghtly.

But most of these feminine rimes occur in two-stress lines, as:

To hear my stóry . . .

Laugh as he háiled us.

The scheme is $aaa_3b_2ccc_3b_2$, in spite of the fact that the *b*-lines often contain three accents, and spondees are not uncommon in the other lines, as in the opening verse:

"Spéak! spéak! thou féarful guést!

A characteristic stanza is the following:

"As with his wíngs aslánt,

Sáils the | fíerce cór | morant,

Séeking some rócky háunt,

With his préy láden, —

So tóward the ópen máin,

Béating to séa agáin,

Through the | wíld húr | ricăne,

Bóre Ì the máiden.

The short lines, triplet rimes, winding constructions —
with appositives, phrase modifiers, and inverted predi-
cates — are jerky, tedious, and more monotonous than the
often-condemned trochees of *Hiawatha*. The meter may
be labeled either "clipped" iambic trimeter or catalectic
trochaic (as one chooses), though the masculine rimes
would seem to indicate the former.

Another illustration of precisely the same meter and
stanza is section XVII, "King Svend of the Forked
Beard," in *The Saga of King Olaf*.

6. THE ANAPEST

We have already observed Longfellow's use of occasional
anapestic feet in his four-stress verse and his ballad measure, the third line of *The Wreck of the Hesperus*, for
instance, being entirely anapestic. In *The Saga of King
Olaf* (written between 1849 and 1860), Longfellow definitely accepted this rhythm, as in section IV, "Queen
Sigrid the Haughty":

The flóor | with tás | sels of fíre | was besprént,

Fíll | ing the róom | with their frág | rant scént.

She héard | the birds síng, | she sáw | the sun shíne,

The áir of súm | mer was swéet | er than wíne.

Incidentally, the number of sibilant alliterations in this
poem is surprisingly large. For example, counting alliterations only in accented syllables:

> She heard the birds *s*ing, she *s*aw the *s*un *sh*ine,
> The air of *s*ummer was *s*weeter than wine.

> Like a *sw*ord without *sc*abbard the bright river lay . . .

> The *sw*ord would be *sh*eathed, the river be *s*panned . . .

> *S*ounded in*c*essantly the waterfall . . .

> And *s*wore to be true as the *s*tars above.

But a complete list is too long to be given here.

Modern poets seldom miss the opportunity of using the galloping anapest for any subject involving fast riding on horseback (*cf.* Freneau's *A New England Sabbath-Day Chace* and Browning's *How They Brought the Good News from Ghent to Aix*). It would be difficult to imagine *Paul Revere's Ride* in any other meter. The main metrical variations of the poem are illustrated in the first few lines, *viz.*, an initial iamb, an initial accented syllable, or a verse partly or completely iambic. The number of syllables, therefore, can range from eight to twelve, but ten is the usual number.

> Lis | ten, my child | ren, and you | shall hear
> Of the mid | night ride | of Paul | Revere, . . .
> He said | to his friend, | "If the Bri | tish march
> By land | or sea | from the town | to-night,
> Hang a lan | tern aloft | in the bel | fry arch
> Of the North | Church tow | er as a sig | nal light, —

The cæsura has a tendency to fall exactly in the middle of the line, or as nearly as possible in the middle of an eleven-syllable verse, dividing it into two sections of two stresses each:

> A hurry of hoofs / in a village street,
> A shape in the moonlight, / a bulk in the dark, etc.

Seldom, though, do we find Longfellow using the ana-pest in this manner.   It is more often found in such rhythms as those of *The Mother's Ghost,* where the number of accents (four) is constant but the placing of the stresses and the number of syllables is variable (hardly as free as in Coleridge's *Christabel,* yet with somewhat the same technique).

7. RIMED TROCHAIC METER

In sections 2 and 3 we raised the question whether the seven-syllable lines of *The Legend Beautiful* and *The Belfry of Bruges* should be scanned as trochaic or iambic. The question would seem to be easy: do the lines *sound* trochaic?   We must admit that they do have a buoyant, lilting cadence similar to unmistakable trochaic verse. Hence, the distinction is largely technical.   The same question arises with respect to Milton's *L'Allegro,* over half of which has seven-syllable, four-stress lines, as in

> Come, and trip it as ye go
> On the light fantastic toe.

Professor Pyre regards these lines as trochaic,[17] but teachers of Milton's poetry frequently call them "clipped" iambic. The fact that nearly half of the lines are plainly iambic octosyllabic couplets makes the "clipped iambic" scan-sion easier, but it does not settle the question.   It seems advisable, therefore, to leave the exact classification open for further debate.

But *A Psalm of Life* begins with trochaic lines, and there appears to be no reason why we should not classify the meter of the whole poem as definitely trochaic:

> Tell me not, in mournful numbers,
> Life is but an empty dream! —

[17] J. F. A. Pyre, *A Short Introduction to English Versification* (New York, 1929), p. 37.

Moreover, every stanza has feminine rimes in the first and fourth lines of each quatrain; so that fifty per cent of the poem is in perfect trochees — for the meter is very regular. Yet the fact that the rhythm is so regularly trochaic makes this one of the most monotonous of poems.

> Life is real! Life is earnest!
> And the grave is not its goal;
> Dust thou art, to dust returnest,
> Was not spoken of the soul.

The trite diction and the metronomic sway lose their lyrical note and remind us of the singsong chanting of a pagan charm, an impression certainly very far from the poet's intention. *Footsteps of Angels* is not much better, except that it is not quite so familiar to most of us. *Flowers* is different only in that it has five feet to the line, a fact which explains why it is slightly less monotonous than *A Psalm of Life*, since the cæsura in a five-stress line cannot divide the verse into two exactly equal parts:

> Spake full well, / in language quaint and olden,
> One who dwelleth / by the castled Rhine,
> When he called the flowers, / so blue and golden,
> Stars, / that in earth's firmament / do shine.

The four-stress trochaic quatrain is perhaps most appropriately used in *Drinking Song*, which has feminine rime throughout. Other trochaic quatrains, with rimes *abcb*, are *Walter von der Vogelweide*, *The Secret of the Sea*, *Gaspar Becerra*, and *Pegasus in Pound*. "Einer Tamberskelver," section XX of *The Saga of King Olaf*, is in 4 + 3 trochaics, and *Seaweed* is in a 4 + 2 form.

Rimed trochees may be said to be fairly characteristic of that period of Longfellow's versification between about 1839, when he wrote *A Psalm of Life*, and about 1845, the date of his unrimed *To an Old Danish Song Book*, a precursor of the *Hiawatha* versification. The influence of these trochaic experiments can be traced throughout most of the remainder of Longfellow's poetic career.

8. UNRIMED TROCHEES

Longfellow's first experiment with unrimed trochees is *To an Old Danish Song Book* (1845), referred to above, in 3-4-4-2-stress quatrains, which are different from the earlier rimed trochees only in their greater tendency to repeat the thought of one line in a following appositive, thus anticipating the parallelism of the later unrimed trochees.

> Welcome, my old friend,
> Welcome to a foreign fireside,
> While the sullen gales of autumn
> Shake the windows.
>   .   .   .   .
> There are marks of age,
> There are thumb-marks on thy margin,
> Made by hands that clasped thee rudely,
> At the alehouse.

Tegner's Drapa, in two- and three-stress six-line stanzas, has many trochaic lines, but it is predominantly iambic, though an occasional stanza has initial trochees in practically every line. The two-stress lines occur anywhere in the stanza except in the final verse. Some stanzas remind us of modern "free verse":

> They laid him in his ship,
> With horse and harness,
> As on a funeral pyre.
> Odin placed
> A ring upon his finger,
> And whispered in his ear.

Here the arrangement in short lines seems purely arbitrary, each sentence containing eight stresses; but only about half of the stanzas break in this manner, parallelism being more common. Yet all of these experiments in trochees and unrimed short lines are merely a preparation

for Longfellow's one sustained effort in this form, *The Song of Hiawatha*, written in 1854–1855.
Many literary battles have been waged over the versification of this poem. In Longfellow's day, his critics accused him of having plagiarized the meter from the Finnish epic, *Kalevala*. And his friend Freiligrath, without of course any charges of dishonesty, wrote, "The very moment I looked into the book I exclaimed, —

> Launawatar, Frau die alte,

and was laughing with you again over the pages of the *Finnische Runen*, as thirteen years ago on the Rhine. The characteristic feature, which shows that you have fetched the metre from the Finns, is the *parallelism* adopted so skillfully and so gracefully in *Hiawatha*." [18] But in his diary Longfellow commented, "He does not seem to be aware that the parallelism, or repetition, is as much the characteristic of Indian as of Finnish song." [19]

Parallelism is apparently found in most primitive poetry, and most translations of the Indian songs have it (*cf.* Mary Austin's *American Rhythms*). It is the main rhythmical principle of biblical poetry. And at the same time that Longfellow was using it in *Hiawatha*, Walt Whitman was composing his first edition of *Leaves of Grass*, in which parallelism and reiteration completely take the place of conventional rime and "meter," though the critics were much quicker to recognize Longfellow's use of repetitive devices (no doubt because they were used with a "meter" that they could recognize).

The versification of *The Song of Hiawatha* is so nearly the same throughout that it makes little difference where we take our illustrations; but section X, "Hiawatha's Wooing," is perhaps the most familiar part. The opening lines have parallel metaphors and similes, balance or antithesis of one half-line against the other, ending with a one-line summary. We may label this parallelism *aabbc:*

[18] II, 117.   [19] *Ibid.*

> "As unto the bow the cord is,
> So unto the man is woman;
> Though she bends him, she obeys him,
> Though she draws him, yet she follows;
> Useless each without the other!"

The pause at the end of each line reminds us of Whitman, notwithstanding the fact that some of Longfellow's verses are enjambed, as in:

> Hardly touched his eagle-feathers
> As he entered at the doorway.

And of course the regularity of meter — it is entirely trochaic throughout the whole poem — is utterly different from *Leaves of Grass.* Furthermore, Longfellow uses less repetition of initial words and phrases than Whitman, and his parallelism is confined mainly to two consecutive lines, or sometimes three, as in the following:

a	Then uprose the Laughing Water,
a	From the ground fair Minnehaha,
a	Laid aside her mat unfinished,
b	Brought forth food and set before them,
c	Water brought them from the brooklet,
b	Gave them food in earthen vessels,
c	Gave them drink in bowls of bass-wood,
d	Listened while the guest was speaking,
d	Listened while her father answered,
e	But not once her lips she opened,
e	Nor a single word she uttered.

a	"After many years of warfare,
a	Many years of strife and bloodshed,
b	There is peace between the Ojibways
(b)	And the tribe of the Dacotahs."
c	Thus continued Hiawatha,
c	And then added, speaking slowly,
d	"That this peace may last forever,
d	And our hands be clasped more closely,
d	And our hearts be more united,

> e Give me as my wife this maiden,
> e Minnehaha, Laughing Water,
> e Loveliest of Dacotah women!"

The antithetical half-lines often form a sort of internal parallelism:

(1) Day is restless,   (2) night is quiet,
(1) Man imperious,   (2) woman feeble; etc.

Oliver Wendell Holmes in his criticism of the versification of this poem appears to sum up pretty well both its advantages and disadvantages: "The eight-syllable trochaic verse of *Hiawatha*, like the eight-syllable iambic verse of *The Lady of the Lake*, and other of Scott's poems, has a fatal facility, which I have elsewhere endeavored to explain on physiological principles. The recital of each line uses up the air of one natural expiration, so that we read, as we naturally do, eighteen or twenty lines in a minute, without disturbing the normal rhythm of breathing, which is also eighteen or twenty breaths to the minute. The standing objection to this is that it makes the octosyllabic verse too easy writing and too slipshod reading. Yet in this most frequently criticized composition the poet has shown a subtle sense of the requirements of his simple story of a primitive race, in choosing the most fluid of measures, that lets the thought run through it in easy sing-song, such as oral tradition would be sure to find on the lips of the story-tellers of the wigwam." [20]

9. THE ODE

In his diary, Longfellow refers to the poem called *To a Child* as "Ode to a Child." And its form is practically the same as that used by Emerson in his "odes," that is, paragraphs of different lengths composed of two-, three-, four-, and five-stress lines, occurring at irregular intervals

[20] "Remarks at Meeting of Massachusetts Historical Society," April 13, 1882. Quoted in "Notes" of the *Poetical Works*, II, 383.

and riming either in couplets or alternately, the alternate
rime being less frequent. The rhythm is iambic, though
many lines have initial trochees.

Rain in Summer differs merely in having fewer five-
stress lines. The eighth section of *To a Child* is very
nearly heroic couplets, but *Rain in Summer* has only an
occasional long line, such as:

> Like a ríver dówn the gútter róars

The ten- and eleven-syllable lines are usually four-stress,
as in:

> From eárth to heáven, from heáven to eárth; . . .
> In the rápid and rúshing ríver of Tíme.

Longfellow's best and probably most famous ode is
The Building of the Ship. It is different from the other
odes in several minor details. One is the use of an opening four-stress trochaic quatrain as a sort of "text,"
which is repeated as a refrain in the middle of the poem:

> "Build me straight, O worthy Master!
> Stanch and strong, a goodly vessel,
> That shall laugh at all disaster,
> And with wave and whirlwind wrestle!"

Where the lines are most irregular, with frequent initial
trochaic feet (or "clipped" iambs), the rhythm is as
monotonous as most of Longfellow's other four-stress
verse, though it has a certain vigor that the trochaic
rhythms lack:

> Day by day the vessel grew,
> With timbers fashioned strong and true,
> Stemson and keelson and sternson-knee,

Some lines are also onomatopoetic:

> And around it columns of smoke, upwreathing,
> Rose from the boiling, bubbling, seething

Caldron, that glowed,
And overflowed,
With the black tar, heated for the sheathing.
And amid the clamors
Of clattering hammers,
He who listened heard now and then
The song of the Master and his men: —

One of the most effective passages is the freest in number of stresses and accentuation:

Long ago,
In the deer-haunted forests of Maine,
When upon the mountain and plain
Lay the snow,
They fell — those lordly pines!
These grand, majestic pines!
'Mid shouts and cheers
The jaded steers,
Panting beneath the goad,
Dragged down the weary, winding road
Those captive kings so straight and tall,
To be shorn of their streaming hair,
And naked and bare,
To feel the stress and strain
Of the wind and the reeling main,
Whose roar
Would remind them forevermore
Of their native forests they should not see again.

Some of the lines are longer than those of Emerson's *Threnody*, but the poem is in the same tradition.

10. DIMETER AND OTHER SHORT LINES

Longfellow used dimeter very little, but "The Challenge of Thor" in *The Saga of King Olaf* (section I) is mainly unrimed two-stress trochaic, though the initial foot is often a dactyl, occasionally an iamb, and some lines have three stresses. There is practically no enjambment, and an abundance of parallelism. The first stanza runs:

> I am the God Thor,
>
> I am the War God,
>
> I am the Thunderer!
>
> Here in my Northland,
>
> My fastness and fortress,
>
> Reign I forever!

The structure and rhythm remind us of the old Anglo-Saxon epic line, with its two stresses to the half-line, the four alliterative accents being divided by a very emphatic cæsura. Longfellow's translation of *Beowulf*, however (see *Beowulf's Expedition to Heort*), is less vigorous, though metrically very much like "The Challenge of Thor." Section XXII, "The Nun of Nidaros," is also in the same rhythm. It contains fewer pure trochaic lines, but the poet was evidently trying to follow the Scandinavian epic rhythms, so that the meter is intentionally rugged and rough. Yet it is interesting to notice the large number of amphibrachs in this poem:

> The Virgin | and Mother . . .
>
> Of war that | thou wieldest! . . .
>
> For rain has | been falling . . .
>
> That God at | their fountains . . .

These unrimed dimeters naturally take their place along with the *Hiawatha* blank trochees as Scandinavian and Germanic influences on American versification. Whether or not they had any influence on the evolution of modern American "free verse" is a complicated question, and inappropriate for the present considerations, but they are, far more than the *Hiawatha* rhythm, a step in the direction of "free cadences."

II. THE HEXAMETER

Since the sixteenth century various English poets have attempted to imitate the classical "quantitative" hexameters, each attempt arousing a new storm of criticism. The study of English prosody, in fact, really began with the criticism of English hexameters. It is not surprising, therefore, that Longfellow's attempts to use this measure should cause great excitement among the scholars and critics.

The most caustic part of Poe's *Rationale of Verse* is devoted to showing that "Dr. Longfellow's" hexameters are simply English dactyls. And Poe was right in his contention that they are not classical,[21] for the very nature of the English language compels our meters to be based primarily on accent, not "quantity" or length of syllables. Our rhythms, in other words, are achieved by the interchange of stressed and unstressed syllables. But the mere fact that the English language is unlike the Greek is no necessary reason for refusing to call Longfellow's six-foot (or six-stress) lines with trochaic substitutions hexameters, that is, *English* hexameters. As a matter of fact, Longfellow's models were not the classical hexameters but those of Goethe's *Hermann und Dorothea*.

The rules of the hexameter prohibit the use of a trochee for a dactyl anywhere except in the last foot, but a spondee

[21] *Cf.* Robert Bridges, *Milton's Prosody*, with *A Chapter on Accentual Verse* (Oxford University Press, 1921), "The Accentual Hexameter," pp. 105–112.

may be substituted anywhere.   In the Latin and Greek hexameter, the fifth foot is regularly a dactyl and the sixth a spondee.   Genuine spondees are, as Poe claimed, rarer in English than in Latin and Greek.   Most of our spondaic words are compounds, such as "ale-house," and we have a tendency to give a primary accent to one element of a dissyllabic compound and a secondary stress to the other (though of course a primary plus a fairly strong secondary stress may be accepted as approximately spondaic).   Yet Poe's objection that scarcity of spondaic words makes English spondees rare is unfounded, since a good spondee is usually composed of two monosyllables, like "cold sky."

Longfellow's early hexameters are represented by his translation of *Children of the Lord's Supper*, from the Swedish poet, Tegner:

Lóve is | lífe, but | hátred is | déath. Not | fáther, nor | móther

Lóved you, as | Gód has | lóved you; | for 't was that | you may

    be | háppy

Gáve He his | ónly | Són. When He | bówed dòwn his | héad in

    the | déath-hóur

Sólemnìzed | Lóve its | tríumph; the | sácrifice | thèn was

    com | pléted.

That the poet himself was not altogether satisfied with these hexameters is indicated by his own comment: "The translation is literal, perhaps to a fault.   In no instance have I done the author a wrong by introducing into his work any supposed improvements or embellishments of my own.   I have preserved even the measure, that inexorable hexameter, in which, it must be confessed, the motions of the English muse are not unlike those of a prisoner dancing to the music of his chains; and perhaps, as Dr. Johnson said of the dancing dog, 'the wonder is not that she should do it so well but that she should do it at all.'" (Introductory note to the poem.)

But to return to the quotation. Four of the six feet of the first line are trochaic; "solemnized" in the last line is a very awkward dactyl; and "bowed down his" in the preceding line is exceedingly questionable, as is, indeed, the accentuation of the whole verse, making the scansion unsatisfactory.

Children of the Lord's Supper was written in 1841. Four years later, Longfellow handled the hexameter with much greater ease, as he himself realized; because in a note in his *Journal* for October 17, 1845, he wrote: "Retouched . . . *To the Driving Cloud* in hexameters, — better than translation from Tegner." The chief differences in the versification of the two poems are (1) more dactyl feet, (2) greater ease in handling the rhythm, (3) fewer full internal stops, and (4) the use of parallelism in *To the Driving Cloud:*

Glóomy and | dárk árt | thóu, Ó | chíef of the | míghty | Ómahàs;
Glóomy and | dárk as the | dríving | clóud, whóse | náme thou
    hást | táken! . . .
Hów canst thou | wálk these | stréets, who hast | tród the gréen |
    túrf of the | práiries?
Hów canst thou | bréathe this | áir, who hast | bréathed the
    swèet | áir of the | móuntains?

Some final spondees are "Elkhorn," "Blackfeet," "red man," "camp-fires," "horse-race," "east-wind," "wig-wams."

Evangéline, written in 1845–1847, shows an even greater mastery of the form. Trochees are still substituted very freely, but we find more spondees, extensive alliteration (one evidence that Longfellow is writing in his natural style), and more control over the cæsuras:

Onward o'er | sunken | sands, through a | wilderness | sombre with | forests,

Day after | day they | glided a down the | turbulent | river;

Night after | night, by their | blazing | fires, en | camped on its | borders.

Now through | rushing | chutes, a | mong green | islands, where | plumelike

Cotton-trees | nodded their | shadowy | crests, they | swept with the | current,

Then e|merged into | broad la | goons, where | silvery | sand-bars

Lay in the | stream, and a | long the | wimpling | waves of their | margin,

Shining with | snow-white | plumes, large | flocks of | pelicans | waded.

Some examples of alliterative pairs are:

> Then in his *p*lace, at the *p*row . . .
> And, as a *s*ignal *s*ound . . .
> . . . *b*lew a *b*last on his *b*ugle.
> Breaking the *s*eal of *s*ilence, . . .
> . . . *d*ied in the *d*istance, . . .
> . . . as of *w*ave or *w*ind in the forest,

An objection sometimes brought against the hexameter is that the cæsura, as in the alexandrine, divides the line too equally. It is noticeable that the cæsuras in *Evangeline* are largely feminine, and that the line has often not one, but two cæsural pauses. This is not ordinarily true of Longfellow's earlier hexameters.

The greatest development in the versification of *The*

Courtship of Miles Standish (1857–1858) is the use of initial reiteration of words and phrases, especially in couplet groups at frequent intervals, such as:

Beautiful were his feet on the purple tops of the mountains;
Beautiful on the sails of the Mayflower riding at anchor, . . .

Meekly, in voices subdued, the chapter was read from the Bible,
Meekly the prayer was begun, but ended in fervent entreaty! . . .

Often the heart of the youth had burned and yearned to embrace him,
Often his lips had essayed to speak, imploring for pardon; . . .

Joined in the talk at the door, with Stephen and Richard and Gilbert,
Joined in the morning prayer, and in the reading of Scriptures,

It is interesting to conjecture whether the biblical tone of much of this poem influenced the use of initial reiteration and parallelism. (See Chapter VIII.)

Toward the end of *The Rationale of Verse*, Poe printed some of Longfellow's hexameters as prose, and commented: "There! — That is respectable prose; and it will incur no danger of ever getting its character ruined by anybody's mistaking it for verse." And it must be admitted that many of the hexameters do read better as prose.

Kreymborg also criticizes the "far-fetched similes or mixed metaphors," which he calls a "fatal facility" that led the poet "into easy lines and lines filled out by sound regardless of meaning." [22] He lists the following examples: "The pewter plates on the dresser caught and reflected the flame, as shields of armies the sunshine." "As in a church, when the chant of the choir at intervals ceases, footfalls are heard in the aisles, or words of the priest at the altar, so, in each pause of the song, with measured

[22] Alfred Kreymborg, *Our Singing Strength* (New York, 1929), p. 104.

motion the clock clicked." "Bent like a laboring oar, that toils in the surf of the ocean, bent, but not broken, by age was the form of the notary public." Somewhat questionable, too, is the euphuistic expanded metaphor of section VI of *The Courtship of Miles Standish.*

The hexameters of *Elizabeth* (1873), the theologian's tale in *Tales of a Wayside Inn,* have fewer eccentricities than the earlier verse in this form, but present no new important metrical characteristics. On the whole, Longfellow's hexameters are appropriate for his purposes, and that is the important thing.

12. BLANK VERSE

Longfellow's lyrics, ballads, and didactic poems are far more familiar to the general reader than his blank verse. It is not commonly known, in fact, that he wrote some exceptionally good unrimed pentameter. Yet even in 1824–1825 he could handle this measure with the ease and skill of Bryant in *Thanatopsis,* though, it must be admitted, without the sonority of Bryant. *Autumn* begins:

> With what a glory comes and goes the year!
> The buds | of spring, | those beau | tiful har | bingers
> Of sunny skies and cloudless times, enjoy
> Life's new | ness, and | earth's gar | niture | spread out;
> And when the silver habit of the clouds
> Comes down upon the autumn sun, and with
> A so | ber glad | ness the | old year | takes up
> His bright inheritance of golden fruits,
> A pomp and pageant fill the splendid scene.

The metrical licenses here are: (1) a redundant syllable or trisyllabic foot, as in the second line; (2) a light ending, such as "with" in the sixth line; (3) an occasional line heavy with spondees, such as the fourth; and (4) the unusual pyrrhic in the seventh line.   Of these licenses, only the third and fourth are especially unusual, though it must be confessed that lines four and seven are hardly in the blank verse tradition.   But such lines as these occur seldom in Longfellow's blank verse.

The enjambment; the long breath-sweeps varied by shorter ones (*cf.* especially lines six, seven, and eight); and easy-flowing rhythm (even where it is difficult to scan) show mastery of the form.   But Longfellow's dramatic blank verse displays an even greater ease and fluency, whatever may be said of these pieces as drama. In *The Spanish Student* (1840), for instance, we find such natural, conversational, smoothly cadenced verse as the following:

> *Don C.*   Nay, not to be won at all!
> The only virtue that a Gypsy prizes
> Is chastity.   That is her only virtue.
> Dearer than life she holds it.   I remember
> A Gypsy woman, a vile, shameless bawd,
> Whose craft was to betray the young and fair;
> And yet this woman was above all bribes.
> And when a noble lord, touched by her beauty,
> The wild and wizard beauty of her race,
> Offered her gold to be what she made others,
> She turned upon him, with a look of scorn,
> And smote him in the face!
>   I, 1.

Occasionally (in the same drama), we find the poet playing with a simile almost in the Shakespearean manner:

> As drops of rain fall into some dark well,
> And from below comes a scarce audible sound,
> So fall our thoughts into the dark Hereafter,
> And their mysterious echo reaches us.
>   I, 3.

The blank verse of the later dramas, however, reveals scarcely any improvements, though it was really depth of thought and not greater facility of versification that the poet needed to improve his dramatic technique. *Michael Angelo, The Masque of Pandora*, and even parts of the much-abused *Christus* contain as excellent blank verse, technically, as can be found in nineteenth-century American poetry.

13. HEROIC COUPLET

Longfellow's heroic couplets are metrically much like his blank verse, with perhaps an average of somewhat more restricted enjambment and less skilfully varied breath-sweeps, two almost inevitable influences of the couplet rimes. Even the early heroic couplets have considerable enjambment and are facile and unaffected. Their greatest fault is the cliché-habit, but none of Longfellow's poetry is entirely free from this blemish. The 1824 (1825?) *Sunrise on the Hills* begins:

> I stood upon the hills, when heaven's wide arch
> Was glorious with the sun's returning march,
> And woods were brightened, and soft gales
> Went forth to kiss the sun-clad vales.[23]

Longfellow's tendency to end the heroic couplet with a spondee, or at least secondary-plus-primary accents, as in "wide arch" and "soft gales," may be labeled an eccentricity. Yet it is not confined to any particular poems. Some other examples are:

> Holding a naked sword in his right hand. . . .
> And rising, and uplifting his gray head, . . .
> Of something there unknown, which men call death.[24]

> And in Thy name refuses to go hence!"
> The Lord replied, "My Angels, be not wroth; [25]

> Thyself unseen, and with an unseen sword,[26]

---

[23] The remainder of this poem is not in heroic couplets, but in alternate pentameter and octosyllabics.
[24] *Tales of a Wayside Inn*, p. 214.   [25] *Ibid.*   [26] *Ibid.*

The main difference between the early heroic couplets and the later ones is an increase of parallelism, as seen, *e.g.*, in *King Robert of Sicily* and *Lady Wentworth*. The former is undated, but was probably written somewhere around 1862. *Lady Wentworth* was finished in 1871, and contains extensive parallelism and epanaphora, as in:

> The robin, the forerunner of the spring,
> The bluebird with his jocund carolling,
> The restless swallows building in the eaves,
> The golden buttercups, the grass, the leaves,
> The lilacs tossing in the winds of May,

In fact, the whole poem makes considerable use of Whitman's favorite device of "changing figures." [27]

Morituri Salutamus, an "occasional" poem written to celebrate the fiftieth anniversary of Longfellow's Bowdoin College class, has often been applauded for its informal ease and grace, praise which applies to the versification as well as to the thought. Take, for instance, the poet's consoling words to his aged friends:

> Chaucer, at Woodstock with the nightingales,
> At sixty wrote the Canterbury Tales; [28]
> Goethe at Weimar, toiling to the last,
> Completed Faust when eighty years were past.
> These are indeed exceptions; but they show
> How far the gulf-stream of our youth may flow
> Into the arctic regions of our lives,
> Where little else than life itself survives.

14. SONNETS

Between 1842 and 1882, Longfellow averaged about two sonnets a year, including translations, all of which are competent and many of which are technically excellent.

---

[27] *Cf.* Chapter VIII, § 11.

[28] A misstatement; Chaucer did not write the *C. T.* at Woodstock. Longfellow was probably thinking of Chaucer's son.

All of his sonnets are in the Italian form (*abba abba cdcdcd,* or *cdecde*).   In his translations, the rime-scheme of the sestet is sometimes erratic, as in *Tomorrow,* from the Spanish of Lope de Vega, which rimes *abba cddc effgeg.* But the original sonnets are very regular, *cdecde* being the favorite sestet rimes.   *Autumn* (1845) is the only exception, the sestet ending with a couplet, *ff.*

Longfellow's sonnets are also typically Italian in the management of full stops and thought-groups.   Each quatrain of the octave ends with either a period or a semi-colon.   Enjambment within the quatrain is used freely, but seldom does the fourth line run on into the fifth.   The octave and sestet divisions are consistently observed.

The 1870 decade may be called Longfellow's "sonnet period," for most of the contents of *A Book of Sonnets* were written during this period, about half of them in 1874.

It is natural that different people should have different choices as to Longfellow's best sonnets.   The *Divina Commedia* sonnets, however, are usually recognized as excellent.   Yet Longfellow was nearly always graceful in using the sonnet form for complimentary and eulogistic purposes; and *Chaucer, Shakespeare, Milton, Keats,* and *The Poets* surely deserve to rank among the poet's best. *Chaucer,* incidentally, is unusual in that the first full stop occurs not at the end of the line but in the middle:

> An old man in a lodge within a park;
> The chamber walls depicted all around
> With portraitures of huntsman, hawk, and hound,
> And the hurt deer. // He listeneth to the lark,

Shakespeare has semicolons after the third foot in the third line and in the middle of the second foot of the fourth line; and the first period in *Milton* comes at the end of the octave.   These minor details show that the late sonnets are not so precise in form as the earlier ones.   The grand sweep of the octave of *Milton* is especially effective and appropriate, reflecting as it does a Miltonic influence on Longfellow's own versification:

> I pace the sounding sea-beach and behold
>   How the voluminous billows roll and run,
>   Upheaving and subsiding, while the sun
>   Shines through their sheeted emerald far unrolled,
> And the ninth wave, slow gathering fold by fold
>   All its loose-flowing garments into one,
>   Plunges upon the shore, and floods the dun
>   Pale reach of sands, and changes them to gold.

Of course the Italian sonnet had been used in English poetry for so long that it was no longer foreign and exotic in Longfellow's day, but undoubtedly the poet's youthful studies in Italian directed him in his choice of this form over the English and Shakespearean. And we are certainly safe in counting the translation of seven sonnets from Michael Angelo and the six written during the translation of the *Divina Commedia* as Italian influences on Longfellow's versification.

15. SUMMARY AND CONCLUSION

No attempt has been made in this chapter to list or discuss all of Longfellow's stanzaic devices or all of his minor metrical forms. His main stanzas, however, including the ballad stanza with variations and different combinations of "tail-rime" stanzas, have been commented upon from time to time, and these are most important. The great bulk of Longfellow's verse is in paragraphs rather than stanzas, including not only his blank verse and heroic couplets but also four-stress couplets, the unrimed trochees of *Hiawatha*, and the several poems in hexameters.

A poem which has not been discussed is the attempted masterpiece, the *Christus* mystery. Though many critics think *The Golden Legend* better than *Evangeline*, almost all agree that the *Christus* is inferior to Longfellow's other poems; and it may, therefore, be dismissed briefly. But it is interesting technically because of its use of the octosyllabic couplet (varied by alternate rime) for narrative and dramatic purposes, a practice unusual in English versification and an evident Goethean influence. Also this drama contains many other short-line (*i.e.*, dimeters, trimeters, etc.) speeches and lyrics, used in the *Faust* manner.

Hence, it is evident that Longfellow's versification was profoundly influenced by the German, as in his *Christus;* by the Italian, in his sonnets; by the Greek, in his hexameters (though much of the Greek influence probably comes indirectly through Goethe's *Hermann und Dorothea*); by the Finnish epic, in *Hiawatha;* by old Norse, in *The Saga of King Olaf;* and by other European poetic techniques in various ways.

Longfellow's specific contributions to American versification are numerous, subtle, and in some respects very difficult to isolate and classify; but we would seem to be safe in listing: (1) His use of the unrimed trochees, accompanied by parallelism and reiteration, a forerunner (even if not a source) of "free verse." No later poet has used this meter in quite the *Hiawatha* manner, yet the precedent has undoubtedly been influential in popularizing the trochee, and the unrimed short lines may have indirectly influenced the trend toward freer rhythmical forms. (2) His popularizing of the hexameter. (3) The effect of his translations, imitations, and subject-matter in directing attention toward poetry in languages and systems of versification hitherto unfamiliar to America. (4) His practice of easy and graceful versification, which influenced other poets in using simple and facile forms — not always, as Holmes pointed out about the meter of *Hiawatha*, an unmixed blessing.

Longfellow's greatest contribution, we may say finally, was not specifically any new theory or practice but a general, broad, and deep influence toward the search for new forms, based on a wide acquaintance with the chief poetic techniques of the world.[29]

SELECTED BIBLIOGRAPHY

TEXT

Longfellow, Henry Wadsworth, *Complete Poetical Works*, etc., ed. by H. E. Scudder. Boston: Houghton Mifflin Company, 1886. (Cambridge edition.)

——, *Complete Works*, Boston: Houghton Mifflin Company, 1886 and 1904. 14 vols.

——, *Henry Wadsworth Longfellow*, ed. by Odell Shepard. (American Writers Series.) New York: American Book Company, 1934. [The best of Longfellow's poetry and prose, with a critical introduction.]

CRITICISM

Elliott, G. R., "Gentle Shades of Longfellow," *The Cycle of Modern Poetry*. Princeton University Press, 1929. V, 64–82. [An excellent re-interpretation.]

Jones, Howard Mumford, "Longfellow," *American Writers on American Literature*, ed. by John Macy. New York: Horace Liveright, 1931. IX, 105–124. [Interpretation of Longfellow's poetry against its European background.]

Kreymborg, Alfred, "The Fallen Prince of Popularity," *Our Singing Strength*. New York: Coward-McCann, 1929. Pp. 97–115.

Saintsbury, George, "American Poets and Prosodists," *History of English Prosody*. New York: The Macmillan Company, 1910. III, 487–490.

---

[29] For the versification of the minor poets of the period see Chapter V, § 11, Chapter VII, § 9, and Chapter IX, § 9.

CHAPTER VII

Oliver Wendell Holmes

I. INTRODUCTION

THERE is almost every reason for us not to expect a prosodic system from Holmes, or even much prosodic thinking at all. He was first of all a physician and professor of anatomy, and most of his poetry is colored to some extent by the scientist, directly in subject-matter and idiom and indirectly in the scientific reserve that always held in check his poetic imagination.

In the second place, he was a "throw back," as most critics have pointed out (though they often over-emphasize it). He says in his note to *Poetry*, "A Metrical Essay" written in 1836, that, "This Academic Poem presents the simple and partial views of a young person trained after the schools of classical English verse as represented by Pope, Goldsmith, and Campbell, with whose lines his memory was early stocked." And in many respects, he remained an eighteenth-century neo-classicist all of his life. But even in this confession we must remember Holmes's statement that the poem, which would of course include the versification, represents only his "partial views." It is plain, however, that this young poet was not headed toward any sort of prosodic revolution.

In the third place, Holmes was always primarily an "occasional" poet, despite the fact that he did write some fine poetry for more serious purposes; and the occasional poet, like the journalistic versifier, may be counted upon to follow the conventions. For new forms divert attention to technique, whereas the "occasional" poet wants all

attention focused on what he has to say. So long, therefore, as Holmes remained the writer of after-dinner verse
(and such he did remain until the end of his days), he was
practically compelled to continue using the familiar octosyllabic couplet, the heroic couplet, ballad meter, and
other simple and accepted forms.

Nevertheless, we do find Holmes now and then specu-
lating on prosodic questions. The most widely known
instance, of course, is "The Physiology of Versification,"
which is typical of Holmes the scientist, and which pro-
claims that there is a vital and necessary connection between the laws of versification and the respiration and the
pulse, "the true time-keepers of the body." He takes as
his starting point the fact that a normal person breathes
about twenty times per minute, and then says:

"The 'fatal facility' of the octosyllabic measure has
often been spoken of, without any reference to its real
cause. The reason why eight syllable verse is so singularly
easy to read aloud is that it follows more exactly than any
other measure the natural rhythm of expiration. In reading aloud in the ordinary way from the 'Lay of the Last
Minstrel,' from 'In Memoriam,' or from 'Hiawatha' . . .
it will be found that not less than sixteen nor more than
twenty-four lines will be spoken in a minute, probably
about twenty. It is plain, therefore, that if one reads
twenty lines in a minute, and naturally breathes the same
number of times during that minute, he will pronounce
one line to each expiration, taking advantage of the pause
at its close for inspiration. The only effort required is that
of vocalizing and articulating; the breathing takes care of
itself, not even demanding a thought except where the sense
may require a pause in the middle of a line. The very
fault with these octosyllabic lines is that they slip away
too fluently, and run easily into a monotonous sing-song." [1]

On the same grounds, Holmes argues that the "heroic

[1] "The Physiology of Versification" in *Pages from an Old Volume
of Life* (Boston, 1892), p. 316.

line" is more difficult to read because only about fourteen verses are pronounced in a minute; so that, "If a breath is allowed to each line the respiration will be longer and slower than natural, and a sense of effort and fatigue will soon be the consequence." Though the cæsura is a "breathing-place," it "entirely breaks up the natural rhythm of breathing." The twelve- and the fourteen-syllable lines are also found difficult for the same reasons.

Now this argument is ingenious and interesting, but it is so "scientific" that it fails to take into account all the facts. Holmes admits that different persons have different respiratory rhythms, and hence his argument may not hold for all people. Moreover, he does not consider the fact that in enjambed octosyllabics, two, three, or several lines are read at one breath-sweep. And in blank verse, which is undoubtedly the most "natural" speaking verse (as Shakespeare's dramas are sufficient to prove), the irregular variation of short and long breath-sweeps gives us the most pleasing effects. But still more important is the fact that this theory is an attempt to explain conventional, classical, accepted prosody, in which end-stopped lines predominate. It is more physiological than prosodic. The attempt to explain prosody on physiological principles is commendable, yet the chief value of the essay for the student of prosody lies in the fact that it is the best proof we could ask that Holmes took conventional prosody for granted.

As late as 1849, Holmes takes Lowell to task for his versification: "You laugh at the old square-toed heroic sometimes, and I must retort upon the rattlety-bang sort of verse in which you have indulged. I read a good deal of it as I used to go over the kittle-y-benders when a boy, horribly afraid of a slump every time I cross one of its up-and-down hump-backed lines. I don't mean that it cannot be done, or that you have not often done it so as to be readable and musical; but think of having to read a mouthful of such lines as this: —

"For the frost's [?] swift shuttles its shroud had spun." [2]

In 1890, Holmes does admit that, "I find the burden and restrictions of rhyme more and more troublesome as I grow older." [3] But here he is probably referring more to his own infirmities than to any intrinsic restrictions of the system; certainly he never seems to have thought of trying to write poetry without the "burden" of rime (except, of course, in blank verse).

And yet, strangely enough, there is in his 1836 preface a doctrine which sounds curiously "modern," even "modernistic" or "cubistic." In defending the "extravagant" in poetry, he says: "A series of hyperbolical images is considered beneath criticism by the same judges who would write treatises upon the sculptured satyrs and painted arabesques of antiquity, which are only hyperbole in stone and colors. As material objects in different lights repeat themselves in shadows variously elongated, contracted, or exaggerated, so our solid and sober thoughts caricature themselves in fantastic shapes inseparable from their originals, and having a unity in their extravagance, which proves them to have retained their proportions in certain respects, however differing in outline from their prototypes." [4]

But this preface is apparently a defence of the poems in the 1836 volume, all of which obey the conventional rules of versification. Apparently Holmes never thought of trying to convey his "hyperbolical images" and "caricature" by a "fantastic" or "exaggerated" technique.

Holmes did make valuable contributions to the practice of American versification, and exerted a powerful influence toward reinstating the French polish and perfection of eighteenth-century English ideals; yet we must study him as a versifier and not as a conscious prosodist.

[2] John T. Morse, Jr. (ed.), *Life and Letters of Oliver Wendell Holmes* (Boston, 1896), II, 110.

[3] Author's note to *Invitâ Minervâ*.

[4] Printed as an introductory note to "Earlier Poems."

2. BALLADS AND BALLAD MEASURE

Though Holmes early began to use practically all the verse forms that he ever used, the ballad measure seems to be most characteristic of his earlier period. He never surpassed *The Spectre Pig*, for instance, in his imitations of the genuine folk ballad, despite the fact that he insisted on placing it in the last section of his collected poems under the heading of "Verses from the Oldest Portfolio." It is difficult to find anywhere a more subtle, ironical, and satirical parody of the thought, diction, and rhythm of the ballad.

> It was the stalwart butcher man,
>   That knit his swarthy brow,
> And said the gentle Pig must die,
>   And sealed it with a vow.
>
> And oh! it was the gentle Pig
>   Lay stretched upon the ground,
> And ah! it was the cruel knife
>   His little heart that found.

These inversions and parataxes are not awkward, as we might expect, but produce a rhythm which is an unmistakable folk ballad tune. We also find the same "tune" in *The Mysterious Visitor*.

Old Ironsides (1830) is in the same ballad measure, yet is different in several details. The eight-line stanzas are fairly regular in meter and have a two-line thought-movement, as in *The Spectre Pig* and the genuine folk ballads; but only four of the twenty-four lines are enjambed, there are comparatively few metrical stresses, and the diction and syntactical constructions are more natural than in *The Spectre Pig*. Occasionally the first foot is reversed:

> Nail to the mast her holy flag,
>   Set every threadbare sail,
> And give her to the god of storms,
>   The lightning and the gale!

The Star and the Water-Lily (1830) contains a generous sprinkling of anapestic feet, a variation which Holmes continued to use intermittently during his whole poetic career.

The sun stepped down | from his gol | den throne,
And lay | in the sil | ent sea,
And the Lil | y had fold | ed her sat | in leaves,
For a sleep | y thing was she;
What is | the Lily dreaming of?
Why crisp the waters blue?
See, see, | she is lif | ting her var | nished lid!
Her white leaves are glistening through!

To an Insect and *My Aunt* (1831), however, are more typical of Holmes's ballad measure, being straight iambic, 4 + 3. *The Cambridge Churchyard* is in precisely the same meter, but is less regular and inclined to singsong because of a skilful variation of stresses, including initial accented syllables, secondary accents, and spondees.

Our ancient church! its lowly tower,
Beneath the loftier spire,
Is shadowed when the sunset hour
Clothes the | tall shaft | in fire;
It sinks beyond the distant eye
Long ere | the glittering vane,
High wheel | ing in the western sky,
Has faded o'er the plain.

Where alternate lines are enjambed, the ballad measure is really seven-stress, the 4 + 3 arrangement being entirely arbitrary. *A Ballad of the Boston Tea-Party* could be printed in seven-stress lines without in any way changing the rhythm, except possibly to tempt the reader to syncopate it.

> The wáves that wróught a céntury's wréck
> Have rólled o'er whíg and tóry;

The Ballad of the Oysterman is arranged in seven-stress lines, but is in the same rhythm as *The Spectre Pig*. These are early poems; later ones are *Nux Postcœnatica* (1848), *Meeting of the Alumni of Harvard College* (1857), and *Post-Prandial* (1881).

3. FOUR-STRESS IAMBICS

Holmes used the four-stress iambic line extensively from his college days (*cf. The Meeting of the Dryads*) until very near the end of his life. His four-stress verse includes simple stanza forms, such as the *abab* quatrain, octosyllabic couplets, and "clipped" four-stress iambic. No new, eccentric, or irregular versification is found in the handling of these forms, and since they are so common anyway, a full discussion of them should not be necessary.

His juvenile *The Meeting of the Dryads* is characteristic of much of Holmes's regular octosyllabic lines, with its inversions, smooth and regular beats, and couplet movement (even with alternate rime):

> "In every julep that he drinks,
>   May gout, and bile, and headache be;
> And when he strives to calm his pain,
>   May colic mingle with his tea.

Under the Violets (1859) is different in its versification only in the greater enjambment of its third stanza, the first four lines being read at one sweep. Rarely are more than two lines enjambed in Holmes's four-stress verse.

The Parting Word is characteristic of the seven-syllable lines:

> I must leave thee, lady sweet!
> Months shall waste before we meet;
> Winds are fair and sails are spread,
> Anchors leave their ocean bed;

Only two lines of this poem depart from the regular pattern, and even this departure (primary-secondary-primary accents) is neither unusual nor especially important:

> When the first sad sun shall set, . . .
> While the first seven mornings last,

However, a few very pretty lines are produced in *Fantasia* partly by this device:

> Kiss mine eyelids, beauteous morn,
> Blushing into life new-born!

Some of the later seven- and eight-syllable couplets contain a good deal of parallelism accompanied by initial repetition and balancing of half-line against half-line, resulting in such a rocking-horse movement as that found in *Programme:*

> Not for glory, not for pelf,
> Not, be sure, to please myself, . . .
> Turn my pages, — never mind
> If you like not all you find; . . .
> Every kernel has its shell, . . .
> Every book its dullest leaf,

In *The New Eden* some of the parallelism is emphasized by alliteration:

> The rippling grass, the nodding grain, . . .
> To scanty sun and frequent rain. . . .
> The food was scant, the fruits were few: . . .
> Austere in taste, and tough at core,

Holmes's most famous four-stress couplets are those of *The Deacon's Masterpiece, or The Wonderful "One-Hoss Shay."* Here anapestic substitution is used very freely:

Have you heard | of the won | derful one | -hoss shay,

That was built | in such a log | ical way?

It ran a hundred years | to a day,

And then, | of a sud | den, it — ah, | but stay,

I'll tell | you what hap | pened without | delay,

Scaring the parson into fits,

Frightening people out | of their wits, —

Have you ev | er heard of that, I say?

The monotonous rime and absurd rhythm are part of the humor of this piece, but the versification is little better than doggerel, especially in such passages as:

> Deacon and deaconess dropped away,
> Children and grandchildren — where were they?
> But there stood the stout old one-hoss shay
> As fresh as on Lisbon-earthquake-day! . . .

> End of the wonderful one-hoss shay.
> Logic is logic. That's all I say.

Parson Turell's Legacy, written in the same year as the *"One-Hoss Shay"* (1858), is, on the whole, more regular, though the rhythm in some passages is broken by short, elliptical sentences, resulting in a colloquialism very characteristic of Holmes's humorous verse:

> Facts respecting an old arm-chair.
> At Cambridge. Is kept in the College there.
> Seems but little the worse for wear.

> Know old Cambridge? Hope you do. —
> Born there? Don't say so! I was, too.

Another colloquial device is the use of abbreviations, with a consequent eccentricity of rhythm, as in *How the Old Horse Won the Bet:*

> The swift g. m., old Hiram's nag,
> The fleet s. h., Dan Pfeiffer's brag,
> With these a third — and who is he
> That stands beside his fast b. g.?

On the whole, *Dorothy Q,* with its very sparing enjambment and monotonous singsong rhythm, is characteristic of Holmes's four-stress couplets. Like Whittier's *Snow-Bound,* it is important for its description, not for its versification, though it is a much smoother and less awkward poem than Whittier's. *At the Pantomime* has greater enjambment, with more skilfully varied pauses, and contains some of Holmes's most pleasing octosyllabic couplets.

4. THE ANAPEST

We have already observed Holmes's use of anapestic feet in both his ballad and his four-stress couplets. *The Stethoscope Song* is not predominantly anapestic, but the use of some anapests is part of the pattern, a pattern which is itself somewhat uneven, individual lines often being as "rough and ready" as limerick verse, as in the first quatrain:

> There was | a young man | in Boston town,
> He bought | him a steth | oscope nice | and new,
> All moun | ted and fin | ished and pol | ished down,
> With an iv | ory cap | and a stop | per too.

But many of Holmes's poems are typically anapestic, such as *The Old Man of the Sea.* Notice also the final repetitions in the first and third lines of each stanza:

Do you know | the Old Man | of the Sea, | of the Sea?
  Have you met | with that dread | ful old man?
If you hav | en't been caught, | you will be, | you will be;
  For catch | you he must | and he can.

Or still more anapestic, with its feminine cæsuras, is
Brother Jonathan's Lament for Sister Caroline, which
begins:

She has gone, | — she has left | us, [:] in pas | sion and pride, —
Our storm | y-browed sis | ter, [:] so long | at our side!

Many of the later "class poems" are in this movement,
as are several pieces in "Bunker-Hill Battle and Other
Poems," 1874–1877. Note, for instance, *Grandmother's
Story of Bunker-Hill Battle*, with its internal double rimes
accompanying the triple rhythm:

'T is like stir | ring liv | ing embers | when, at eight | y, one |
    remembers
All the achings | and the quakings | of "the times | that tried |
    men's souls;"
When I talk | of *Whig* | and *Tory*, | when I tell | the *Reb* | el story,
To you the words are ashes, | but to me | they're burning coals.

The 1874 *At the "Atlantic" Dinner* contains three-
and four-syllable rimes:

    I suppose it's myself that you're making allusions to
    And bringing the sense of dismay and confusion to.
    Of course *some* must speak, — they are always selected to,
    But pray what's the reason that I am expected to?
    I'm not fond of wasting my breath as those fellows do
    That want to be blowing forever as bellows do;

> *Their* legs are uneasy, but why will you jog any
> That long to stay quiet beneath the mahogany?

Though Holmes did use this meter fairly frequently, especially in his later period, he apparently adopted it merely as a variation to relieve the monotony of his octo-syllabics and heroics. No one realized better than the poet himself that his style was limited, as he confesses in the anapestic *For Whittier's Seventieth Birthday* (1877):

> Yes, — "the style is the man," and the nib of one's pen
> Makes the same mark at twenty, and three-score and ten;

5. HEROIC COUPLET

We have already seen that Holmes admitted his eight-eenth-century prosodic background, and that he seemed to resent Lowell's laughing "at the old square-toed heroic." In *Poem Read at the Dinner Given to the Author by the Medical Profession*, he proudly admits his allegiance to this measure:

> And so the hand that takes the lyre for you
> Plays the old tune on strings that once were new.
> Nor let the rhymester of the hour deride
> The straight-backed measure with its stately stride;
> It gave the mighty voice of Dryden scope;
> It sheathed the steel-bright epigrams of Pope;
> In Goldsmith's verse it learned a sweeter strain;
> Byron and Campbell wore its clanking chain;
> I smile to listen while the critic's scorn
> Flouts the proud purple kings have nobly worn;

This passage is also a good illustration of the metrical regularity of Holmes's heroics. Each line has exactly ten syllables, inverted feet are used sparingly, spondees rarely (but *cf.* "proud purple"), and each couplet is closed or "couplet moulded" in the eighteenth-century manner. Extra syllables can in nearly every case be accounted for by the usual rules of elision, as, for example, in the follow-ing lines from the 1836 *Poetry*, "A Metrical Essay"·

(1) Elision of "open vowels":

> Would wail its req*uie*m o'er a poet's grave! . . .
> And carve in language its ether*e*al form,

(2) "Pure *l*":

> The hot-cheeked rev*elle*r, tossing down the wine

(3) "Pure *n*":

> The infant, list*en*ing to the warbling bird;

(4) "Pure *r*":

> Scenes of my youth! awake its slumb*er*ing fire!
> Ye winds of mem*or*y, sweep the silent lyre!

Holmes used this measure extensively, both for serious and "familiar" verse. Most of his long poems are in this form. His "Five Stories and a Sequel," which he collected under the heading of "Readings Over the Teacups," are all in heroic couplets. They include *To My Old Readers, The Banker's Secret, The Exile's Secret, The Lover's Secret, The Statesman's Secret, The Mother's Secret,* and *The Secret of the Stars.* These poems are not so well known as Holmes's four-stress couplets of the *"One-Hoss Shay,"* yet they contain some good versification, such as *The Secret of the Stars,* which has some beautiful cadences, held in check only by the rime and a corresponding tendency toward the full stop after the completion of the rime. Many of the first lines of couplets, though, are enjambed:

> In vain the sweeping equatorial pries
> Through every world-sown corner of the skies,
> To the far orb that so remotely strays
> Our midnight darkness is its noonday blaze;
> In vain the climbing soul of creeping man
> Metes out the heavenly concave with a span,

These lines are less "couplet moulded" than the average eighteenth-century English heroics, but the neo-classical model is apparent. It is in this measure, however, that the eighteenth-century influence on Holmes's versification is strongest.

The pentameter in alternate rime is so nearly like the heroic couplets in versification that it need not be analyzed here. The most popular instance is *The Iron Gate*, in *abab* quatrains. *Homesick in Heaven* is sometimes highly praised. And some other examples are *For the Commemoration Services* and *My Aviary*.

6. BLANK VERSE

Holmes wrote comparatively little blank verse, probably because it is not a very convenient form for "occasional" poems; and his few attempts are perhaps less known than any other poetic form that he used. But the little blank verse that he did write is, so far as versification goes, unusually good. The 1864 *A Sea Dialogue* contains some awkward lines, the worst being:

> Friend, you seem thoughtful. I not wonder much
> That he who sails the ocean should be sad.

Yet the 1872 *Wind-Cloud and Star-Drifts* shows complete mastery of the form. Especially commendable are the long breath-sweeps, permitting sustained cadences in the best blank verse tradition.

> With quickened heart-beats I shall hear the tongues
> That speak my praise; / but better far the sense
> That in the unshaped ages, / buried deep
> In the dark mines of unaccomplished time
> Yet to be stamped with morning's royal die
> And coined in golden days, / — in those dim years
> I shall be reckoned with the undying dead, /
> My name emblazoned on the fiery arch, /
> Unfading till the stars themselves shall fade. //

However much Holmes's heroic couplets may be in the eighteenth-century tradition, his blank verse is certainly

not, for it shows scarcely a trace of the couplet influence.
Yet it is more in the tradition of Freneau than of Bry-
ant, since it echoes the good workmanship of Freneau (*cf.
The Rising Glory of America*) and lacks the sonority of
Bryant's *Thanatopsis*.

7. *THE CHAMBERED NAUTILUS*

The popularity of *The Chambered Nautilus* and the
poet's own undisguised pride in this poem make a discussion of it almost imperative. In a letter to George Ticknor, Holmes declares, "I am as willing to submit this
[poem] to criticism as any I have written, in form as well
as substance, and I have not seen any English verse of
just the same pattern." [5]
In none of his other poems do we find Holmes using
such freely varied accents as in *The Chambered Nautilus*.
There are, in fact, so many reversed feet and interpolated
spondees that no one stanza accurately indicates the underlying rhythmical pattern. Stated simply, the pattern
is composed of iambic pentameter, trimeter, and a final
alexandrine, in the following scheme: $a_5a_3b_3bb_5c_3c_6$. But
to illustrate the basic pattern we must build up a composite stanza:

Its webs of living gauze no more unfurl; . . .   (a)

That spreads his lustrous coil; . . .   (a)

The venturous bark that flings . . .   (b)

Let each new temple, nobler than the last, . . .   (b)

In gulfs enchanted, where the Siren sings, . . .   (b)

Before thee lies revealed, —   (c)

Its irised ceiling rent, its sunless crypt unsealed!   (c)

[5] *Life and Letters, op. cit.*, p. 278.

The following stanza is as typical as any:

Year af | ter year | beheld | the sil | ent toil
  That spread | his lus | trous coil;
    Still, as | the spir | al grew,
He left | the past | year's dwell | ing for | the new,
Stole with | soft step | its shin | ing arch | way through,
    Built up | its id | le door,
Stretched in | his last | -found home, | and knew | the old | no
  more.

While the first element of the compound, such as "last-found," is usually given primary stress, with secondary stress on the second element (as scanned above), this phrase and others, like "sea-maids," are nearly spondaic. "Sea-maids" is especially interesting. In the phrase "the sea-maids rise" the normal accentuation would be $(\times \nearrow \searrow \nearrow)$; but "the cold sea-maids rise" contains a conflict, the preceding monosyllable "cold" tending to reduce the accentuation of "sea" to secondary stress. Perhaps the whole line is normally pronounced as follows:

Where the cold sea-maids rise to sun their streaming hair.

The poem contains an abundance of alliteration, much more, in fact, than we find in most of Holmes's poetry. Several examples are:

  On the *s*weet *s*ummer *w*ind its purpled *w*ings . . .
  Its irised *c*eiling rent, its *s*unless crypt un*s*ealed! . . .
  *S*tole with *s*oft *s*tep its *s*hining archway through, . . .
  Build thee *m*ore *s*tately *m*ansions, O my *s*oul, . . .
  *L*eaving thine outgrown *s*hell by *l*ife's unresting *s*ea!

It is probably unsafe to press very far a search for symbolism in the form of this poem, yet one wonders whether the rhythms (including the combinations of pentameter, trimeter, and alexandrine in the novel stanzaic arrangement) were not intended to symbolize the crenulated and scalloped shell of the chambered nautilus. At any rate, the form is, as Holmes himself believed, very unusual, and perhaps unique.

8. OTHER STANZA FORMS

Next to *The Chambered Nautilus*, Holmes perhaps took most pride in *The Last Leaf*, at least among his stanzaic poems. Certainly it is the only other poem which he believed he had written on an original model. His own explanation of why he happened to use the "somewhat singular measure" is amusing. "I had become a little known as a versifier, and I thought that one or two other young writers were following my efforts with imitations. . . . I determined to write in a measure which would at once betray any copyist." He mentions Campbell's *Battle of the Baltic* as having probably suggested the form, "But I do not remember any poem in the same measure, except such as have been written since its publication." [6]
It is a little puzzling why Holmes took so much pride in the form of this poem, but his handling of it is easy and dexterous.

> I saw him once before,
> As he passed by the door,
> And again
> The pavement stones resound,
> As he totters o'er the ground
> With his cane.

The rhythm does have a lilt which is more musical than anything else Holmes ever wrote. The only trouble is

[6] Introductory note to the poem. (See Cambridge ed.)

that it is almost too musical, the "tune" obtruding itself into the reading so much that the poem is mostly sound. Still, it is a competent lyric. And its music is reminiscent of the seventeenth-century English lyrics.

Holmes's most peculiar stanza is the unrimed trochaic quatrain of *De Sauty*, composed of three six-stress and one three-stress lines. This is unique in his poetry, for his only other unrimed verse is regular blank verse, and no other poem of his is so predominantly trochaic.

Mány | thíngs thou | áskest, | jáckknife | -béaring | stránger,

Múch-conjécturing mórtal, pórk-and-tréacle-wáster!

Prétermit thy whíttling, whéel thine éarflap tóward me,

　Thóu shalt héar them ánswered.

Whén the chárge galvánic tíngled thróugh the cáble,

Át the pólar fócus óf the wíre eléctric

Súddenly appéared a white-fáced mán amóng us:

　Cálled himsélf "DE SAUTY."

Though the great bulk of Holmes's poetry is in couplets and alternate rime (often paragraphed as stanzas), he did use several stanza arrangements. But since most of them are fairly conventional, and none of those not already discussed are of any special importance, it should be sufficient merely to list the main forms.

The quatrains have already been discussed, but we may add the form aab_5b_3, in *But One Talent* and *To the Eleven Ladies*.

The tail-rime stanza appears to have been a favorite with Holmes. Examples of the main combinations are: $aa_3b_2ccc_3b_2$, *International Ode;* $ab_2bcc_4abdb_2$, *Too Young for Love;* $ABcc_4B_2$, *Martha;* $aa_4b_3ccc_4b_3$, "The World's Homage," in *Two Poems to Harriet Beecher Stowe;* $abab_4cc_3d_4ee_3d_4$, *Lexington;* $a_5a_3bbccd_5a_3$ (var.), "At the Summit," in *Two*

Poems to Harriet Beecher Stowe; abaa₅b₃, The Rose and the Fern; and *abbcc₃a₂, The Peau de Chagrin of State Street.* The *Two Sonnets: Harvard* (1878) and the sonnet sequence to Longfellow, *Our Dead Singer* (1882), show that Holmes could handle the Italian form with ease and facility, and it is surprising and regrettable that he did not write more sonnets. These five adhere closely to the form, but the first obeys most strictly the quatrain divisions of the octave. Its opening quatrain is as follows:

> To God's Anointed and His Chosen Flock:
> So ran the phrase the black-robed conclave chose
> To guard the sacred cloisters that arose
> Like David's altar on Moriah's rock.

To judge by Holmes's random stanzas, his sonnets, his blank verse, and his few excellent lyrics, he could have achieved success in almost any conventional meter; yet as we have seen, he always remained essentially a poet of octosyllabics and the heroic couplet. In this connection, it is interesting to recall Lowell's qualified praise, whether or not we agree with it:

> He has perfect sway of what I call a sham metre,
> But many admire it, the English pentameter,
> And Campbell, I think, wrote most commonly worse,
> With less nerve, swing, and fire in the same kind of verse,
>
> *A Fable for Critics*

While Holmes won considerable fame and distinction in his day, it is doubtful whether he has had much influence on American versification, (1) because he used the old measures without contributing anything new to their handling except an urbane unself-consciousness and an epigrammatic polish, and (2), and consequently, because his method called attention to content rather than technique.

9. THE FAMILIAR VERSE OF SAXE, FIELD, BUNNER

Since Holmes was preëminently a poet of *vers de société* —
or, as Brander Matthews prefers to call the type, "familiar
verse," — we may properly consider here some of the
minor familiar versifiers of the period. In his anthology
of *American Familiar Verse* Brander Matthews includes
Benjamin Franklin's *Paper*, Freneau's *The Parting Glass*
and *To a Caty-Did*, Paulding's *The Old Man's Carousal*,
Bryant's *Robert of Lincoln*, Emerson's *The Humble-Bee*,
Whittier's *The Barefoot Boy*, Longfellow's *Catawba Wine*,
and selections from many other American poets, both
major and minor. Indeed, most poets at one time or another write light lyrics which may be called familiar verse,
but Holmes is the only major American poet with whom
this verse was especially characteristic.

Likewise the number of significant minor poets who are
distinguished chiefly for their familiar verse is small. In
fact, we find only three of special importance. They are
John Godfrey Saxe (1816–1887), Eugene Field (1850–1895),
and Henry Cuyler Bunner (1855–1896). Matthews says
that Saxe "is not only the earliest, he is also the most old-
fashioned in his method and the least individual in his
outlook. His verse is modelled upon Praed's, to whose
dazzling brilliance he could not attain; and he borrowed
also the pattern of Hood in his more broadly comic lyrics." [7]

Saxe himself made no secret of his imitation of Hood
and Praed. He even labelled *The Beauty of Ballston*, for
instance, as "After Praed." And it is also true, as Matthews says, that Saxe was conventional in his methods,
as in his simple ballads, *The Briefless Barrister*, *Captain
Jones's Misadventure*, and *The Cold Water-Man;* in his
heroic couplets, as in *The Times*, with its balance and antithesis of half-line against half-line; in the rollicking but

[7] Brander Matthews, "Writers of Familiar Verse," *Cambridge History of American Literature* (New York: G. P. Putnam's Sons, 1918),
Vol. II, p. 242. By permission of The Macmillan Company, publishers.

smoothly flowing anapestics of *A Benedict's Appeal to a Bachelor;* and the playful triplet and quadruplet feminine rimes of *The Devil of Names* can be parallelled in the humorous verse of many other poets. But *The Cold Water-Man* is a skilful burlesque of the folk ballad, though hardly so successful as Holmes's *The Spectre Pig.*

One special characteristic of Saxe's versification is his fondness for "tail-rime." Some examples are: *A College Reminiscence, aa$_4$b$_2$cc$_4$b$_2$; The Proud Miss MacBride, aaa$_4$-b$_3$ccc$_4$b$_3$;* and many simple arrangements in the "Love Poems." We also find three-stress blank trochees in *Rhyme of the Rail.* Saxe's "Love Poems" is perhaps the most significant group for verse technique, being the most truly lyrical. His use of burdens, repetitions, and frequent iterations of the same rimes in these poems is analogous to the versification of the seventeenth-century English madrigals — and possibly to the late nineteenth-century adaptations of the fourteenth-century French forms, as practiced by both Swinburne and later Austin Dobson. One interesting example is *To My Love,* riming *abbBa abbBa abbBa* — apparently an original type of the rondel. *Roger Bontemps, The King of Normandy,* and *The Poet of this Garret* are translations and adaptations from Béranger.

The sentimentality of Eugene Field, is so out of fashion today with educated Americans that his smooth, facile, and melodious versification is generally unappreciated. But most of his poems have a truly musical lyricism hardly equalled by any other minor American poet of his time. His ballads, lullabys, and dialect poems are as singable as the original English ballads which he deliberately tried to imitate. He uses alternate rime, especially in trimeters and quatrameters, but his characteristic measure is the ballad. *Father's Way* is in seven-stress couplets, but the poem has an unmistakable ballad tune, as do likewise the long-line dialect poems, such as *Casey's Table D'hote,* which begins:

Oh, the days on Red Hoss Mountain, when the skies wuz fair
   'nd blue,
When the money flowed like likker, 'nd the folks wuz brave 'nd
   true!
When the nights wuz crisp 'nd balmy, 'nd the camp wuz all astir,
When the joints all throwed wide open 'nd no sheriff to demur!

The singing quality of Field's poems is partly the result
of his extensive use of couplet and alternate rime. But
sometimes the excessive reiteration of similar rime sounds
results in undesirable singsong — probably Field's greatest
weakness. His best poems could all be set to folk ballad
tunes. *Long Ago, Little Boy Blue, Dutch Lullaby,* and
Cornish Lullaby are essentially songs anyway.

Practically all of Bunner's poems in conventional
measures are distinguished for their grace, ease, and clever
manipulation of meter to produce fresh and novel effects;
but he is particularly important in the history of American
versification for his adaptation and use of the fourteenth-
century French forms which Austin Dobson had recently
used so successfully in English. The American interest in
these forms may be dated from the spring of 1878. In
May of that year Brander Matthews reviewed one of
Dobson's volumes for the *Nation,* and then in June he
published "Varieties of Verse" (an essay on the history
of these forms) in *Appleton's Journal.* Thereafter Matthews, Bunner, and many others began writing triolets,
rondels, rondeaus, and ballades. Eugene Field wrote one
ballade, called *Ballade of Women I Love,* but Bunner's experiments in the French forms are the most important
ones of the period.

An example of the triolet is Bunner's *A Pitcher of Mi-
gnonette,* riming *ABcAcbAB.* *O Honey of Hymettus Hill* is
a rondel on Dobson's variation, *viz., ABab baAB ababAB.*
She was a Beauty rimes *ABab baAB babaAB.* Some rondeaus
are *An April Fool, Les Morts Vont Vite, Saint Valentine,
That New Year's Call.* *Behold the Deeds* is a chant royal,
one of the most complicated forms aside from the sestina.

Bunner was perhaps the cleverest of all the minor American poets of the late nineteenth century, but the *tour de force* apparently interested him more than the content of his poems. Some of his cleverest work is in *Home, Sweet Home, with Variations*, in which he cleverly burlesques the versification of Swinburne, Bret Harte, Dobson ("As Austin Dobson Might Have Translated it from Horace if it Had even Occurred to Horace to write it"), Oliver Goldsmith at 19 and Alexander Pope at 52, and Walt Whitman. These parodies also indicate that Bunner was a profound student of versification. Many of his lyrics are also reminiscent of Heine and Herrick.

SELECTED BIBLIOGRAPHY

Oliver Wendell Holmes

Text

Holmes, Oliver Wendell, *The Complete Poetical Works*, etc., ed. by H. E. Scudder. Boston: Houghton Mifflin Company, 1895.

——, *Life and Letters*, ed. by John T. Morse. Boston: Houghton Mifflin Company, 1896.

——, "The Physiology of Versification," in *Pages from an Old Volume of Life*. Boston: Houghton Mifflin Company, 1913. (Riverside edition.)

Criticism

Kreymborg, Alfred, "Dr. Holmes and the New England Decline," *Our Singing Strength*. New York: Coward-McCann, 1929. Chapter XI, pp. 134–150.

Matthews, Brander, "Writers of Familiar Verse," in *Cambridge History of American Literature*. New York: G. P. Putnam's Sons, 1918. Vol. II, Chapter XXIII, pp. 224–244.

Untermeyer, Louis, *American Poetry from the Beginning to Whitman*. New York: Harcourt, Brace and Company, 1931. Pp. 401–405.

Minor Poets

Cohen, Helen Louise, *Lyric Forms from France*. New York: Harcourt, Brace and Company, 1922.
[A History and Anthology of the Ballads, Chants Royal, Rondels,

Rondeaus, Triolets, Villanelles, and Sestinas in English and American verse.]

Matthews, Brander, *American Familiar Verse*. New York: Longmans, Green, and Company, 1904.

——, "Varieties of Verse," *Appleton's Journal* (June, 1878), 19, 565–567.

White, Gleeson, *Ballades and Rondeaus*. London: Walter Scott Publishing Company, Ltd., 1887.
[An anthology of English and American Ballades, Rondeaus, Chants Royal, Sestinas, Villanelles, etc., with a critical and historical Introduction.]

CHAPTER VIII

Walt Whitman

1. INTRODUCTION

THE one thing that every one knows about Whitman is
that he started a *new* mode, style, or type of versification.
He is famous (or in some quarters still infamous) as
America's most revolutionary and prosodically original [1]
poet. Yet if we ask what was "new" about Whitman's
prosody, we learn only that it does not have conventional
meter or rime.

Part of the misunderstanding began with Whitman
himself. In his 1855 Preface, he let the world know in no
unmistakable terms that he thought the time had come
for a new poetry (including, of course, a new prosody);
and he left no doubt that he intended to fulfill the need.
But his own theory, embracing as it did a new æsthetic
as well as a new prosody, suggested rather than defined
new principles.

In fact, it is never easy to determine when Whitman's
critical words on his poetic art apply to his versification
and when to the thought of his poems. His written words
do not anywhere show a clear distinction in his own mind
between his thought and his manner of expressing it. Yet
this is not to say that he himself did not understand the
distinction (though of course that is possible, too).

His one most consistent rationalization of his technique
was that the thought and the form must always exactly

[1] We speak of Whitman's *prosody* because his whole poetic technique was based on a deliberate attempt to start a new "school" of
American versification.

217

coincide; but this rationalization is so broad and general that it can be of little help to the student of prosody. It even seems at times that Walt Whitman deliberately attempted to conceal the specific principles of his prosody. To his friend Traubel (who, as Whitman very well knew, was preparing to be his Boswell), he once said:

"I have never given any study merely to expression: it has never appealed to me as a thing valuable or significant in itself: I have been deliberate, careful, even laborious: but I have never looked for finish — never fooled with technique more than enough to provide for simply getting through; after that I would not give a twist of my chair for all the rest." [2]

But just how, one may ask, was he "deliberate, careful, even laborious"? Careful and laborious about *what?* Traubel was quoting Whitman when he wrote:

"The style of these poems, therefore, is simply their own style, just born and bred. Nature may have given the hint to the author of the 'Leaves of Grass,' but there exists no book or fragment of a book which can have given the hint to them. All beauty, he says, comes from beautiful blood and a beautiful brain. His rhythm and uniformity he will conceal in the roots of his verses, not to be seen of themselves, but to break forth loosely as lilacs on a bush, and take shapes compact, as shapes of melons, or chestnuts, or pears." [3]

Traubel himself was neither scholar nor critic and his own judgment is worth nothing on this subject, but this quotation is important because it represents Whitman's own attitude. In his 1872 Preface, Walt says (concerning the early edition of *Leaves of Grass*), "I fulfilled in that an imperious conviction and the commands of my nature as total and irresistible as those which make the sea flow,

---

[2] Horace Traubel, *With Walt Whitman in Camden* (New York, 1914), III, 84.

[3] Traubel, Bush, and Harned, *In Re Walt Whitman* (Philadelphia, 1893), p. 16.

or the globe revolve." Again in his 1876 Preface, he declares anew, "Thus my form has strictly grown from my purports and facts, and is the analogy of them."

Even when Whitman did attempt to analyze his method, however, he never got further than an insistence on his care in the choice of words. "I take a good deal of trouble with words . . . but what I am after is the content not the music of words. Perhaps the music happens — it does no harm." [4] But can any one conscientiously read and compare Whitman's rejected lines with the ones retained for his text without doubting his statement that he was "not after the music of words"? Certainly many of his revisions are not for the thought. Once when Traubel discovered the MS. of "The Sobbing Bells," which showed considerable signs of revision, Whitman exclaimed: "Some of my enemies who think I write in the dark without premeditation ought to see that sheet of paper." [5]

Hence, Whitman's own analyses never penetrate deeper than a mere insistence (1) that his "form has strictly grown from his purports and facts, and is the analogy of them," and (2) that he is profoundly careful in the choice of his words. Of the two explanations, only the latter is of any specific value to the student of Whitman's versification, and how naïve that is!

But then his whole *American Primer* [6] is nothing but the same naïve assertion of the poetic and oratorical value of words. "Names are magic," he declares. "One word can pour such a flood through the soul." *An American Primer* is really a treatise (of course fragmentary, for it was never finished) on craftsmanship for the American writer and orator. Yet the sole theme is that words are magic, and the whole work is composed largely of catalogs of "magic words," without any hints on how to apply the cantraps.

<hr/>

[4] Traubel, *op. cit.*, I, 163.   [5] Traubel, *op. cit.*, II, 136.
[6] *An American Primer* (Boston, 1904), Traubel ed.

It is possible, as many people believe, that Whitman was guided by intuitive principles which he himself did not fully understand; but we should not base this conclusion on his own words, such as those quoted here, since in these (as always) Whitman was speaking as a poet and not as a prosodist. And of course he used the method of the poet: suggestion, metaphor, *indirection*, as he himself would have said; for that was his own word.

But just such words as have been quoted here have thrown many investigators off the right track. In a comparatively modern book on Whitman we are told that, "His own wild music, ravishing, unseizable, like the song of a bird, came to him, as by his own principles it should have come, when he was not searching for it." [7] To some extent this is true of every real poet, and it should not blind us to a basic and preconceived technique. Yet even to the present day the main interpretations of the critics are based on the cues that Whitman gave them: that (1) he has no art except the art of nature, and (2) he is careful in the choice of his words and in the length of his lines.

It has been necessary to dwell at some length upon these facts because of the hold that they seem to have upon the popular imagination. It is impossible, in other words, to discuss Whitman's versification in the same way that Freneau's, Bryant's, and Poe's have been treated in this book, because the general public is too well acquainted with certain superficial and preconceived notions regarding Whitman's "new" and "free" rhythms.

The truth of the matter is that they are not new, since they are, to go no farther back, at least as old as Hebrew poetry; nor are they free, for they have laws as rigid in their own way as the versification of *Beowulf*, or *The Rime of the Ancient Mariner*. Precisely where Whitman derived the laws of his versification is uncertain and not altogether germane to the present discussion, yet there are many

[7] Basil de Selincourt, *Walt Whitman, a Critical Study* (New York, 1914), p. 73.

evidences that Professor Bliss Perry was right when he
declared that the "essential model . . . was the rhythmical pattern of the English Bible . . . [in which he]
found the charter for the book he wished to write." [8] At
any rate, the analogy of Old Testament versification [9]
provides us with certain specific principles which enable
us to analyze and explain Walt Whitman's poetic technique. This is the important thing, and not whether he
borrowed his technique from the Bible, the *Bhagavad-Gita*,
or caught it in a mystic trance.

Our task is somewhat simplified by the fact that only
the versification of *Leaves of Grass* need be examined, for
Walt Whitman's reputation as a poet does not in any
way rest upon his youthful, imitative, conventional poems
in rime and meter (in the usual sense). In fact, we today
know these juvenile poems [10] only because the same poet
later wrote *Leaves of Grass*.

2. "PARALLELISM"

The first rhythmical principle of *Leaves of Grass* is that
of parallel structure: *the line is the rhythmical unit*, each
line balancing its predecessor, and completing or supple-
menting its meaning. This "parallelism" may be called
"a rhythm of thought." As we shall see later, it also
produces a phonetic recurrence similar to the rhythm we
ordinarily speak of as meter, but the first and most fundamental principle is a thought-rhythm.

The fact that Whitman intended his line to be considered as the unit is, as Ross has pointed out,[11] indicated by

[8] Bliss Perry, *Walt Whitman, A Biography* (Boston, 1906), p. 96.
[9] For a detailed comparison see Gay W. Allen's "Biblical Analogies
for Walt Whitman's Prosody," *Revue Anglo-Américaine* (August, 1933),
X, No. 6, 490–507.
[10] *Uncollected Prose and Poetry*, edited by Emory Holloway (New
York, 1921), I.
[11] E. C. Ross, "Whitman's Verse," *Modern Language Notes* (June,
1930), XLV, 363–364.

the punctuation; *i.e.*, practically every line ends with a comma or a period. Because of this fact, Ross has correctly observed that "A run-on line is rare in Whitman — so rare that it may be considered a 'slip.'" [12] (Miss Wiley says, "In more than 10,500 lines in *Leaves of Grass*, there are, by my count, only twenty run-on lines." [13]) This is one evidence that parallelism is Whitman's first rhythmical principle.

The second evidence is that the verses of *Leaves of Grass*, like those of Old Testament poetry, are composed of four types of parallelism:

(1) *Synonymous* — the second line enforces the first by repeating the thought. (There may or may not be repetition of words. See § 5.)

> How solemn they look there, stretch'd and still,
> How quiet they breathe, the little children in their cradles.
>
> *The Sleepers*, Sec. 1

> I too am not a bit tamed, I too am untranslatable,
> I sound my barbaric yawp over the roofs of the world.
>
> *Song of Myself*, Sec. 52

(2) *Antithetical* — the second line denies or contrasts the first. (Used very sparingly in *Leaves of Grass*.)

> A woman waits for me, she contains all, nothing is lacking,
> Yet all were lacking if sex were lacking . . .
>
> *A Woman Waits for Me*

(3) *Synthetic* or *Cumulative* — the second line, or several consecutive lines, supplements or completes the first:

> I celebrate myself, and sing myself,
> And what I assume you shall assume,
> For every atom belonging to me as good belongs to you.
>
> *Song of Myself*, Sec. 1

[12] E. C. Ross, "Whitman's Verse," *Modern Language Notes* (June, 1930), XLV, 363–364.

[13] Autrey Nell Wiley, "Reiterative Devices in '*Leaves of Grass*,'" *American Literature* (May, 1929), I, 161, note 2.

(4) *Climactic*, or "ascending rhythm" — each succeed-ing line adds to its predecessor, usually taking up words from it and completing it:

When lilacs last in the dooryard bloom'd,
And the great star early droop'd in the western sky in the night,
I mourn'd, and yet shall mourn with ever-returning spring,

Ever-returning spring, trinity sure to me you bring,
Lilacs blooming perennial and drooping star in the west,
And thought of him I love.

When Lilacs Last, etc., Sec. 1

The most common of these four types in *Leaves of Grass* is the synonymous, which is used extensively in practically every poem, and may extend in number from two to sixty-two consecutive lines. (*Cf.* second strophe of the *Song of the Broad-Axe.*) It is also often difficult to distinguish the synthetic from the climactic parallelism, yet the fact that parallel structure is being used is always obvious.

Frequently we find not only line-parallelism but internal parallelism, as in:

(a) I celebrate myself,
(a) and sing myself,
(b) And what I assume
(b) you shall assume,
(c) For every atom belonging to me
(c) as good belongs to you.

Or, perhaps more common:

(a) I too am not a bit tamed,
(a) I too am untranslatable,
(a) I too sound my barbaric yawp
over the roofs of the world.

Parallelism does group the lines, but the number of consecutive parallel verses is not particularly important. It should be observed, however, that we find couplets, triplets, quatrains, and longer groups — such as the second strophe of *Song of the Broad-Axe* already referred to.

Examples of couplet parallelism are:

I cannot aid with my wringing fingers,
I can but rush to the surf and let it drench and freeze upon me.
The Sleepers, Sec. 4

No shutter'd room or school can commune with me,
But roughs and little children better than they.
Song of Myself, Sec. 47

Triplet:

I throw myself upon your breast, my father,
I cling to you so that you cannot unloose me,
I hold you so firm till you answer me something.
As I Ebb'd with the Ocean of Life

The quatrain may contain synonymous parallelism (indicated *aaaa*); alternate parallelism, resembling "common meter" (*abab*); or other parallel combinations (such as *abba*, *abbb*, and *abac*).

(a) Each of us inevitable,
(a) Each of us limitless — each of us with his or her right upon
        the earth,
(a) Each of us allow'd the eternal purports of the earth,
(a) Each of us here as divinely as any is here.
Salut au Monde, Sec. 11

(a) Allons! with power, liberty, the earth, the elements,
(b) Health, defiance, gaiety, self-esteem, curiosity;
(a) Allons! from all formules!
(b) From your formules, O bat-eyed and materialistic priests.
Song of the Open Road, Sec. 10

(a) O liquid and free and tender!
(a) O wild and loose to my soul — O wondrous singer!
(b) You only I hear — yet the star holds me, (but soon will
        depart,)
(b) Yet the lilac with mastering odor holds me.
When Lilacs Last, etc., Sec. 13

3. THE "ENVELOPE"

Another parallelistic device which we find used extensively in *Leaves of Grass* is what biblical prosodists call the "envelope." [14] In this combination the parallelism may be either of figures or of thought. First, we should understand the latter. In the envelope of thought-parallelism, the initial line states an idea or a proposition, succeeding lines state parallel thoughts regarding the first line, and the final line states a concluding thought. The introduction and conclusion may be two or three lines instead of one, but in *Leaves of Grass* it is usually only one line. Sometimes the whole poem is one envelope, as *O Me! O Life!*, or *Joy, Shipmate, Joy!*:

(a) Joy, shipmate, joy!
    (Pleas'd to my soul at death I cry,)
(b) Our life is closed, our life begins,
(b) The long, long anchorage we leave,
(b) The ship is clear at last, she leaps!
(b) She swiftly courses from the shore,
(a) Joy, shipmate, joy!

The envelope is frequently used for a series of lines which Whitman has grouped separately, apparently intending this device to serve as a sort of stanza. *Passage to India* is an example of a poem characterized by such groupings:

Passage to more than India!
Are thy wings plumed indeed for such far flights?
O soul, voyagest thou indeed on voyages like those?
Disportest thou on waters such as those?
Soundest below the Sanscrit and the Vedas?
Then have thy bent unleash'd.

                           Sec. 9

In the biblical envelope either the introduction or the conclusion may be omitted, making the parallelism either

[14] See Richard G. Moulton, *Literary Study of the Bible* (Chicago, 1895), pp. 53–54.

abbb . . . or *aaaa* . . . *b.* Perhaps "incomplete envelope" is a misnomer for this form, but it can be assigned
for convenience, since the device is used so frequently in
Leaves of Grass that we need some name for it. It is
found even more frequently than the complete envelope.
Good examples are so easy to find that it is almost superfluous to cite particular ones, though convenient instances
are *The Mystic Trumpeter, So Long,* and *Song at Sunset.*
Repetitions of words may or may not be used; but it is
"thought rhythm" that we are observing just at present.
In the following strophe the envelope conclusion is missing:

> (a) Good in all,
> (b) In the satisfaction and aplomb of animals,
>   In the annual return of the seasons,
>   In the hilarity of youth,
>   In the strength and flush of manhood,
>   In the grandeur and exquisiteness of old age,
>   In the superb vistas of death.
>
> *Song at Sunset*

A partial list of poems in both the complete and the
incomplete envelope may be useful. In *Song of the Broad-
Axe,* either the complete or incomplete form is the strophic
model for practically every section; in *I Sit and Look
Out,* we have the perfect envelope; in *When Lilacs Last
in the Dooryard Bloom'd,* there is an extraordinarily effective use of the envelope, with the complete form in sections
8 (arranged *abcccccccccd*), 11, and 12, and the incomplete
form in sections 5 and 13 (introduction missing); in
Assurance and *Weave in My Hardy Life,* perfect envelopes are employed; and in *Miracles,* we find a double
envelope.

Many of the shorter poems which Whitman wrote in
his old age are composed of a single envelope, as in
Election Day . . ., *Old Salt Kossabone, Thanks in Old
Age, After the Supper and Talk, Osceola,* and *On, On the
Same, Ye Jocund Twain!*

As an example of the fact that parallelism, or "thought rhythm," is the first rhythmical principle of *Leaves of Grass,* let us observe its use in *When Lilacs Last in the Dooryard Bloom'd,* which is not only rhythmically characteristic of Whitman's special technique but is also widely recognized as his best poem. The following is a tabulation of the parallelism of the poem down to the song of the bird:

1. *aaa* — synonymous
   aaa "
2. *aaaaa* "
3. *abcccd* — synthetic
4. *abccb* "
   aab "
5. *aaaaaab* — synonymous
6. *aabbbbbbbbbac* — envelope
7. *abc* — synthetic
   aabcdd — climactic
8. *abcccccccccd* — envelope
9. *abbcc* — climatic
10. *aaa* — synonymous
    aabc — synthetic

11. *aab* — synthetic
    abbbbbaa — envelope
12. *abbbbbbbba* "
13. *aab* — synonymous
    aa "
    aabb "
14. *abbbbbbbbbcdefffghh* —
    mainly envelope: note,
    c modifies *d*, *d* completes *a*, *e* concludes *a*
    and *d*
    aab — synthetic
    aab "
    abc "

4. INTERNAL PARALLELISM

An analysis of Whitman's parallelism by lines reveals only the broader aspects of this "thought rhythm." The internal parallelism has already been referred to incidentally, yet it is not incidental in the total effect. Sometimes we cannot analyze it satisfactorily, though it rests entirely on the principles which we have already observed in the line-by-line analysis. An excellent example for dissection is the short poem, *To Rich Givers.* First, let us observe the line parallelism:

(a) What you give me I cheerfully accept,
(b) A little sustenance, a hut and garden, a little money, as I rendezvous with my poems,

(b) A traveller's lodging and breakfast as I journey through the
    States, — why should I be ashamed to own such gifts?
    why to advertise for them?
(c) For I myself am not one who bestows nothing upon man
    and woman,
(c) For I bestow upon any man or woman the entrance to all
    the gifts of the universe.

In a general way, the first line states the main proposition; lines two and three elaborate it, listing by synonymous parallelism what is given; and lines four and five
state the reasons for the "cheerfully accept" in the first
line, making the whole passage synthetic parallelism. But
if we break up the poem into groups of parallel ideas, we
have the following arrangement:

(a) What you give me
(b)   I cheerfully accept,
(a) A little sustenance,
(a) a hut and garden,
(a) a little money,
(c)   as I rendezvous with my poems,
(a) A traveller's lodging and breakfast
(c)   as I journey through the States, —
(b)   why should I be ashamed to own such gifts?
(b)   why to advertise for them?
(d)   For I myself am not one
(e)   who bestows nothing upon man and woman,
(d)   For I bestow upon any man or woman
(e)   the entrance to all the gifts of the universe.

When arranged in this manner, the poem has parallelism arranged in almost the order of the rime-scheme of
a sonnet, but this, of course, is partly coincidence. However, the very fact that the parallelism has a recurrence
similar to the recurrence of rime in a sonnet is excellent
proof that the poem has a very definite rhythmical scheme.

5. PHONETIC RECURRENCE

The second main rhythmical principle of *Leaves of Grass* is what we shall call "phonetic recurrence." Rhythm is repetition; in conventional "meters," it is composed of repetitions in a certain order (conforming either rigidly or in a general way to a pattern) of speech accents, or the interplay of stressed and unstressed syllables. The repetition of thoughts or ideas in a schematic order is also a rhythm, as has been demonstrated in the preceding section, and is actually *felt* as a rhythm once the mind has been trained to expect it.

But since thoughts are expressed by means of spoken sounds (or symbols that represent spoken sounds), it is possible for a poem to have two rhythms, one of thought and the other of sounds. Whether or not one necessarily implies the other need not bother us here, yet it is a fact that in *Leaves of Grass* parallel thoughts have a tendency to slide into parallel manners of expression, including both grammatical constructions and similar phonetic recurrences.

We find these reiterations of sounds (*i.e.*, words or phrases) in modern conventional "meters." Tennyson, for example, repeats consecutively the same word or a phrase throughout many passages; and the refrain and repetend, as in Poe, is the same thing in a slightly different manner. These reiterations may, as has been pointed out (see Chapter I, § 2), set up a rhythm of their own, either syncopating or completely distorting the regular metrical pattern. But there is this very important difference between reiteration in rime and meter and reiteration in *Leaves of Grass:* in the former the poem has a set pattern (iambic, trochaic, anapestic, dactylic, or a combination of these), whereas in Whitman's verse there is no set pattern of sounds until the reiterations produce one.

Yet in every emotionally and intellectually pleasing poem in *Leaves of Grass*, these phonetic recurrences do set up a rhythmical pattern of sounds. Since the line is not bound by a specified number of syllables, the rhythm may give an untrained reader the impression that it is entirely "free" and lawless. To a certain extent, Whitman's rhythms are freer than those of classical and conventional versification; and therein lie their advantages. Still, they are no freer than the rhythms of the best musical compositions. They can, of course, become so free that the pattern is difficult to discover; and then the poet has failed, as Whitman many times does. But in his best poems — such as *Out of the Cradle Endlessly Rocking*, *By Blue Ontario's Shore*, and *When Lilacs Last in the Dooryard Bloom'd* — the combined "thought" and "phonetic" rhythms obey principles as definite as those of *Paradise Lost* or *Samson Agonistes*.

6. INITIAL REITERATION

The first of the phonetic recurrences we shall call *Initial Reiteration* (epanaphora is a less familiar term), which means repetition of a word or phrase at the beginning of the line.

> *Out of the* cradle endlessly rocking,
> *Out of the* mocking bird's throat, the musical shuttle,
> *Out of the* Ninth-month midnight.
>
> *Out of the Cradle Endlessly Rocking*

Even though these lines are of unequal length, the initial reiteration sets up a cadence which carries through the whole line. The same cadence, of course, is seldom present through many consecutive lines, and it would be monotonous if it were. But Whitman is especially skilful in interweaving his cadences, as in *Give Me the Splendid Silent Sun*. In this poem, the first cadence is distinguished by the reiteration of "give me." In the second strophe, the cadence is varied by brief repetitions; the second main cadence rings out clear and bold in the first four lines of section two and is achieved mainly by the reiteration of "keep your . . ."; and then the poet quickly shifts to the first cadence for several lines, and plays variations throughout the remainder of the poem.

7. MEDIAL AND FINAL REITERATION

The word or phrase may also be repeated within, or at the end, of the line:

> I will know if I am to be less *than they*,
> I will see if I am not as majestic *as they*,
> I will see if I am not as subtle and real *as they*,
> I will see if I am to be less generous *than they*.
> *By Blue Ontario's Shore*, Sec. 18

Or the reiteration may have several positions:

> Over the breast of the spring, the land, *amid* cities,
> *Amid* lanes and through old woods, where lately the violets
>   peep'd from the ground, spotting the gray debris,
> *Amid* the grass in the fields each side of the lanes, *passing* the
>   endless grass,
> *Passing* the yellow spear'd wheat, every grain from its shroud
>   in the dark-brown fields uprisen,
> *Passing* the apple-tree blows of white and pink in the orchards,
> Carrying a corpse to where it shall rest in the grave,
> Night and day journeys a coffin.
> *When Lilacs Last*, etc.

The use of these reiterations in both the initial (epanaphora) and the medial and final (epanalepsis) places may be summarized briefly as follows: (1) to produce cadence — *i.e.*, the musical rhythms of the line depend largely upon phonic reiterations, (2) to band lines together into strophes or stanzaic divisions, and (3) to achieve purely oratorical effects. Catel [15] thinks that Whitman's poetry should be regarded largely as oratory, and there is no denying the fact that parallelism and reiteration are

[15] Jean Catel, *Rythme et langage dans l'édition des "Leaves of Grass,"* *1855* (Montpellier, 1930?).

characteristically oratorical rhythms.   But the analogy of
oratory should not be carried too far.   The second use (as
given above) need not be emphasized a great deal.   It is
true that initial and final repetitions do often mark the
beginning and ending of a strophe.   Yet this is less important than the fact that they are responsible for the beginning and ending of cadences.   In other words, the most
important use of phonetic reiterations is rhythmical and
musical.

8. GRAMMATICAL RHYTHM

A special sort of reiteration not covered by the phonetic
recurrences already discussed is the repetition of a certain
sort of speech or grammatical construction.   This we may
appropriately call *grammatical rhythm*.   Examples are:

Flow on, river! *flow* with the flood-tide and *ebb* with the ebb-tide!
Frolic on, crested and scallop-edg'd waves!
Gorgeous clouds of the sunset! *drench* with your splendor me, or
     the men and women generations after me!
Cross from shore to shore, countless crowds of passengers!
Stand up, tall masts of Mannahatta, etc.
Crossing Brooklyn Ferry, Sec. 9

The fact that it is difficult to scan some of the poems
of *Leaves of Grass* in the orthodox manner is no sure indication that they do not have rhythmical patterns, but
this is a convenient place for a demonstration that reiteration (whether of the same words or of parallel grammatical constructions) does often produce a line so regular
in its rhythms of speech stresses that we can actually
scan it.   *E.g.*,

Lóng and lóng has the gráss been grówing,

Lóng and lóng has the ráin been fálling,

Lóng has the glóbe been rólling róund.
Song of the Exposition

The song is to the singer, and comes back most to him,

The teaching is to the teacher, and comes back most to him,

The murder is to the murderer, and comes back most to him.

Song of the Rolling Earth, Sec. 2

Of course, the parallel reiteration in these examples is unusually regular. In addition to the "long" reiteration, for instance, we have the parallel nouns "grass," "rain," and "globe," and the present participles "growing," "falling," and "rolling." We also have a fairly regular rhythmical pattern in:

O to sail to sea in a ship!

To leave this steady unendurable land,

To leave the tiresome sameness of the streets, the sidewalks and

the houses,

To leave you O you solid motionless land, and entering a ship,

To sail and sail and sail!

A Song of Joys

At times the reiterations produce two half-lines with different stresses, the first being accentuated more firmly and the second half lighter, sometimes as faint as an echo:

Great are the myths — I too delight in them;
Great are Adam and Eve — I too look back and accept them.

Great Are the Myths

9. WHITMAN'S PARENTHESES

Whitman's use of the parenthesis has puzzled many students of his poetry, for it is often employed where the passage is not parenthetical in thought. Careful examination, however, shows that usually the parenthesis indicates a break in the rhythm set up by the phonetic recurrences. The rhythm is momentarily suspended, broken off completely, or in some manner varied by the passage inside the parenthesis.   Sometimes the parenthetical marks bracket a passage at the very beginning of the poem, so that it could not be parenthetical in thought; but these cases are rare.   A fairly characteristic specimen is:

To the leaven'd soil they trod calling I sing for the last,
(Forth from my tent emerging for good, loosing, untying the
    tent ropes,)
In the freshness of the forenoon air . . .
To the fiery fields emanative . . .
To the leaven'd soil . . .
To the Alleghanian hills . . . etc.

To the Leaven'd Soil They Trod

10.   IMAGERY AND FIGURES

From his 1855 Preface until the end of his life, Whitman preached a doctrine which, among other things, insisted that the American poet (by which, undoubtedly, he meant himself) should free his art from all literary imitations. Among the things which he was to give up were allusions, inversions, and all the usual poetic tricks.   Simplicity was, to be sure, a virtue which he demanded in life, manners, philosophy, and, naturally, prosody.   Yet he taught that the method of *indirection* was to be the method of the poet, and indirection does not make for simplicity.

Our key to this paradox is Walt Whitman's attitude toward words, already referred to in the Introduction to this chapter.   Almost any passage from *An American Primer*, his would-be treatise for the orator and poet, reveals what words do to him.

"Some words are fresh smelling like lilacs, roses to the soul, blooming without failure, — The name of Christ — all words that have arisen from the life and death of Christ, the divine son, who went about speaking perfect words, no patois — whose life was perfect, the touch of whose hands and feet was miracles, — and who was crucified — his flesh laid in a shroud, in the grave." [16]

After rhythm (or perhaps before), it is largely figures of speech which separate poetry from prose. There are scarcely any literary allusions in *Leaves of Grass*, but these poems are as rich in metaphors and figures as any poetry. The 1855 Preface itself is full of poetic figures and metaphors:

When the long Atlantic coast stretches longer and the Pacific coast stretches longer he [the American poet] stretches with them north or south. He spans between them also from east to west and reflects what is between them. On him rise solid growths that offset the growths of pine and cedar and hemlock and liveoak and locust and chestnut and cypress and hickory and limetree . . . and tangles as tangled as any canebreak or swamp . . . and forests coated with transparent ice and icicles hanging from the boughs and crackling in the wind . . . and sides and peaks of mountains . . . and pasturage sweet and free as savannah or upland or prairie . . . with flights and songs and screams that answer those of the wildpigeon and highhold and orchard-oriole . . .

Already we can see what sort of figurative language Whitman is going to use. (And incidentally, it is worthwhile to remember that in this Preface, in just such passages as the one quoted above, he is also setting forth indirectly a new prosodic theory.) First, it will be observed that the objects named are simple and concrete. Second, the poet is content for the most part merely to name the object without attempting to describe it further. True, the forests are "coated with transparent ice and icicles hanging from the boughs and crackling in the wind," but that is merely a piling up of other concrete objects, which man can see and feel and hear.

This discussion cannot go into the psychology of the problem, but one hint may be apropos. The imagery of

[16] Pp. 18–19.

Leaves of Grass is a brilliant illustration of the James-Lange theory:[17] it expresses emotion either by naming the sensations of which the emotion consists, or it indirectly portrays the emotion by naming the concrete objects which may be counted upon to produce the sensation. Whitman's long catalogs of specific objects are explained by this theory.

Interlink'd, food-yielding lands!
Land of coal and iron! land of gold! land of cotton, sugar, rice!
Land of wheat, beef, pork! land of wool and hemp! land of the
    apple and the grape!
Land of the pastoral plains, the grass-fields of the world! land
    of those sweet-air'd interminable plateaus!
Land of the herd, the garden, the healthy house of the adobie!
                                Starting from Paumonok, Sec. 14

To Whitman each of these simple, concrete names carries with it an emotional experience; so, to produce the same emotional experience in the reader, he simply chants the names of the objects. Whatever we may think of the psychology (and art) of such a procedure, it is Walt Whitman's technique, and the explanation given here is important not only in understanding his poetry but also his prosody. For this technique affects his versification in a most profound manner. Indeed, the discovery of the catalog method of producing an imaginative response was probably the beginning of Walt Whitman's "new" system of prosody.

11. "CHANGING FIGURES"

The actual simile is not found so often in *Leaves of Grass* as in most other poetry, yet we do have it occasionally:

> As a strong bird on pinions free,
> Joyous, the amplest spaces heavenward cleaving,
> Such be the thought I'd think of thee, America,
> Such be the recitative I'd bring for thee.

[17] See William James, *Psychology* (New York, 1899), II, 452 ff.

Beautiful world of new superber birth that rises to my eyes,
Like a limitless golden cloud filling the western sky,
Emblem of general maternity lifted above all, . . .

Thou Mother with Thy Equal Brood

Fecund America — today,

. . . .

As some huge ship freighted to water's edge thou ridest into
    port,
As rain falls from the heaven and vapors rise from earth, so have
    the precious values fallen upon thee and risen out of thee;
Thou envy of the globe! thou miracle!

The Return of the Heroes

In this passage, Whitman uses the word *recitative*, and
he often refers to his poems as "these recitatives."
Whether or not the word had any special connotation for
him, it is impossible to determine, but it is interesting
that the biblical recitatives consist, as do Walt Whitman's,
of a series of changing figures. *Cf. Joel* I.11:

> The vine is withered
> And the fig tree languisheth
> The pomegranate tree,
> The palm tree also, and the apple tree,

Give me the splendid silent sun . . .
Give me the juicy autumnal fruit ripe and red from the orchard,
Give me a field where the unmow'd grass grows,
Give me an arbor, give me the trellis'd grape,
Give me fresh corn and wheat, . . .

Give Me, etc.

This is Whitman's method. Whether he was capable
of no other or whether he adopted it deliberately does not
concern us here. It is appropriate to observe, however,
that it was not entirely a poetic device, since much of
his prose reveals the same technique of composition.
Once when the editor of the *North American Review*
asked Whitman to write an essay on American literature,
he promised to do so provided he would be allowed to

"put down some mélanged cogitations regarding the matter." Professor Foerster has quite correctly observed that "mélanged cogitations" aptly describes Whitman's style, in poetry as well as prose.[18]

That poetry should be expressed by the method of *indirection* follows Whitman's theory. Some of his poems are all metaphor, all suggestion, and are scarcely intelligible to many readers. He fails, not because his poetry lacks figures, but because it is too figurative. However, since Whitman thought of himself as a modern prophet, perhaps it is appropriate that he should have played the Christ-rôle even to the point of speaking parables, for that is precisely what this technique amounts to. What, after all, is *Leaves of Grass* but a composite parable to which the reader must supply his own interpretation and conclusion? Such Whitman always insisted it was.

12. CHRONOLOGICAL DEVELOPMENTS

The purpose of this chapter has been merely to trace and illustrate the basic principles of Walt Whitman's rhythms and implied prosody, without regard to chronological developments, yet several observations on chronology may be helpful.

Whitman's juvenile versification has already been mentioned disparagingly, and a sample ought to show why:

> Behold around us pomp and pride:
>   The rich, the lofty, and the gay,
> Glitter before our dazzled eyes,
>   Live out their brief but brilliant day;
> Then, when the hour for fame is o'er
>   Unheeded pass away.[19]

It is obvious here that Gray and the lesser "graveyard poets" were the young poet's masters. Metrically, this piece (and it is probably one of his best) is better than it

[18] Norman Foerster, *American Criticism* (Boston, 1928), p. 158.
[19] *Uncollected Prose and Poetry*, I, 13.

is poetically, with its borrowed, diluted, and trite thought;
but of course it is also inferior in versification too, with
its monotonous *te-dum, te-dum, te-dum* movement.

> At night, go view the solemn stars,
> Those wheeling worlds through time the same —
> How puny seem the widest power,
> The proudest mortal name! [20]

The remainder of Whitman's juvenile poems are in this
same chop-stick versification, utterly without verbal melodies, felicitous variations, fresh rimes, or anything to
make them genuine poetry.

Our first indication of a change is in a poem which
Whitman is said to have written and presented to his host,
"Farmer Johnson," at Blennerhasset Island, in the Ohio
River, where it is claimed that Whitman spent a night about
1849. It is called *Isle of La Belle Rivière*, and begins:

> Bride of the swart Ohio;
> Nude, yet fair to look upon,
> Clothed only with the leaf,
> As was innocent Eve of Eden.
> The son of grim old Alleghany
> And white-breasted Monongahela
> Is wedded to thee, and it is well.
> His tawny thighs cover thee
> In the vernal time of spring,
> And lo! in the autumn is the fruitage. [21]

After this, the lines sweep into longer lengths and freer
rhythms, not altogether unsuccessful. It is evident that
by 1849 Whitman was beginning to find his style. He
had abandoned rime, set metrical patterns, and was writing what the French were later to call *vers libre*. His

[20] *Uncollected Prose and Poetry*, I, 13.

[21] See Emory Holloway's biography, *Whitman* (New York, 1926),
pp. 79–81. The poem appears in *Uncollected Prose and Poetry*, I, 24–25.
Jean Catel, in *Walt Whitman, la Naissance du poète* (Paris, 1929),
p. 288, thinks these verses are spurious. He bases his judgment on
internal evidence.

lines were mainly end-stopped, yet he had not yet completely acquired the knack of composing by line-units, with parallelism and phonetic reiteration as his guiding principles. Parallelism of a sort was used, though the lines tended to march in pairs, and the music was a little uncertain.

But the young poet was apparently working on his technique during these years, for in 1851 a speech which he delivered to the Brooklyn Art Union contained some of his own verses in the style of *Leaves of Grass*. And by 1855 his "new" method was ready to show to the public.

Song of Myself is Whitman's longest poem, and it suffers from what is perhaps the greatest danger of the poet's new method. It lacks organization, in many places has poor coherence, and is unduly prolix. Yet what else could be expected from a first poem written in a line-by-line parallelism in the style of changing figures? It was so easy for the enthusiastic young poet, composing (as he apparently was) without a logical scheme in mind, to strike one chord after another, as he might stack one brick on top of another, until he had tired himself out.

This description is no exaggeration. It seems to have been literally the way Whitman wrote *Leaves of Grass*. Later he became more discriminating, and eventually wrote the marvelously and subtly melodious *When Lilacs Last in the Dooryard Bloom'd;* but the basic prosodic principles of this poem are the same as those of *Song of Myself*.

During his old-age invalidism, Whitman did not have the physical and emotional energy to write long, sustained poems. As a result, his later poems are not only shorter but also more compact, though the difference is one of degree rather than kind. It is for this reason that a poem written in 1876 is merely an expanded metaphor:

The Beauty of the Ship

When, staunchly entering port,
After long ventures, hauling up, worn and old,

Battered by sea and wind, torn by many a fight,
With the original sails all gone, replaced, or mended,
I only saw, at last, the beauty of the ship.

Different periods of the poet's work, to be sure, had
their own special peculiarities and interests, but these
include mainly differences in subject-matter and minor
stylistic idiosyncrasies, indicated to a great extent by
Whitman's names for the different groups of his poems,
such as "Inscriptions," "Children of Adam," "Sea-
Drift," "Drum-Taps," "Sands at Seventy," etc. Yet
few of these differences affect his versification to any
great extent, and none of them alter the basic principles
which have been explained in this chapter.

We might guess from *O Captain! My Captain!* that
about 1865 Whitman's versification tended to become
more metrical and conventional. But this poem, with its
fairly regular iambic meter, its rimes, and its refrain, is
almost an anomaly in the volume, *Leaves of Grass.* These
very uncharacteristic features have made it unjustly
popular in school readers, but it is not what the lovers of
Walt Whitman prize most, and even the poet himself
seems to have regretted that he ever wrote it, after he
realized that it was becoming more famous than his
other poems. Perhaps he did not realize that a poet is
seldom celebrated for his best poems. *O Captain! My
Captain!* and *Beat! Beat! Drums!* are on a par with
Poe's *Bells* in respect to undeserved renown.

The one technical feature of *Leaves of Grass* which does
show an important chronological development (that is,
after 1855) is that of phonetic recurrence. Miss Wiley
says, "Whitman's use of the reiterative devices shows a
constant increase from 1855 to 1881. From a frequency
of approximately twenty-two per cent in 1860, the use of
the repetitive patterns increases to thirty-two in 1867
and 1871 and thirty-eight per cent in 1881." [22] After
1881, she finds only twenty-two per cent, which is ex-

[22] Wiley, *op. cit.*, p. 170.

plained by the fact that phonetic reiteration is more essential in the longer poems; and after 1881, Whitman wrote hardly any poems over ten lines in length, though not, it should be repeated, because of any change in prosodic theory or intentional variation of practice.

We must conclude, finally, that sometime around 1851, Walt Whitman discovered a poetic technique which was peculiarly adapted to his own abilities. He preached his "new" literary theory (including a new prosody) as the medium to be used by the future poet of Democracy, but he was really defending his own most natural style of versification. Precisely where he learned this new manner so well suited to him we do not know, but it was, whatever its source, a rediscovery of a verse technique some five thousand years old rather than the invention of an entirely new method. From Whitman it passed to France (or at any rate it soon appeared in France) and from France back to America, where we still have it in modified and transmuted forms.[23]

SELECTED BIBLIOGRAPHY

Text

Whitman, Walt, *Leaves of Grass*, ed. by Emory Holloway. Garden City, New York: Doubleday, Doran and Company, 1929. [Inclusive authorized edition.]

——, *American Primer*. Boston: Small, Maynard and Company, 1904.

——, *Walt Whitman*, ed. by Floyd Stovall. (American Writers Series.) New York: American Book Company, 1934. [Selections of Whitman's best poetry and prose, with a suggestive introduction and helpful notes.]

---

[23] After 1855 Whitman wrote a few poems with conventional versification, even using regular rime and meter; but they form so minor a part of his usual technique that it has not seemed necessary to discuss them here. See Lois Ware, "Poetic Convention in Leaves of Grass," *Studies in Philology* (January, 1929), XXVI, 47–57.

CRITICISM

Allen, Gay W., "Biblical Analogies for Walt Whitman's Prosody," *Revue Anglo-Américaine* (August, 1933), X, No. 6, 490–507.

Catel, Jean, *Rythme et langage dans l'édition des "Leaves of Grass," 1855.* (Thèse complémentaire.) Montpellier: Causse, Graille et Castelman, 1930 (?).

Erskine, John, "Whitman's Prosody," *Studies in Philology* (1923), XX, 334–344.

Jannaccone, P., *La Poesia di Walt Whitman e L'Evoluzione delle Forme Ritmiche.* Torino, Italy: 1898.

Ross, E. C.: "Whitman's Verse," *Modern Language Notes* (June, 1930), XLV, 363–364.

Scott, Fred Newton, "A Note on Whitman's Prosody," *Journal of English and Germanic Philology*, VII, 134–153.

Ware, Lois, "Poetic Convention in Leaves of Grass," *Studies in Philology* (January, 1929), XXVI, 47–57.

Wiley, Autrey Nell, "Reiterative Devices in 'Leaves of Grass,'" *American Literature* (May, 1929), I, No. 2, 161–170.

CHAPTER IX

James Russell Lowell

I. INTRODUCTION

WE might expect from one of America's most prolific literary critics and from an outstanding poet who followed in Longfellow's academic footsteps at Harvard an important contribution to American prosody. We know from Lowell's essays on Milton, Dante, and Spenser that he was a serious and competent student of versification, and throughout his writings both in prose and in verse there are many remarks on the art and form of poetic composition. Yet nowhere do we find anything like a "system" or a theory of prosody. His remarks on poetics, however, do reveal great impatience with the eighteenth-century standards and a predilection for those of the near-contemporary poets of England. Of all American poets, Lowell's prosodic attitudes and his versification are probably nearest those of post-Wordsworthian England.

A detailed study of his literary and æsthetic theories and criticisms might enable us to concoct a prosody which would be in agreement with both his own practices and his literary and artistic beliefs; but lack of space forbids any such attempt here, even if it were advisable. Furthermore, scholarly opinions regarding Lowell as a poet and literary critic are considerably at variance, so that almost any conclusions that we might draw would probably be controversial. Professor Reilly,[1] for instance, finds Lowell no critic at all but a mere impressionist, whereas Professor Foerster [2] regards him as the most dis-

---

[1] Joseph J. Reilly, *James Russell Lowell as a Critic* (New York, 1915).
[2] Norman Foerster, *American Criticism* (Boston, 1928), pp. 111–156.

tinguished American critic, and an Aristotelian. Professor Clark [3] finds three stages of development in Lowell's work: humanitarianism, nationalism, and humanism; and the argument is so well substantiated that no future surveys of Lowell's thought can fail to take into account the poet's progressive development. Professor Pritchard [4] attempts to trace Lowell's debt to Horace's *Ars Poetica*. Possibly most of these views could be reconciled, but it seems fairly obvious that any attempt to trace a "system" in Lowell's thinking on poetic form and technique must overcome many difficulties, not the least of which is the poet's own pleasantly garrulous inconsistency. A few illustrations may serve to indicate these difficulties to which we refer; and though the following discussion is not intended to outline either genetically or comprehensively Lowell's ideas on poetics, it may at least indicate the type of man with which we are dealing.

On numerous occasions, Lowell stipulated that poetry should be philosophical. For example, he censured former versions of the Prometheus story and defended his own by saying that, "So much of its spirit as poets in former ages have attained . . . was by instinct rather than by reason." [5] When he frequently referred to his own "radicalism," he apparently meant his attempts to keep reason uppermost in his poetry. "The proof of poetry is," according to Lowell, ". . . that it reduce to the essence of a single line the vague philosophy which is floating in all men's minds, and so render it portable and useful and ready to hand . . . no poem ever makes me respect its author which does not in some way convey a truth of philosophy." [6]

[3] Harry Hayden Clark, "Lowell — Humanitarian, Nationalist, or Humanist?," *Studies in Philology* (July, 1930), XXVII, No. 3, 411–441.

[4] John Paul Pritchard, "Lowell's Debt to Horace's *Ars Poetica*," *American Literature* (Nov., 1931), III, No. 3, 259–276.

[5] Charles Eliot Norton (ed.), *Letters of James Russell Lowell* (New York, 1894), I, 72.

[6] *Ibid.*, p. 73.

If English poets of any age have been predominantly philosophical and "reasonable," they were the eighteenth-century poets. And certainly no other poet in the English language has reduced so many vague philosophical thoughts floating in all men's minds to the "essence of a single line" as did Pope. Yet Lowell was always at war with the eighteenth-century standards. Is not "common-sense" the "vague philosophy which is floating in all men's minds"? At least it is the basis of such philosophical thoughts as "all men" may be said to have. But in *The Cathedral*, Lowell calls common-sense "Poor Richard slowly elbowing Plato out." He regards it as the great blot upon Dryden's work [7] and as the eighteenth-century drought upon the very springs of poetry.

Even his definition of a lyric appears to exalt reason over emotion: "My notion of a true lyric is that the meaning should float steadfast in the centre of every stanza, while the vapory emotions (protean in form as you will) float up to it and over it, and wreathe it with an opal halo which seems their own, but is truly its own work. The shades of emotion over, there floats the meaning, clear and sole and sharp-cut in its luminous integrity . . ." [8]

Again there seems to be a contradiction between Lowell's demand for finish and form and his inspirational notion of poetic composition. Nothing short of the most perfect control over technique could reduce philosophical thoughts to a single line, or leave clear-cut meaning shining through the emotion of a simple lyric. Such achievements are the result of long practice and much polishing. The same is true of style, which Lowell demanded along with thought.[9]

Still, we know that not only in theory but also in practice he believed in the spontaneous, inspirational method of poetic composition. "Second thoughts are prose," he

---

[7] *Latest Literary Essays and Addresses* (Boston, 1892), pp. 4–5.
[8] *Letters*, I, 282.
[9] *The Function of the Poet* (Boston, 1920), p. 147.

says in *The Cathedral*. And on numerous occasions he explained that when he did revise his poems, he invariably found his first draft best. At other times, he could not revise at all. But then, despite the paradox, finish and polish were not what he wanted anyway. In the *Fable for Critics*, Bryant was set down because:

> He's too smooth and too polished to hang any zeal on:

Whittier, who was anything but a careful craftsman, was more to Lowell's liking:

> There was ne'er a man born who had more of the swing
> Of the true lyric bard and all that kind of thing;

Yet Whitman's crudities were too much for the Harvard professor-poet — perhaps because he did not understand them.

If there is any solution to the paradoxes in Lowell's prosodic and critical opinions, it probably lies in his easy impressionability and the nature of the recent English poetry with which he was most familiar. The idea that poetry is the medium for the expression of philosophical thoughts is, as we have pointed out, typically eighteenth-century, but even Wordsworth and Coleridge emphasized philosophy in poetry: the main difference is that theirs is an idealistic philosophy, whereas Pope's is "common-sense," the kind that Lowell seems to demand but apparently does not mean. Of course Lowell's whole inspirational attitude toward poetic composition is typically transcendental, and he has been classified as a transcendentalist.[10] It was also characteristic of his age to believe that intuition rather than revision and "fundamental brain-work" could produce perfection of form, as Lowell states regarding the song (by which he means lyric): "The best part of a song lies often not at all in the words, but in the metre, perhaps, or the structure of

---

[10] George Willis Cooke, *The Poets of Transcendentalism* (Boston: Houghton Mifflin Company, 1903), pp. 10–11, 44–52.

the verse, in the wonderful melody which arose of itself from the feeling of the writer, and which unawares throws the heart into the same frame of thought." [11] He censured Ben Jonson for writing without inspiration, and declared that "Herrick is perhaps the best and most unconscious." [12]

This attitude, and apparently a congenital distaste for revision, are no doubt partly responsible for some of the crudities in Lowell's versification. Yet we must not accuse him of not trying to reason out the best forms to use (*cf.* his note to the Harvard *Ode*). And when he calls pentameter a cold "and almost glacier-slow measure," [13] he is merely asserting his prosodic heritage. That his versification should be less classically regular than that of Holmes, who admired the "neo-classical" poets, is less surprising than that it is as regular as it is.

But Lowell, himself, insisted that his irregularities of meter were intentional and studied, and no doubt they were, in principle if not in actuality in every case: "I may," he says, "be a bad poet (I don't mean to say I *think* that I am), but I *am* a good versifier. I write with far more ease in verse than in prose; I have studied the subject, and I understand it from beginning to end. There is not a rough verse in my book that isn't intentional, and if my critics' ears were as good as they are long, they would perceive it. I don't believe the man ever lived who put more *conscience* into his verses than I do." [14]

On another occasion, the poet reported that, "R.[obert] animadverted on the irregular metre of the T.[hrenody], but, as I think, very unphilosophically and without much perception of the *true* rules of poetry. In my opinion no verse ought to be longer than the writer can sensibly make it. It has been this senseless stretching of verses to make them octo- or deka-syllabic or what not, that has

[11] *Early Prose Writings of James Russell Lowell* (The Bodley Head, London and New York, 1903), p. 75.   [12] *Ibid.*, p. 90.
[13] *Letters*, I, 318.   [14] *Ibid.*, I, 121–122.

brought such an abundance of useless epithets on the shoulders of poor English verse." [15]

In other words, the poet must be free to choose the versification best suited to the thought that he wants to express and the emotion he wishes to convey; he will not let his thought and emotion be bound by a "system" or by "rules" of versification. Lowell is thus theoretically in the line of the American prosodic rebels. But he carried out his revolt only in his free choice of the number and the placing of the accents in the line, while allowing himself, of course, the most freedom in his odes and kindred forms (especially with respect to the length of the line). His versification is in many respects as "modern" as Shelley's, which very likely influenced him profoundly; but he can hardly be classed with such *bona fide* rebels as Whitman and Amy Lowell, or even Emerson and Emily Dickinson. Lowell is simply a nineteenth-century poet revolting against eighteenth-century prosody.

2. THE ODE AND IRREGULAR MEASURES

Lowell's most original versification is found in his odes and other poems written in lines of irregular lengths. It is also in these poems, as we have anticipated, that his own theories are best exemplified. His verse in other and more regular forms, moreover, contains few peculiarities of style or versification not found in these measures.

The poet himself used the word *ode* more to signify thought and content than metrical form, for some of the poems that he called odes are in regular iambic pentameter or octosyllabic lines. Yet when we speak here of the ode as a metrical form, we mean a poem in lines of different length, usually without stanzas in any unified sense (though it may be "paragraphed"), and ordinarily riming alternately and in couplets. This is the pseudo-Pindaric ode, used by both Emerson and Longfellow. Lowell used

[15] *Letters*, I, 38.

it off and on during most of his life, but the two outstanding examples are *Threnodia* (1839) and *Ode Recited at the Harvard Commemoration* (1865).

Though Lowell's only justification of the meter of *Threnodia* is merely that "no verse ought to be longer than the writer can sensibly make it," he rationalizes his metrical freedom in the Harvard *Ode, viz.*, that the poem was intended to be read in public and that lines of irregular length are more readable than those in "a long series of uniform stanzas." He also reports that he tried writing some of this poem in "mixed rhymed and blank verse of unequal measures, like those in the choruses of 'Samson Agonistes,'" but found that his ear was better pleased with the rime coming at infrequent intervals.

However, since *Threnodia* was evidently not intended for public reading, it would seem that the form appealed to the poet merely as convenient and pleasing. The lines range from two to five stresses, preponderantly iambic, but with some trisyllabic feet, and a considerable number of spondees, inversions, etc. They are grouped into twelve strophes, ranging from fourteen to over fifty verses each. The short lines are distributed singly and in groups throughout the strophes, with apparently some attempt at balance. As fair samples of the versification, we might list the following:

> Gone, gone from us! and shall we see
> Those sibyl-leaves of destiny,
> Those calm eyes, nevermore? . . .
> Oh stern word — Nevermore! . . .
> . . . .
>
> How peacefully they rest,
> Crossfolded there,
> Upon his little breast,

Those small, white hands that ne'er were still before,
But ever sported with his mother's hair,
Or the | plain cross | that on her breast she wore!
. . . .
He did but float a little way
Adown the stream of time,
With dreamy eyes | watching | the rip | ples play,
Or hearkening their fairy chime;
His slender sail
Ne'er felt the gale;
He did but float a little way,

The accentuation of these lines does not raise any difficult problems. The reader may mark the feet of the
fourth line any way he chooses, since the accents will not
be affected. The contraction of "ne'er" was apparently
made to avoid a trisyllabic foot, though the poet may
have used it not for any metrical reason at all, but simply
because he regarded the contraction as "poetic diction."
We wonder, then, whether "hearkening" should be read
with a metrical stress on "-ing," making the line four-
stress (most of Lowell's predecessors would elide "-ening"
— elision of "pure *n*"). The inversion of "on her breast
she wore" for the sake both of maintaining the even beat
and making a rime for "before," the stilted "He did but
float," and the archaic "adown" are indications that this
is either an early poem or that the poet has not been completely emancipated by the Wordsworthian reform of
poetic diction. As a matter of fact, it is a fairly early
poem, but Lowell later used even more inversions, poetic
tags, and clichés, though no more than Whittier, Longfellow, or Holmes.

Summer Storm, written the same year as *Threnodia*
(1839), is more characteristic of Lowell's versification in
general. It is iambic with many "headless" lines, ranging
from two- to five-stress. But more important, there are
feminine rimes such as:

> The thunder is rumbling
> And crashing and crumbling, —

The poem is lyrical, onomatopoetic, and spirited, yet
some of the lines are a bit heavy and not easy to read.
Such verses as these are characteristic of much of Lowell's
versification:

> But up the west, like a rock-shivered surge,
>
> Climbs a great cloud edged with sun-whitened spray;
>
> Huge whirls of foam boil toppling o'er its verge,
>
> And falling still it seems, and yet it climbs alway.

Two spondees in a pentameter are rather unusual, and
the sense of the line seems to demand a primary stress on
"boil."   Perhaps "great" in the preceding line should
also be read with primary accent.   At any rate, the lines
unmistakably labor with the elements, which is possibly
the poet's intention.

The rhythm of *To Perdita, Singing* (1841) is characterized by primary-secondary-primary accents, with an occasional spondee.

> The green, bright grass of childhood bring to me, . . .
>
> The joy, that, like a clear breeze, went
>
> Through and through to old time! . . .
>
> Peace sits within thine eyes,
>
> With white hands crossed in joyful rest,

We also find the archaic *-ĕd*, which Lowell definitely
adopted in his versification, though he used it sparingly:

Grows from behind its black, clear edg | ëd bound,

Memoriæ Positum is different in having a general stanzaic pattern, which is $a_2b_4b_4a_3cc_5a_3dd_5a_3$. But the four-
and five-stress lines vary, and some are difficult to scan.
In an introductory note, Lowell says, "Perhaps I was
wrong in stiffening the feet of my verses a little, in order
to give them a kind of slow funeral tread." This "stiffening" results in such lines as:

But the | high soul | burns on | to light | men's feet

"High soul" may be a doubtful spondee, for "high"
could receive secondary stress, as seems to be desirable in:

In the mere wreck of nobly-pitched designs,

Ode (1841) is in pentameter lines, but the usual spondees and primary-secondary-primary accentuation is
found:

In the old days of awe and keen-eyed wonder,

The Poet's song with blood-warm truth was rife; . . .

To know the heart of all things was his duty,

And especially light, since a metrical stress on "the"
would be absurd, is:

His soul was led by the eternal law;

Ode (written for the Celebration of the Introduction of
the Cochituate Water into the City of Boston) is simply
four-stress, riming *ababcc*. *Ode to Happiness* is also four-
stress, riming in couplets and alternately. *Love's Clock*
is two-stress, the only excuse for the occasional four-stress
verses being the economy of rime:

"Early or late,
When lovers wait,
And Love's watch gains, if Time a gait
So snail-like chooses,

> Why should his feet
> Become more fleet
> Than coward's are, when lovers meet
> And Love's watch loses?"

But Lowell's three great odes are in the irregular form. In *Ode Recited at the Harvard Commemoration* the strophes range from fourteen lines (strophe I) to fifty-nine (VI). It begins with a dimeter and ends with a pentameter line, and many passages contain trimeter and tetrameter. The rimes are alternate and couplet. The basic rhythm is iambic, though there are numerous inversions, trisyllabic feet, and juxtapositions of three stressed monosyllables. The irregular meter makes it doubtful whether metrical stresses should be marked at all. For instance, in the examples below the meter and not the sense demands the metrical stress on the unemphatic "and" and "of":

> In manly hearts to come, and nerves them and dilates:
>
> Nor such thy teaching, Mother of us all.

Typical lines are:

> Whither the brave deed climbs for light: . . .
>
> Bringing our robin's leaf to deck their hearse
>
> Who in warm life-blood wrote their nobler verse,

"Warm life-blood wrote" can be read so many ways that it is probably foolish to try to scan it. The cæsura, after "blood," is so emphatic that it could be counted as a "metrical silence," consuming the time of an unaccented syllable.

Double rimes are common in this poem, but identical rime of the second syllable is rarer:

> What were our lives without thee?
>
> What all our lives to save thee?

We réck not whát we gáve theè;
We will not dáre to doùbt theè,

Agassiz (1874) is less irregular than the Harvard *Ode*,
though the two are technically a good deal alike. Yet
Ode Read at Concord (1875) and *An Ode* (1876) are more
regular still. In an introductory note the poet says,
"The sentiment of the Concord Ode demanded a larger
proportion of lyrical movements, of course, than the
others. Harmony, without sacrifice of melody, was what
I had mainly in view." The chief metrical difference is
the greater use of three- and four-stress lines. Also each
strophe has one characteristic measure, with fewer inser-
tions of variant lines than in most of the other odes.
Some of the cadences are prosy:

Whose choíce decídes a mán lífe's sláve or kíng?

The last strophe (X) has so many anapestic substitutions that some lines are characteristically anapestic:

Whŏ wĭll mín | glĕ hĕr lífe | wĭth ŏur dúst
And mákes | ŭs dĕsérve | tŏ bĕ frée!

Under the Old Elm ranges from three to six-stress, but
has fewer short-line passages than the earlier odes. In
fact, it is more regular all around, though, like the *Concord
Ode*, it has many anapestic feet.

A chronological study of Lowell's irregular measures
does not reveal any startling advancements or changes in
his versification. The anapest is used more freely in the
later poems, and the poet apparently gave increasingly
more attention to harmony; but the "kittle-y-bender"
lines, to use Holmes's term (see Chapter VII, § 1), are
found in the later poems almost as frequently as in the
earlier ones. On the other hand, there is a certain appropriateness in the irregularities of *Summer Storm* which
we do not find in most of the later odes and lyrics.

The versification of *The Vision of Sir Launfal* is a little difficult to classify, since it begins with iambic pentameter, shifts to octosyllabic couplets, develops into irregular four-stress verse with frequent trisyllabic substitutions, and in certain places varies from four to ten syllables to the line. The poem is predominantly four-stress, but the irregularity of the meter seems to make it more appropriate to discuss the versification under the section of irregular forms, though it is distinctly different from the structure of the pseudo-Pindaric ode.

The opening lines indicate what the poet is attempting to do:

> Over his keys the musing organist,
> Beginning doubtfully and far away,
> First lets his fingers wander as they list,
> And builds a bridge from Dreamland for his lay:

Lowell does not let his fingers wander, however, for the prelude to the first part is very carefully fingered; but there is an analogy between the poem and a musical composition. In no other poem does Lowell display such virtuosity in the handling of rhythms and yet keep so closely to a basic pattern (in this case, four-stress iambic). The pattern may be illustrated by:

> Daily, with souls that cringe and plot,
> We Sinais climb and know it not.

Yet the cadences quickly spread out to include trisyllabic feet and feminine rime:

> Earth gets its price for what Earth gives us;
> The beggar is taxed for a corner to die in, . . .
>
> 'T is heaven alone that is given away,
> 'T is only God may be had for the asking;

Then the cadence is modified by the entrance of spondees:

And the heart | in her | dumb breast | flutters and sings;
He sings | to the | wide world, | and she to her nest, —
In the | nice ear | of Nature which song is the best?

The prelude to Part II begins with:

Down swept the chill wind from the mountain peak,
From the snow five thousand summers old;

And toward the end, the lines vary in the ode manner:

But the wind without was eager and sharp,
Of Sir Launfal's gray hair it makes a harp,
        And rattles and wrings
        The icy strings,
Singing, in dreary monotone,
A Christmas carol of its own,
Whose burden still, as he might guess,
Was "Shelterless, shelterless, shelterless!"
The voice of the seneschal flared like a torch
As he shouted the wanderer away from the porch,

In Part II the poet-organist resorts to less versatile
devices and metrical *legerdemain*, but the rhythms have
a suggestiveness fully equal to the other parts of the poem.
Especially effective for tone and color are such lines as:

The bare boughs rattled shudderingly; . . .
A single crow on the tree-top bleak
From his shining feathers shed off the cold sun;

Or notice the appropriateness of the cæsural pause and
the contrast of anapest against iamb in:

Again | it was morning, | but shrunk | and cold,

No American poet had hitherto achieved more varied and subtle effects with meter, and indeed Lowell scarcely ever succeeded so well again himself. But even this poem, we must remember, has some of the "kittle-y-benders" [16] which Holmes so much objected to.

3. FOUR-STRESS VERSE

Lowell used the four-stress line more than any other metrical form. Under this head, we may include not only the octosyllabic couplet (and alternate rime) but also the four-stress stanzas, combinations of three- and four-stress lines, the four-plus-three measure, and the much rarer four-plus-two form. Since there are no important chronological developments in Lowell's four-stress versification, we may concern ourselves only with the different forms.

The Beggar and *My Love* are examples of the regular eight-syllable couplet combined with alternate rime, the former grouped in stanzas of from four to eight lines and the latter in five-line stanzas, riming *abccb*.

Serenade is an example of the nine-syllable couplet. The extra syllable may occur anywhere in the line, but of course the cæsura provides a convenient place for it, as the following extract shows (the last line is a refrain):

> From the close | -shut windows gleams no spark,
>
> The night is chill | y, the night | is dark, . . .
>
> Under the win | dow I sing | alone,
>
> Alone, alone, ah, woe! alone!

There is an extra syllable in the last foot:

> The darkness is pressing coldly around,

[16] Holmes's example: "For the frost's swift shuttles its shroud had spun."

In *Ambrose*, the number of syllables varies from eight (in regular iambic feet) to twelve (anapestic line). The base is iambic, as in:

Than Ámbrose, sìnce the wórld begán;

But the anapestic feet range from one to three:

Some sáwn in twáin, | thăt hĭs heárt's | desíre, . . .

Sŏ hĕ sét | himsélf | bў thĕ yóung | màn's síde, . . .

Bŭt thĕ heárt | ŏf thĕ st́rán | gĕr wăs hár | dĕned ĭndeéd,

In such versification as this, it is sometimes difficult to decide whether the rhythm should be labeled iambic or anapestic, and the number of predominant feet does not always settle the question, for one or two anapestic feet can make the whole line (or passage) sound anapestic. *A Parable* is a good example.

Many of Lowell's four-stress couplets are headless, *i.e.*, they have only seven syllables, as in *The Ghost-Seer*. The only thing unusual about his use of this common device is his consistent repetition of it in a long passage without the occasional variation of a normal eight-syllable line. Practically the only variation at all from the regular headless iambic tetrameter pattern is his use of an initial metrical stress, frequently followed by another in the third foot:

Tŏ | a bléssing frŏm the líght; . . .

Ŏf | the trúst he hăs betráyed, . . .

'T ĭs | a póet whŏ was sént . . .

Bў | compélling ĭt to see . . .

But on the whole, few of Lowell's poems adhere as strictly to one set pattern as his seven-syllable couplets, including (in addition to *The Ghost-Seer*), *On Burning Some Old Letters*, *Eleanor Makes Macaroons*, and *Scherzo*.

The Pregnant Comment and *Credidimus Jovem Regnare* have both eight- and seven-syllable lines. Other octosyllabics have occasional headless lines. The opening couplet of *St. Michael the Weigher* is headless, despite the fact that it has eight syllables, the eighth being the unstressed syllable of a feminine rime and therefore extrametrical:

Stóod | the táll Árchángel wéighĭng ⁽ˣ⁾

Áll | màn's dréaming, dóing, sáyĭng, ⁽ˣ⁾

If the feminine rime were used throughout, we might call the rhythm trochaic; but there is no question that it is iambic when all the other lines are seven-syllable with masculine rime.

4. DIMETER AND TRIMETER

Lowell's versification in his two- and three-stress verse is different in several minor respects from his handling of longer measures. The general structure of *The Fountain*, for example, is very simple, consisting of two-stress lines riming *abcb* and sometimes *abab*, with *a* and *c* occasionally forming assonance. Yet the rhythm is difficult to tabulate. Every line begins with an accented syllable and over half of them end with feminine rime, so that the rhythm is predominantly "falling"; but it could be scanned in various ways. Syntactically, the structure is elliptical; there is not a complete sentence in the entire poem. Each stanza is also parallel in thought, in punctuation and in rhythm, the balance applying to lines as well as to stanzas. The first stanza:

Ìnto the súnshìne,

Fúll of the líght,

Léaping and fláshing

From mórn till níght;

Six of the eight quatrains contain one enjambed line,
each quatrain being stopped by a semicolon (except, of
course, the last), and the other lines by commas. This
is probably the most rigidly schematized poem in the
whole bulk of Lowell's work.
The Fountain of Youth is much less regular. The
rhythm is definitely "rising," the two-stress line apparently being the base, though a number are three-stress,
with much use of feminine rime in both lengths. There is
also little enjambment, fewer ellipses than in *The Fountain*, and more use of pairs of nouns and epithets:

> Than blackbirds and thrushes, . . .
> And gurgles and flashes,
> To the maples and ashes . . .
> Then, silent and glossy,
> Slips winding and hiding

The following is a typical passage:

> The soft, noiseless metre,
>
> The pause and the swell
>
> Of that musical motion:
>
> I recall it, | not see it;
>
> Could vision be clearer?
>
> Half I'm fain to draw nearer
>
> Half tempted to flee it;
>
> The sleeping Past wake not,
>
> Beware!

Not even Lowell's odes contain more irregular versification than this. *A Mood* and *In the Twilight* are in similar
forms.

Among the trimeter poems are *Midnight*, *A Requiem*,
and *Song* ("O Moonlight deep and tender"), all of which

are fairly regular, the chief variation being the substitution of an occasional trisyllabic foot, reversed feet, etc. There are many anapestic feet in *After the Burial, The Dead House,* and *An Ember Picture.* But *Under the October Maples* is strictly six-syllable. *Jonathan to John* (in the *Biglow Papers* series) has an interesting rime-scheme, $A_4bAbcdedd_3$.

Some of the Biglow poems are in four-stress couplets (*The Two Gunners, Leaving the Matter Open, Festina Lente,* and "Thrash away, you'll hev to rattle"[17]), but the versification of the dialect poems presents no metrical characteristics not already discussed. The whole tone (possibly even the cadences) is affected by the dialect idiom with its slurred syllables, drawls, and rhetorical stressing of ordinarily unaccented syllables, yet none of these have any appreciable effect upon the scansion of the line.

Extreme Unction, Above and Below, and *Lines* are examples of alternate rime. These particular poems are in eight-line stanzas, or groupings. An example of the four-stress triplet is *For an Autograph.* Some of the chief four-stress, stanzaic forms are: *abab, The Falcon; abcb, A Parable; abaab, An Invitation; ababcc, The Nest; aaaBcccB, The Rose; A Ballad* and *Rosaline.*

Only a few poems are three- and four-stress, such as *The Moon* and *The Shepherd of King Admetus.* *The Changeling* is mainly three-stress, and *The Finding of the Lyre* mainly four-stress. The scheme in *Auf Wiedersehen* is $abab_4C_3$, and in *Gold Egg; A Dream Fantasy,* $a_4b_3cc_4b_3$. In the 4 + 3 measure we have *An Interview with Miles Standish, Longing,* No. IV of *Biglow Papers, The Courtin', The Singing Leaves* (irregular), *Godminster Chimes,* and *At the Burns Centennial.* None of these are imitations of the folk ballad. One of Lowell's most musical lyrics is *Song,* "Violet! sweet violet!" in a four- and two-stress combination.

In *The Voyage to Vinland,* Lowell experimented with

---

[17] First line of the poem.

blank dimeter. To a friend the poet wrote, "I have written [part of this poem] in an unrimed alliterated measure. . . . It does not aim at following the law of the Icelandic alliterated stave, but hints at it and also at the *assonante*, without being properly either. But it runs well and is melodious, and we think it pretty good here, as does also Howells. Well, after that, of course, I was all for alliteration." [18]

> Looms there the New Land:
> Locked in the shadow
> Long the gods shut it,
> Niggards of newness
> They, the o'er old.

It will be noticed that the alliteration is used not only for the short line ("looms" — "land," "niggards" — "newness," etc.), but there is also a cross-line alliteration, as in the "l's" of the first three lines, or in "shadow" and "shut." Yet if this poem is compared with Longfellow's *The Saga of King Olaf*, it will be found that Longfellow used alliteration both more and better than Lowell in this experiment. Nevertheless, the short-phrased, alliterative, two-stress versification of *The Voyage to Vinland* has a vigor which reminds us of the Icelandic and certain parts of the Anglo-Saxon *Beowulf*.

Lowell did not, however, despite his enthusiasm, use alliteration to any great extent after the composition of this poem (1850?). Alliteration belongs to those devices of melody and reiterations of sound which are on the whole quite uncharacteristic of his versification. No one has ever called Lowell "melody mad"!

[18] *Letters*, II, 2 (letter to C. E. Norton); quoted in introductory note to *The Voyage to Vinland* in the Cambridge edition of the *Poems*.

5. SEVEN- AND EIGHT-STRESS VERSE

Metrically there is almost no difference between Lowell's 4 + 3 measure and his seven-stress verse, as, for instance, in *An Incident of the Fire of Hamburg:*

It séemed a wóndrous fréak of chánce, so pérfect, yèt so róugh,

A whím of Náture crýstallízed slówly in gránite tóugh;

The variations from the pattern are simply the insertion of trisyllabic feet in the iambic rhythm (as in *A Second Letter from B. Sawin, Esq.*[19]); the inverted foot; and the light line, *i.e.*, six stresses instead of seven (or a metrical stress so light that it is questionable to count it, as in *On the Capture of Fugitive Slaves near Washington*):

Sháme on the cóstly móckery of píling stóne on stóne

To thóse who wón our líberty, the héroes déad and góne.

Several numbers of the *Biglow Papers* are in this measure — Nos. II, VIII, and IX in the first series, and Nos. I and III in the second series.

The chief difference between the eight-stress line and the seven-stress one (or the eight-stress and an octosyllabic couplet) is that this longer line has a tendency to syncopate as, for example, in *The Present Crisis:*

Rùns a thríll of jòy prophétic, trèmbling ón from èast to wést,

Ànd the sláve where'èr he cówers, fèels the sóul withìn him clímb

Anti-Apis has both eight and seven-stress lines, usually eight when the first syllable is stressed. But it does not syncopate quite so easily as *The Present Crisis:*

Láw is hóly; but nót yòur láw, yè who kéep the táblets whóle

Whìle ye dásh the Làw to píeces, shàtter ìt in lífe and sóul;

[19] *Biglow Papers*, No. VIII.

Some lines, however, can be read with greater syncopated
accentuation:

Bearing up the Ark is lightsome, golden Apis hid within,

6. THE ANAPEST

To a Pine-Tree echoes Shelley's *Cloud* both in rhythm
and thought, but whereas Shelley's poem is iambic with
anapestic substitutions, Lowell's is anapestic with iambic
substitutions. Of course no poem of Lowell's can compare
in melody and lyrical beauty with *The Cloud*, yet *To a
Pine-Tree* does make at least one reader wonder just how
much influence Shelley's versification had on Lowell.
Metrically, the only similarities between the two poems
are the double rimes and the triple rhythms, but there are
other echoes difficult to analyze.

Many lines of *To a Pine-Tree* are unquestionably anapestic:

In the storm, | like a pro | phet o'ermaddened,

But

The wild storm | makes his lair | in thy branches,

contains two decidedly rough anapests, for neither "wild"
nor "storm" can be read as unstressed syllables, and it is
possible to read the first half-line several ways. The rest
of the stanza is:

Swooping thence on the continent under;

Like a lion, crouched close on his haunches,

There awaiteth his leap the fierce thunder,

Growling low with impatience.

A Fable for Critics is more regular in meter, though the
rhythm is not sufficiently uniform to have the rocking-
horse gallop of some of Freneau's and Bryant's anapests.

Lowell's introduction, printed as prose, illustrates the rhythms: "The waterfall, scattering its vanishing gems; the tall grove of hemlocks, with moss on their stems, like plashes of sunlight; the pond in the woods, where no foot but mine and the bittern's intrudes, where pitcher-plants purple and gentians hard by recall to September the blue of June's sky . . ."

It will be noticed that several of these anapestic feet are composed, not of two unstressed syllables and a stressed one, but of secondary stress, unstress, plus primary stress, as in the second and third feet of:

the tall | grove of hem | locks with moss | on their stems,

And this is the special characteristic of many of Lowell's anapestic poems, though we also find in *The Fable for Critics* such couplets as this one on Emerson:

In the worst of his poems are mines rich of matter,

But thrown in a heap with a crash and a clatter;

The Wind-Harp illustrates the running over of an anapestic foot from one line to another, a trick which Lowell may have learned from Byron: [20]

"One lover still waits 'neath the green-wood tree

But 't is dark," and they shuddered, "where li | eth she

Dark | and cold! Forever must one be taken?"

The anapestic *The Flying Dutchman* contains some of Lowell's most amusing double rimes, *e.g.*: "Dutchman" — "clutch, man"; "idea" — "see a"; "legend" — "wedge-end"; "newer" — "Jew were."

Anapestic rhythm is also used in the following numbers of the *Biglow Papers:* first series, III, IV, V; second series, IV and V.

[20] Especially the *Bride of Abydos; cf.* Johannes Andersen, *The Laws of Verse* (Cambridge University Press, 1928), p. 26.

7. IAMBIC PENTAMETER

Despite Lowell's objection to iambic pentameter as an "almost glacier-slow measure," he used it considerably, both in the rimed and unrimed form. He even tried his hand at the much-abused heroic couplet (in *An Epistle to George William Curtis, Endymion, Fitz Adam's Story, Tempora Mutantur*, and in the second series of the *Biglow Papers*, Nos. II, VI, XI). These heroic couplets are conventional, fairly regular, and have most of the lines stopped by commas; they are not, however, couplet-moulded. That is, they do not have a full stop at the end of each couplet.

Nor do we find any important peculiarities in the versification of Lowell's pentameter in alternate rime, or alternate combined with couplet rime. He still uses double rime, but this variation goes at least as far back in American versification as Freneau. Other variations of both poets include a free use of metrical stresses, and the pyrrhic followed by a spondee, *e.g.*, in *Bibliolatres:*

And think | ing the | great God | is thine alone, . . .

Thinking the cisterns of those Hebrew brains . . .

Lowell also continues the use of the archaic past participle (*–ĕd*) in his rimed iambic pentameter, such as "revealĕd" in *Irené* and "gnarlĕd" in *The Oak*. The last poem that he wrote was *On a Bust of General Grant* (1891),[21] with the scheme $ababacdcde_5e_6$, but there is nothing at all unusual in the final alexandrine. The eighteenth-century English poets introduced the practice of ending a passage of heroic couplets with the alexandrine, and many poets have used it to close a pentameter stanza. Lowell also adopted it in other combinations: $abcb_5b_6$, *The Birch Tree*; $abb_5a_6a_5$, *The Pioneer;* and $ababcc_5b_6$, *An Indian-*

---

[21] *I.e.*, the last poem of which the date of composition is definitely known.

Summer Reverie. The "Venus and Adonis" stanza (*ababcc₅*) is also found in Lowell's last poems (*cf. An April Birthday at Sea*).

Other important forms are *ab₅a₃ba₅c₅cdd₅*, *To the Dandelion; a₅b₄a₅b₃, To the Memory of Hood; ab₃a₅b₄cd₃c₅d₄efefgg₅, The Search; ab₄a₅bc₄c₅, To Lamartine;* combinations of three- and five-stress lines, *Si Descendero in Infernum, Ades* and *To the Past.*

Lowell also wrote around fifty sonnets, all in the conventional Italian form except the youthful *Sonnets* (sequence) of 1827, which are in a combination of Italian and English rime-schemes, the favorite scheme being *abbaaccadedeff,* though some of the final couplets are *ee, gg, hh,* etc. Only five of the twenty-six sonnets in the sequence do not end with couplets. In the Italian sonnets the poet almost invariably preserves the unity of the quatrains of the octave and the distinctive "turn" or "break" between the octave and the sestet. He was apparently careful to smooth out the rhythm as much as possible. The versification is adequate, though not brilliant.

Lowell did not write many poems in blank verse, less than twenty-five in all, but this form includes several of his better known poems, such as *Prometheus, A Chippewa Legend, Columbus, Under the Willows, The Parting of the Ways,* and the still more widely known *The Cathedral.* One of the first differences that we notice between the versification of the rimed pentameter and the blank verse is that in the latter the word-order is more natural. Some of the earlier poems, however, such as *Love* and *L'Envoi,* have little enjambment, no internal stops, and are more couplet-moulded than Lowell's actual heroic couplets. But in *Prometheus* and *Rhoecus,* we find more enjambment, a few internal stops, and much better control of the breath-sweeps. Many of the breath-sweeps of *A Glance Behind the Curtain* extend over several lines, yet Lowell's control over typical blank-verse movement was distinctly limited. *The Cathedral* is fairly smooth and regular, but the cadences are somewhat monotonous, partly the result of insufficient variation of pauses and enjambment, no doubt aided by the didactic nature of most of the poem. Some of the poet's most successful versification is in *Under the Willows*, of which the following extract is characteristic:

> And Winter suddenly, like crazy Lear,
> Reels back, and brings the dead May in his arms,
> Her budding breasts and wan dislustred front
> With frosty streaks and drifts of his white beard
> All overblown. Then, warmly walled with books,
> While my wood-fire supplies the sun's defect,
> Whispering old forest-sagas in its dreams,
> I take my May down from the happy shelf
> Where perch the world's rare song-birds in a row,
> Waiting my choice to open with full breast,
> And beg an alms of springtime, ne'er denied
> Indoors by vernal Chaucer, whose fresh woods
> Throb thick with merle and mavis all the year.

Lowell's blank verse frequently bursts into the pleasing cadences of the first sentence of this passage, always to sink back into the comfortable line-by-line or clause-by-clause movement of the succeeding lines — good blank verse, though not to be compared with that of the great English masters.

8. LOWELL'S CONTRIBUTION

In conclusion, we must decide that Lowell made no direct contribution to American prosodic thought, but his versification introduced into American poetry the freedom which we find in the first two or three decades of nineteenth-century English poetry; and the Shelley influence on Lowell seems especially important. This freedom includes a more varied placing of accents and the combination of different kinds of feet to produce a suggestiveness of tone and cadence. Double rime had been used in

America for a long time, but never so extensively as in Lowell's poetry.

Yet at the same time that we acknowledge these contributions of Lowell to American metrical practice (all tending toward a greater emphasis of melody and harmony), we must also recognize the fact that he was not a great verbal musician; for instead of being more musical, many of his lines are more difficult to read than those in the conventional versification of Freneau and Bryant, or even Holmes.

Most important to American versification, therefore, are those poems of Lowell's which display the greatest metrical freedom, such as *The Vision of Sir Launfal* and the odes in irregular lines. These may be said to be in the tradition of late nineteenth-century versification, and probably exerted some influence even on Lowell's twentieth-century kinswoman.[22] At any rate, Lowell's versification is more important for the lessons it teaches than for the poetic beauty it achieved.

9. MINOR POETS OF THE LATER NINETEENTH CENTURY

One of Poe's most important contributions to American prosody was his deliberate artistry. In fact, he was the main founder in America of a tradition which has its English counterpart in Tennyson. But for a time this tradition almost died out in America because of the dominance of the transcendental theory of poetry and prosody, which emphasized intuitional methods at the expense of conscious artistry. Thus, in a sense, American prosodic history met a crossroad with Poe, for Emerson and Whitman were fundamentally at variance with most of his theory and practice. Holmes worked in an older tradition than Poe's and was apparently little influenced by the inspirational methods of the transcendentalists, but

[22] Amy Lowell was the leading figure in the "Imagism" movement. See p. 319, footnote 19.

both Whittier and Lowell (different as they were) shaped their art in conformance to intuitional principles — though influenced by several English poets. Lanier had much in common with Poe, but it is especially in the work and beliefs of the minor poets of the latter part of the nineteenth century that we encounter again a strong adherence to fine form as a thing desirable in itself.

The poet whom we should consider first in this group is Thomas Bailey Aldrich (1836–1907). His first volume of verse, *The Bells* (1855), reveals him as a student of Chatterton, Keats, Tennyson, Poe, Willis, and Longfellow. By the publication of his *The Ballad of Babie Bell and Other Poems* (1859) Tennyson may be regarded as his great guiding star. [*Songs and Sonnets* (1906) was published too late to be discussed here.] It is not surprising that a great admirer of Tennyson should object to "Kiplingese" and what Professor Foerster terms the "négligée dialect of James Whitcomb Riley." [23]

Aldrich's practice of versification was above all neat, precise, and delicate, but it was in no sense pedantic. He availed himself of most of the metrical freedoms found in the work of the nineteenth-century English poets, but these do not extend beyond free use of the trisyllabic foot in iambic measures, use of the *Christabel* meter, and lightening or stiffening the line to suit the context. *Palabras Cariñosas* is in easy-flowing but regular octosyllabics. But *When the Sultan Goes to Ispahan* is in four-beat free-stress rhythms, as is also the narrative *Friar Jerome's Beautiful Book*. *The Guerdon* is pentameter, but has free use of the minor ionic, the metrical stress in the third or fourth foot, reversed stress, and similar freedoms. *Pauline Pavlovna* is in strictly ten-syllable blank verse, but the metrical stress is used frequently to give a light line with only four normal speech stresses. In the *Ode on the Un-*

[23] Norman Foerster, "Later Poets of the Nineteenth Century," *Cambridge History of American Literature* (New York, 1921), III, 37. By permission of The Macmillan Company, publishers.

veiling of Shaw Memorial short lines predominate, but the versification is fairly conventional.

Bayard Taylor (1825–1878) also belonged to the Tennyson cult, and, like Aldrich too, despised dialect verse. But he should probably be compared to Longfellow rather than Aldrich, for both in scholarship and verse technique he resembled Longfellow. Goethe was his great master, and he will probably be remembered longest for his translation of *Faust* into English, preserving the original measures. He wrote in almost every meter and type of poetry, including lyrics, pastorals, idylls, odes, dramas, and translations. But he made few contributions to the history of American versification. In some of his verse, especially his early lyrics, we find the "kittle-y-benders" to which Holmes objected in Lowell's versification.[24] Some of the more unusual examples of Taylor's verse practices are: *The Bison Track*, in eight-stress trochees that do not syncopate; *Cupido*, two-stress (∕ × × ∕ ×) with a final four-stress line arranged in stanzas of alternate rime; *Napoleon at Gotha*, alexandrine couplets with an epic cæsura occurring regularly in each line; "Home Pastorals" and the fourth section of *Improvisations* are in six-stress unrimed dactyls — a form perhaps suggested to Taylor by Goethe's hexameters. Realizing that the heroic measure is one of the most monotonous forms for a long poem, Taylor sought in *The Picture of St. John* to prevent monotony by using an eight-line stanza with a variable rime-scheme. The poet says that he himself counted seventy different rime-schemes in the poem.

R. H. Stoddard (1825–1903) was neither unusual nor significant for his admiration for Keats, but as a member of the Aldrich-Taylor group he helped foster the ideal of artistry in versification. His *Autumn* has been pointed out as almost a copying of Keats's poem *Autumn*. He was a great admirer of the Orient, but his oriental poems

[24] See p. 195.

are in conventional meters. His most significant poems
are probably his short-line lyrics, such as *A Catch*, three-
stress; *The Flight of the Arrow*, two-stress; *Abraham
Lincoln*, aa_4bb_3; and "The Sea" in *Melodies and Catches*,
which has a cretic base. Toward the end of the century
there was almost a vogue of dimeters and trimeters in
American verse.

Clarence Edmund Stedman has been discussed elsewhere [25] for his Civil War poems, but he should be
mentioned here as one of the poet-scholars who also
followed in Longfellow's footsteps as an adapter of foreign
rhythms. *The Reapers* is a translation from Theocritus in
hexameters — which are mainly dactyllic. Stedman also
translated fragments from Homer, Bion, and Moschus.
Although a friend of Walt Whitman, most of his versification is conventional. Tennyson exerted a considerable
influence upon his work.

Richard Watson Gilder (1844–1909) was a disciple of
Milton in early youth and some Miltonic overtones are
to be found throughout much of his work, but he is particularly important in the history of American prosody
because his versification shows a very strong influence of
Rossetti. He wrote *The New Day* (pub. 1875) after reading Rossetti's translation of *Vita Nuova*. Professor
Foerster says of *The New Day*, mainly a collection of
Italian sonnets in the typical Rossetti manner: "With its
slow, heavily-freighted lines, its solemn music and carefully composed imagery, its intense feeling not fully
articulate, its occasional vagueness of meaning, it contrasts with the obvious and more lively American poetry
of that day and the day before." [26] This criticism applies,
it will be noticed, to general aspects of versification, not
to new meters, novel rhythms, or unconventional practices. But the "slow, heavily-freighted lines" and
"solemn music" are achieved by the difficult and subtle

[25] See p. 150–151.
[26] Foerster, *op. cit.*, p. 49. By permission of The Macmillan Company, publishers.

technique of vowel arrangements, shifting of accentuation to achieve just the nuance desired, phrasing, etc.

Edward Rowland Sill (1841–1887) also shows that the Rossetti and Præ-Raphaelite influence was becoming stronger in America toward the end of the century. His requirement of a poem was that it should "be full of lovely images," that it should "be in every way musical." Here we have both the Lanier ideal and what may very well have been the seeds of twentieth-century "imagism." And it is perhaps significant that some of his short poems resemble Father Tabb's, another forerunner of the twentieth-century American lyric.

But not all of the American poets of the later nineteenth century belonged to this cult of artistic form, for meanwhile the Western dialect versifiers were in their heyday. James Whitcomb Riley (1849–1916) is the most famous. Early in life he read Quarles and later Burns, but his versification is not greatly indebted to either. As a matter of fact, his forms and rhythms are characteristic of most of the American versification of his time, however different his subject-matter and poetic ideals were. His poems are perhaps more closely related to balladry and song than those of the average contemporary, but for the minor poets it was chiefly a lyric age. *Ike Walton's Prayer* is in the popular two- and four-stress movement; *A Life-Lesson*, two- and three- and four-stress; *Knee-Deep in June*, four-stress with various tail-rime arrangements; *The Old Man and Jim*, $a_4b_2cbdefdAa_4BG_2$; and *Little Orphan Annie*, in a seven-stress, syncopated ballad movement.

Bret Harte (1836–1902) wrote in ballad meters, anapests, and clipped octosyllabic couplets, with frequent feminine and double rimes, but two unusual forms should be mentioned. One is the six-stress unrimed dactyls of *Chiquita* — possibly intended for hexameters. The other is the dimeter and monometer dramatic monologue, as in *Jim*.

Joaquin Miller (1841–1913) was called the "Oregon Byron," and reflected Præ-Raphaelitism in his belief that "a poem is a picture," but he used the typical forms and conventions of his age. *Kit Carson's Ride* is in four-stress anapestic couplets, *Columbus* in four-stress iambics in alternate rime. His two other most famous poems, *Westward Ho!* and *Juanita*, are also four-stress, and *Dead in the Sierras* two-stress.

But perhaps no one is more characteristic of the better minor poets of the closing nineteenth century than Richard Hovey (1864–1900). He was a great admirer of Walt Whitman, of the Elizabethans, and of Verlaine, Mallarmé, and the later symbolists. He also translated Maeterlinck. Here we find good craftsmanship, somewhat in the manner of the "Eastern Group," but also a general drifting with the prosodic taste of the times. Like Lanier and others he attempted musical effects in poetry, though he never went so far as to attempt to identify the two arts. *The Call of the Bugles* has many short lines, some of them monometers. In form the poem is related to the transcendental odes, but the rhythms are finer and general technique more finished. *Dartmouth Winter-Song* contains many cretics. Hovey wrote many lyrics, or songs as they deserve to be called, in the short measures becoming so increasingly popular. His technique is essentially that of the best modern American lyricists.

SELECTED BIBLIOGRAPHY

JAMES RUSSELL LOWELL

TEXT

Lowell, James Russell, *The Complete Poetical Works*, etc., ed. by H. E. Scudder. Boston: Houghton Mifflin Company, 1896. (Cambridge edition.)

——, *Letters*, ed. by C. E. Norton. New York: Harper & Brothers, 1894. 2 vols.

——, *Early Prose Writings*. London and New York: The Bodley Head, 1903.

Lowell, James Russell, *The Function of the Poet*. Boston: Houghton Mifflin Company, 1920.

——, *Latest Literary Essays and Addresses*. Boston: Houghton Mifflin Company, 1892.

CRITICISM

Foerster, Norman, "Lowell," in *American Criticism*. Boston: Houghton Mifflin Company, 1928. Pp. 111–156.
[Lowell's literary criticism as a guide to his prosodic thinking.]

Lovett, Robert Morss, "Lowell," in *American Writers on American Literature*, ed. by John Macy. New York: Horace Liveright, 1931. XIV, 177–189.

Pritchard, John Paul, "Lowell's Debt to Horace's *Ars Poetica*," *American Literature* (November, 1931), III, No. 3, 259–276.

Reilly, Joseph J., *James Russell Lowell as a Critic*. New York: G. P. Putnam's Sons, 1915.
[Mr. Reilly regards Lowell primarily as an impressionist.]

MINOR POETS

Foerster, Norman, "Later Poets of the Nineteenth Century," *Cambridge History of American Literature* (New York: G. P. Putnam's Sons, 1921), III, 37 ff.

CHAPTER X

Sidney Lanier

I. *THE SCIENCE OF ENGLISH VERSE*

THERE are probably many literary historians and critics who would challenge Lanier's right to be called one of the chief American poets, but he merits a detailed analysis in this survey of American theory and practice of poetic technique because in addition to writing a handful of poems in unusually interesting and original forms of versification he also published an important treatise on prosody.

The Science of English Verse is significant both in the history of American prosodic thought and as a guide in interpreting and evaluating Lanier's own versification. A thorough discussion of this work would necessitate excursions into the fields of physics, phonetics, the history of the English language, music, and æsthetics, for the treatise is not only concerned with these subjects but is actually based on such knowledge of them as Lanier could rake together (and he was a reasonably thorough, if somewhat haphazardly prepared, scholar). It is obvious, therefore, that the present discussion must be confined to main principles.

Lanier's thesis is that the laws governing versification and music are not only similar (as most prosodists would agree) but that they are precisely the same laws. Though of course he recognizes that the tones of a musical instrument, such as the violin, do not convey the intellectual *meaning* that spoken words do,[1] he nevertheless regards sound-relation as the only important factor in verse, a

---

[1] *Cf. Music and Poetry* (New York, 1898), pp. 6–7.

doctrine which, if carried to the ultimate logical conclusion, would end up with some such theory as Gertrude Stein's and other "ultra-moderns" of her group.

To avoid misrepresenting Lanier, it is best to quote his own words: "If, therefore, the ear accepts as perfect verse a series of words from which ideas are wholly absent, — that is to say, a series of sounds, — it is clear that what we call 'verse' is a set of specially related sounds, at least in the case of a formal poem repeated aloud . . . when we hear verse, we *hear* a set of relations between sounds; when we silently read verse, we *see* that which brings to us a set of relations between sounds; when we imagine verse, we *imagine* a set of relations between sounds." [2]

It would appear that he is here using "verse" in a technical manner (*i.e.*, as sound-patterns in poetry), but he even defines a poem in the same terms: "*A formal poem is always composed of such sounds and silences (or of the signs, or of the conceptions of such sounds and silences) as can be coördinated by the ear.*" [3] Still, Lanier's own practice proves he does not mean that *vocalizing* is the whole of poetry, though, as we shall see later, he leans far enough toward this attitude to affect very seriously his own versification.

For the present, however, we need not go beyond Lanier's fundamental assumption, namely, that "there is absolutely no difference between the sound-relations used in music and those used in verse." [4] This concept is based on a confusion of *song* and *poetry*. It is generally believed that poetry originated as song, and poems today are frequently written to be sung. The lyric is still usually regarded as a species of song, but the articulation (which of course includes "sound-relations") of words spoken or read and of those which are sung is distinctly different. The time relations between spoken English

[2] *The Science of English Verse* (New York, 1880), pp. 21–23.
[3] *Ibid.*, p. 33.   [4] *The Science of English Verse*, p. 48.

syllables are very complicated and precarious (as we shall have occasion to illustrate); whereas in singing, the time relations are fixed by the musical composition, the voice modulating the pronunciation to fit the music (*e.g.*, a syllable may be "held" for several seconds). Pitch, intensity, etc., vary in the same way, irrespective of normal speech habits.

Lanier attempts to make his theory scientific by approaching his problem from the point of view of physics. He carefully defines (1) duration, (2) intensity, (3) pitch, and (4) tone-color. Only the latter definition need be given here: "as in studying colors we find purple composed of red and violet, and the like, so many sounds have been discovered to be made up of other sounds (*tone-color*)." [5] The pronunciation of the vowel *a*, for instance, comprises several different sounds, but we treat the composite sound as if it were one. *Timbre* is the more accepted word today for this phenomenon. Lanier is less scientifically correct when he says that, "Each 'sound,' for the purposes of verse, is represented by one syllable [6] [for which he prefers the term 'verse-sound']"; but in scanning verse we still use the syllable as the unit of measure; so we need not challenge this definition.

Lanier's desire to explain English versification by the principles of music leads him astray, however, when he takes the stand (which is logical after his first fundamental but erroneous assumption) that *time* is the only important element in the rhythm of verse.[7] "'Accent' can effect nothing, except in arranging materials already rhythmical through some temporal recurrence. Possessing a series of sounds temporally equal or temporally proportionate, we can group them into various orders of larger and smaller

---

[5] *The Science of English Verse*, p. 24.

[6] *Ibid.*, p. 59. Stetson and Hudgins have demonstrated that breath movements are more important in syllabification than sounds. See "Breath Movements in Speech," *Archives Néerlandaises de Phonétique Expérimentale* (1930), Tome V, p. 4 ff.   [7] *Ibid.*, p. 65.

groups . . . by means of accent, but the primordial temporalness is always necessary." [8]

That the pronunciation of syllables does consume units of time and that, therefore, time is one important element in verse is so obvious that it is trite; but laboratory experiments have shown that the actual time covered in the pronunciation of syllables in English verse varies so greatly that it is impossible either to write or read (naturally) a passage so that the series of sounds are even proportionately equal.[9] Thus accent, instead of merely being convenient in marking sounds already rhythmical, is the *only* element in English verse which is sufficiently rhythmical for us to measure outside the laboratories of the physicist and the applied psychologist.

Lanier speaks frequently of his own laboratory experiments at Johns Hopkins, but such a theory of English prosody as he held was based on an hypothesis *ad hoc*. And it is essentially the same as Poe's, despite Lanier's belief that he disagreed with Poe. For one of the cardinal doctrines of *The Rationale of Verse* is that every foot is equal in time to every other foot in the line of verse. After reminding us that "In a strain of music any bar is exactly equal to any other bar in the time it occupies," [10] Lanier proceeds to substitute "bar" for "foot" in his analysis of verse-rhythms. In music the first note of a bar is accented or given greater stress than the other notes of the bar; but Lanier regards the accent in a "bar" (*i.e.*, foot) of verse as the same thing. Hence, as in music, he begins counting time only when the accented

---

[8] *The Science of English Verse*, p. 65.

[9] *Cf.* Paull Franklin Baum, *The Principles of English Versification* (Cambridge, Mass., 1923), pp. 56–65. The most important laboratory work on this problem has been done by Professor Ada L. F. Snell, for whose reports see *Publications of Modern Language Association* for September, 1918, pp. 396–408, and September, 1919, pp. 416–435. See also Miss Snell's *Pause; a Study of its Nature and its Rhythmical Function in Verse* (Ann Arbor, 1918).

[10] *The Science of English Verse*, p. 67.

syllable is sounded. In other words, the first syllable in an iambic foot is simply not counted in the analysis. Pauses, of course, are counted as part of the rhythm, because they occupy part of the time of the bar.

Briefly, the rhythms in Lanier's system are as follows:

(1) The *temporal relation* is "primary" rhythm, that is, the time covered by each separate sound ("verse-sound," or syllable) and the pauses and silences.[11]

(2) *Accent*, which indicates the beginning of a new bar, forms a "secondary" rhythm.[12]

(3) But English speech is not pronounced in syllable or sound groups but in "phrases," necessitated by the dependence of human speech upon respiration. Thus the *phrase* forms a "tertiary" rhythm.[13] Subheads of tertiary rhythm are alliteration, rhetorical emphasis (which includes both intensity and pitch accent), and logical accent.

(4) The "fourth order of rhythmic groups" is the *line* — meter is the number of verse-sounds in a line.[14] Rime also has a rhythmic function because it marks the end of the line.[15]

(5) The "fifth order of rhythmic groups" is the stanza. This rhythm, of course, is ordinarily marked by rime-schemes, but may be indicated by phrases and full stops.[16]

Lanier tried out his "system" extensively on Anglo-Saxon verse, which contains usually four accented syllables to the line but an indefinite number of unaccented ones. By giving a time value to pauses and silences, he demonstrated that the Anglo-Saxon line can be read with equivalent duration for each bar. (Professor William Ellery Leonard has also investigated this principle.[17]) A short quotation from *The Battle of Maldon* will illustrate not

[11] *The Science of English Verse*, p. 74.
[12] *Ibid.*   [13] *Ibid.*, p. 78.
[14] *Ibid.*, p. 88.
[15] *Ibid.*, p. 92.   [16] *Ibid.*, p. 94.
[17] See "*Beowulf* and the Nibelungen Couplet," *University of Wisconsin Studies in Language and Literature* (September, 1918), No. 2, 99–152.

only Lanier's analysis of Anglo-Saxon poetry but his theory in general:

us   sceal   ord   and   ecg   ær   ge - se - man,

grimm   guth - pleg - a   ær   we   gaf - ol   syll - on.[18]

We notice that the single syllable "grimm" is given the equivalent time of the five syllables "guth-pleg-a ær we," for each composes one bar. There is no doubt that Anglo-Saxon verse can be sung (and possibly was) in this manner.[19] But whether modern poetry, based only partly on Anglo-Saxon traditions and usually not intended to be sung, should be *read* to such a scheme as this is a different matter. Coleridge's *Christabel*, however, is more in the Anglo-Saxon tradition than poetry written in the classical scheme with a specific number of syllables to the line. Lanier finds no difficulty in fitting *Christabel* to his system:[20]

'Tis   the mid- | dle   of night | by the cas | - tle clock.
And   the owls | have   a - wa- | ken'd the crow | - ing cock.

Tu-whit!   Tu - whoo!

---

[18] "Us shall point and blade rather persuade, grim, war-play, ere we tribute give [you for peace]."

[19] Professor Baum, however, denies any necessity for scanning Anglo-Saxon alliterative verse as song. By assuming that it, like most modern poetry, was written to be read, he greatly simplifies the metrical analysis. See "The Character of Anglo-Saxon Verse," *Modern Philology* (1930–1931), XXVIII, 143–156.

[20] *The Science of English Verse*, p. 197.

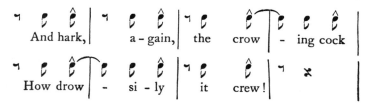

But the objection to this scheme is that the reader needs Lanier's musical notations to guide his reading of the poem. Probably not one person in one hundred, reading naturally, will "time" the "bars" — even proportionately — as the above notations demand. It is the artificiality of the system which is objectionable. This objection, though, applies merely to the attempt to reduce English versification to the science of music, and especially to the view that time is both more important and easier to analyze than accent.

The last part of Lanier's treatise is concerned with "Colors of Verse." There is a slight scientific discrepancy in applying "tone-color" both to the phenomenon of *timbre* and the combination of characteristic tone-colors of a line; but since metrists still use the term "tone-color" for the latter, this discrepancy is not of much importance.

Under "colors of English verse," Lanier includes the use of vowel and consonant sounds for musical effects, rime, reiteration, phonetic syzygy (*i.e.*, the use of consonant sounds which may be easily yoked together in the pronunciation [21]), etc.

It is primarily in this part of the book that Lanier assumes the rôle of teacher, telling the student-poet what is desirable and undesirable in versification. It is significant, however, that in this section of the treatise he is usually not dogmatic. The only rule he lays down regarding alliteration, for example, is that it must never become conspicuous *per se*. But his ideas regarding rime are

[21] *N.B.* Classical *syzygy* is something different — applying to feet.

more severe: "the resources of our tongue are so great
that we are entitled to hold every poet down to the strict-
est measure of the law which forbids the least intrusion
of the rhyme as rhyme — that is, as any thing less than
the best word in the language for the idea in hand." [22]
And again, "If the rhyme is not perfect, if it demands the
least allowance, it is not to be tolerable: throw it away." [23]
This injunction apparently applies both to the thought
and the sound of the rime-word. Some further rules
regarding rime are very commendable. "As to the position of rhymes in English verse there is no law but the
poet's own ear." [24] The student is warned that rimes of
more than two syllables are likely to produce a comic
effect and should be used only in humorous verse. [25] Also,
"neighboring rhymes which are very nearly alike in tone-
color" should be avoided. [26] Finally, "rhymes involving
sweet, sonorous, and dignified vowel-colors, such as 'ore'
and 'restore,' 'name' and 'blame,' 'harm' and 'alarm,' and
the like, are in general to be favored beyond those of more
finical color, as 'pity' and 'witty,' 'seem' and 'gleam,'
'hid' and 'kid,' and so on." [27] Precisely what Lanier's
criteria are here it is difficult to understand. Apparently
they are based on mere personal taste, for under desirable
vowels he includes both "front" and "back" ones, though
he seems to indicate a preference for back vowels. [28] If
there is a phonetic distinction, it is very subtle.

The theme of the last chapter in the book is that, "For
the artist in verse there is no law: the perception and love
of beauty constitute the whole outfit. . . . In all cases,
the appeal is to the ear. . . ." [29] And this attitude, commendable as it is, is cut from the same cloth as Lanier's desire to reduce English versification to musical composition.
In summing up Lanier's contribution to the *science* of

---

[22] *The Science of English Verse*, p. 297.   [23] *Ibid.*, p. 298.
[24] *Ibid.*, p. 299.   [25] *Ibid.*   [26] *Ibid.*, p. 300.   [27] *Ibid.*, p. 301.
[28] *I.e.*, articulated in either the front or back of the mouth.
[29] *The Science of English Verse*, p. 315.

American prosody, we must emphasize his intentions more than his actual accomplishments (though one great tribute to his actual accomplishments is the fact that metrists still find his treatise useful). Yet he deserves great credit for approaching his subject scientifically, and (as part of the scientific method) experimentally. That his experiments were not sufficiently extensive and complete is of course true, and his own musical talent and predilections caused him to set up an untenable major hypothesis, but a great part of his treatise is scientifically correct, and all of it is challenging and suggestive. We must also remember that Lanier labored under the disadvantage of an insufficient knowledge of phonetics,[30] of the nature of the English language, and of the scientific aspects of speech rhythms.[31]

As for the importance of time in English versification, the quantity-accent battle raged intensely for some time after Lanier's death, and has not completely subsided yet. But it is doubtful whether any other prosodist has presented the quantity argument with so much clarity and force as we find in *The Science of English Verse*.

2. LANIER'S USE OF METER

While most of Lanier's meters in individual lines are fairly regular and conventional with respect to number of syllables and accentuation, and are, therefore, easy to scan, any analysis of his body of poetry by metrical form

[30] *E.g.*, The "phoneme," discovered only recently, might have modified some of his views. For definitions, see Ida C. Ward, *The Phonetics of English* (New York, 1929); D. Jones and M. Trofimov, *The Pronunciation of Russian* (Cambridge University Press, 1924).

[31] Professor W. M. Patterson, in *The Rhythm of Prose* (Columbia University Press, 1916), says: "Experimental work upon the rhythm of speech virtually begins with Brücke," Chap. II, p. 17. Thus the attempt to understand rhythm of speech scientifically was very literally in its infancy when Lanier wrote his treatise, for E. W. Brücke's *Die Physiologischen Grundlagen d. neuhochd. Verskunst* appeared at Wien in 1871.

(the method used in most chapters of this book) would be unduly complicated, because Lanier's prosodic theory led him to combine different measures in a single poem, especially in his later verse. Thus, a brief section may be in one meter, the following in a different measure, and a third line in still another form. Furthermore, though meter is important in showing how Lanier attempted to apply the technique of musical composition to his versification, it is by no means the only important (or perhaps most important) element in his poetic technique. Hence, it seems desirable that we should first learn what meters Lanier used, and give some attention to their appropriateness, without over-emphasizing them by a too elaborate analysis.

Chronology is very important in studying Lanier's versification, for his theory of the identity of the laws of music and verse either did not crystallize early enough to affect his first poems or else several years of practice were necessary for learning how to embody the theory in rime and meter. In fact, we can easily follow the genesis and growth of the theory in his own practice of versification, for however we may judge the result, few prosodists have ever striven more earnestly to follow their own doctrines.

In an introductory note to "Unrevised Early Poems," Lanier's editor (his wife) says, "These unrevised poems are not necessarily exponents of Mr. Lanier's later teaching, but are offered as examples of . . . his earlier methods and his instructive growth . . . none of these poems would have been republished by him without material alterations, the slightest of which no other hand can be authorized to make." It is fortunate for the student that this batch of "unrevised" poems has been left.

All except one of them are in iambic rhythm, though there is some anapestic substitution even in the earliest one,[32] *The Tournament,* "Joust First" (1862); in fact,

[32] *Resurrection* is undated, but internal evidence points to a later date.

there are so many anapestic feet that they could be counted as part of the pattern:

> To the tóurnament únder the ládies' éyes,
>
> Where the joústers were Héart and Bráin . . .
>
> They chárged, they strúck; both féll, both bléd . . .

Metrical stresses on "to" and "where" would not alter very much the essentially bounding and leaping rhythm. The second part of the poem, written 1865, has similar versification, and so does *To* — (1863).

The Dying Words of Stonewall Jackson (1865) shows an early preference for the simple stanza with a short final line (the scheme is abb_5a_3). But still more characteristic is the triplet, in various measures, including the four-stress *Nilsson* (1871); the pentameter *A Birthday Song* (1866); *Nirvâna* (1869), aaa_5B_3; and *The Golden Wedding of Sterling and Sarah Lanier* (1868), $aaabcccb_4$. *Laughter in the Senate* (1869) is characteristic of the latter part of this period:

> In the Sóuth lìes a lónesome, húngry Lánd;
>
> He húddles his rágs with a crípple's hánd;
>
> He mútters, próne on the bárren sánd,
>
> What tíme his héart is bréaking.

Here meter is used to achieve suggestive cadences, but there is nothing the least unconventional in the technique for 1868. The undated *Our Hills*, with its dimeter couplets plus pentameter triplet, is more in the style of Lanier's later (or "middle") period of versification.

The Jacquerie — a Fragment (1868) is an unsuccessful experiment in blank verse (with the opening lines in heroic couplets), though the meter is regular enough, and perhaps even too regular with its insufficient variation of pause and breath-sweep. But Lanier never learned to handle blank verse with mastery; the measure was unsuited to his lyricism.

Some of the songs for this unfinished blank verse poem, however, are interesting, especially the one called *Song for "The Jacquerie,"* since it is in short-line trochaics:

> Máy the máiden,
>
> Víolet-láden
>
> Óut of the víolet séa,
>
> Cómes and hóvers
>
> Óver lóvers,
>
> Óver thée, Márie, and mé.

The obvious "tune" of this song seems to demand a pause (or "hold," as we would call it in singing) after "thee," thus anticipating the poet's later teaching.

Among those poems revised and published by the poet himself are two written in 1868, the four-stress *Life and Song* and *The Ship of Earth,* in "poulter's measure." The former has a few trisyllabic feet, but the latter is more irregular:

> "Thóu Shíp of Éarth, with Déath, and Bírth, and Lífe, and Séx
>
> abóard,
>
> And fíres of Desíres búrning hótly ĭn the hóld,
>
> I féar thēe, Ò! I féar thēe, fŏr I héar the tóngue and swórd
>
> At báttle ŏn the déck, and the wíld mútinēers are bóld!

Yet there is nothing particularly unusual in the pyrrhic followed by the spondee (lines two and four), and aside from this one irregularity the passage can be scanned by use of metrical stresses.

The dialect poem, *Thar's More in the Man than Thar*

is in the Land (1869), is a combination of anapestic and iambic feet, the anapestic predominating, so that we may regard the iambic feet as substitutions.

And the lón | ger he swore | the mad | der he got,

But note:

So hím | and Tóm | they hìtched úp | the múles,

My Springs (1874) has an octosyllabic base, yet we find such lines as:

In the héart of the hílls of lífe, I knów

During 1874–1875, Lanier wrote several sonnets, including *Acknowledgment* (composed of four Shakespearean sonnets), *In Absence* (also with four in the English form), *Martha Washington* (a Shakespearean sonnet), and *To Charlotte Cushman* (in the unnamable form of *aaaabbbbccccdd*). All of these are conventional in technique, except the one eccentric rime-scheme. The sonnet, however, is one of the most rigid of all metrical forms and offers a limited number of experiments with meter, though it does serve as a severe test of a poet's ability to control meter.

During this "middle period" of Lanier's versification, there was considerable growth in the use of rime, reiteration, and tone-colors (subjects to be discussed in another section), yet the only new meter we find is "poulter's measure," and the only pronounced difference in accentuation is the somewhat freer use of the trisyllable.

There is no distinct dividing line between Lanier's "middle period," as we call it for convenience, and his later versification, but *Corn* (1874) may be considered as on the border-line of the new style. It is composed mainly of pentameter lines, despite the fact that it has a large number of short lines which vary all the way from monometer to tetrameter. Typical lines (for meter) are:

Today the woods are trembling through and through
With shimmering forms, that flash before my view, . . .
Soul filled like thy long veins with sweetness tense,
    By every godlike sense . . .
  So thou dost reconcile the hot and cold, . . .
And many a heart-perplexing opposite,
       And so,
  Akin by blood to high and low . . .
That manfully shall take thy part,
    And tend thee,
    And defend thee,
With antique sinew and with modern art.

Though this technique is metrically similar to the irregular ode as written, for example, by Lowell, actually no poet
in America had hitherto used meter to produce such various cadences in one poem. *The Symphony*, composed in
the following year (1875), deliberately runs the gamut in
versification. It begins with octosyllabic couplets, with
anapestic substitution ranging from a single foot to three
out of four feet. This part attempts to represent the
rhythms and cadences of the violins. It ends with heroic
couplets. The flute begins in a two-stress line, extends
to four-stress lines, then varies like an ode, and comes
back to the octosyllabic, giving way to the violins, which
begin anew with pentameters but include this passage:

      Change thy ways
      Change thy ways;
   Let the sweaty laborers file
     A little while,
     A little while,
  Where Art and Nature sing and smile.

The flute answers in a few four-stress couplets, which the clarionet continues, the rhythm rising into pentameter again. But the horn renews the four-stress rhythm, and continues for thirteen stanzas in the scheme $aaa_4a_3B_1$, the refrain being the amphibrach,

$$\grave{\text{F}}\text{air l}\acute{\text{a}}\text{d}\overset{\times}{\text{y}},$$

The horn ends with an heroic couplet. Then the hautboy returns the rhythm to four-stress, with some dimeter and monometer lines, and finally closes the poem with a four-stress quatrain.

Yet *Psalm of the West* (1876) contains more metrical forms than any other poem Lanier wrote. They are: (1) five-stress anapestic, with some short lines; (2) pentameter triplets; (3) four-plus-three measure; (4) pentameter in alternate rime; (5) four-plus-three; (6) pentameter triplets; (7) four-plus-two in alternate rime, six-line stanza; (8) alexandrines; (9) eight Italian sonnets; (10) headless octosyllabic couplets; (11) pentameter triplets; (12) octosyllabic couplets, some headless and some with an extra syllable; (13) pentameter triplets; (14) headless octosyllabic couplets; (15) four-plus-three quatrains; (16) headless octosyllabic couplets; (17) pentameter triplets; and (18) a four-stress stanza, riming *ababcc*. It is important to notice that this poem is iambic except for the beginning anapests, and that the different meters are not interwoven; *i.e.*, the poet passes directly from one measure to another, and irregularities within a particular meter are rare.

After these experiments, Lanier attempted more complicated uses of meter to produce music of words. The next, and simplest of the later important poems, is *Song of the Chattahoochee* (1877). The meter is mainly iambic, but most of the lines have one or two anapestic feet, sometimes the whole line being headless anapestic, as in:

$$\text{Spl}\acute{\text{i}}\text{t} \mid \overset{\times}{\text{at}} \overset{\times}{\text{the}} \text{r}\acute{\text{o}}\text{ck} \mid \overset{\times}{\text{and}} \overset{\times}{\text{togeth}} \mid \text{er} \overset{\times}{\text{ag}}\acute{\text{a}}\text{in,}$$

Each stanza begins and ends with the half-line repetend:

> . . . the hills of Habersham,
> . . . the valleys of Hall.

These lines are always headless, as at the beginning of the poem:

> Óut | of the hílls of Hábershàm
> Down the valleys of Hall,

And they are always very closely parallel, both in thought and words. The cadences of the other lines of each stanza are subtly varied by skilful arrangement of the trisyllabic feet and initial truncation, the whole being worked out so that each stanza has a slightly different basic cadence from the other four.

The Marshes of Glynn (1878) is anapestic, but the shifting of accents, initial truncation, and the frequent shifting of the number of syllables in the line from one to seventeen prevents the rhythm from becoming monotonous. All of these metrical devices are unmistakably intended primarily to produce the varying cadences of a musical composition. Few lines have precisely the same cadence, yet the meters (and other devices to be discussed later) give each verse a characteristic cadence, and the total effect is that of interlaced cadences. Some examples are:

> Émerald twilíghts, —
> Vírginal shy líghts,
> Wróught of the léaves to allúre to the whísper of vóws, . . .
> Of the dím sweet wóods, of the deár dàrk wóods, . . .
> Ye héld me fást in your heárt and I héld you fást in míne; . . .
> As the mársh-hèn sécretly búilds on the wátery sód,
> Behóld I will búild me a nést on the greátness of Gód:

But here it is impossible to determine just how much the meter, the repetition, or the tone-color is responsible for the music, so inextricably are they bound up together. With the exception of *Individuality*, which is basically iambic, the other marsh "hymns" are also anapestic. *Marsh Song — at Sunset* (1879–1880) has such a singing rhythm that it is difficult to read it without giving it a "tune." For instance:

> Over the humped and fishy sea,
>   Over the Caliban sea
> O cloud in the West, like a thought in the heart
> Of pardon, loose thy wing, and start,
>   And do a grace for me.

It is interesting that this stanza seems to justify to some extent Lanier's theory of equal time for each bar (regardless of number of syllables and accents); since the reader will probably find that the tripping rhythm of the first three lines causes him to read the two last iambic lines with a special emphasis and pause after each accent, in such a way as to preserve much of the time-value of the anapestic foot (or "bar"). Of course this observation is based on a purely subjective phenomenon which may not be true for all readers, but no doubt every one will agree that the anapestic rhythm does affect the reading of those lines which scan as iambs.

The same phenomenon will probably be experienced by most readers of *Sunrise* (1880), which combines iambic and anapestic feet in a much more irregular manner, in lines ranging from one to sixteen syllables; yet the anapestic rhythm predominates and has various and subtle effects on the few iambic lines, as in,

> Like as the lips of a lady that forth falter yes,
>   Shaken with happiness:
>   The gates of sleep stood wide.

But no isolated passage can fully illustrate. And a mere examination of meter itself is inadequate to reveal either the main characteristics of Lanier's versification, or (and most especially) his successes and failures in identifying the sound-patterns of music and verse. The study of feet and measures is merely a necessary preliminary foundation for understanding the special contribution which Lanier made to American versification in his attention to sound as the most important element in poetic technique.

3. PHONETIC REITERATIONS (INCLUDING "COLORS OF VERSE," ETC.)

In his treatise, under the head of "Colors in Verse," Lanier includes rime, alliteration, predominant vowel and consonant sounds in a line, phonetic linking (syzygy), and similar devices. All of these are repetitions either of the same or of similar (and, as with syzygy, blending) sounds; hence, it is safe, and perhaps less confusing, to use the general term of *phonetic reiteration* to cover all of these phenomena.

Rime may be disposed of first, since it is the most definite of all the phonetic reiterations. Lanier states in his volume that one of the chief functions of rime is to mark the end of the line or "measure" (see § 1 of this chapter). This particular function, however, seems much less important in his own verse than that of repeating sounds for a purely musical effect. We have already seen that triplet rime was an early favorite with Lanier, but he also used it extensively in his later poetry (*cf. Psalm of the West*, which also has some quadruplet rime). Couplet rime was always a favorite of his, too, even in lines of irregular lengths, thus indicating that the couplet rime was used more for the repetition of a sound than because of any necessity for binding the lines together. In fact, about the only time that Lanier's rimes ever seem to be used for joining verses is when the final rime of one stanza is repeated in the first line of the following stanza, as in the first two strophes of *Sunrise*.

Feminine rime made its appearance in Lanier's early poems, never to be abandoned. It is perhaps used most extensively in *The Symphony*, a present participle occurring in one passage as the rime-word for five consecutive lines. Most of these feminine rimes are, of course, trochaic words, but two-word rimes occur in some places. In *Our Hills* we even find such three-word rimes as "bled for us," "dead for us," and "lead for us," but this is unusual; and later in the treatise, as we have noticed, Lanier advises against such rimes except for humorous poems.

Since in his prosodic theory he is so insistent ón avoiding any rime the least bit imperfect, it would be entirely fair to subject Lanier's own rimes to microscopic analysis; and it is not surprising that this has been done. A good example is Professor Kent's article,[33] which commends Lanier in most respects but is severe on his "bad" rimes, like those in *Huntingdon's Miranda*, "rare: hair and flare: air."[34] In *To* —, "The imperfect rhyme say: pay: day, is not to be commended."[35] "Heaven" and "given"[36] are also criticized in *Golden Wedding*, perhaps justly, but most American poets before Lanier had used it. As to the other bad rimes, however, it would appear that Professor Kent either had a very peculiar notion of what constitutes a correct rime, or that he himself had a dialect pronunciation which actually prevented, for example, "say," "pay," and "day" from riming for him.

A liberty which we might not expect Lanier's theory to condone is the practice of riming final –*y*, for instance, with either *eye* or *me*. In *The Symphony* we find: "me," "charity"; "sky," "mystery"; "absently," "thee"; "cry," "remedy." And in the same poem, "fed" rimes

---

[33] Charles W. Kent, "A Study of Lanier's Poems," *Publications of the Modern Language Association* (1892), VII, 33–63.
[34] *Ibid.*, p. 49.   [35] *Ibid.*, p. 51.   [36] *Ibid.*, p. 49.

with "solicited"; while in *Laus Mariæ*, "uprise" rimes with "indifferencies." But despite Lanier's injunctions, these distortions of "light" rimes do not seem to be of special importance, for they were and still are firmly established in the versification of most of our best poets. This is practically the only respect in which Lanier's rimes do not conform to his teaching. Occasionally there is a slip, such as "have" and "brave" ("eye rimes," as they are sometimes called) in *Golden Wedding*, but these slips are rare. Lanier was too keenly interested in the sounds of his verse to be careless with his rimes.

The horn-passage in *The Symphony* is a good example of contrasting tone-colors in rimes. The first rimes (not counting the refrain) use back vowels (*i.e.*, vowels pronounced in the back of the mouth): "horn," "lorn," "scorn," "morn," and "wrong," "song," "long," "long." Then they shift to front vowels, return to back vowels ("long" *o*'s), and play variations on front vowels during the rest of the passage, the final couplet "away" and "fray" possibly being intended to represent a final flourish in a higher key.

The reiteration of a word or a phrase at the beginning of the line is analogous to rime, the only difference being (aside from position) that in reiteration consonants as well as vowels are repeated, while in rime there is only a similarity of primary vowel-tone (provided the rime is masculine) and repetition of part of the consonant sounds. Initial reiteration also makes parallelism of thought and grammatical structure almost inevitable. This device is used so extensively in most of Lanier's poetry that it cannot be discussed or illustrated exhaustively here, but the following examples indicate its nature and effectiveness:

> (1) A-many sweet eyes wept and wept,
>   A-many bosoms heaved again;
>   A-many dainty dead hopes slept.
>
> *The Tournament*

(2) Gold crushed from the quartz of a crystal life,
     Gold hammered with blows of human strife,
     Gold burnt in the love of man and wife,

The Golden Wedding

(3) And he rolled up his breeches and bared his arm,
     And he picked all the rocks from off'n the groun',
     And he rooted it up and he plowed it down,

Thar's More to the Man, etc.

(4) And ever Love hears the poor-folks' crying,
     And ever Love hears the women's sighing,
     And ever sweet knighthood's death-defying,
     And ever wise childhood's deep implying,
     But never a trader's glozing and lying.

The Symphony

(5) The blood that made you has all bled for us,
     The hearts that paid you are all dead for us,
     The trees that shade you groan with lead, for us!

Our Hills

In (2), (3), and (5), we also have what has been called elsewhere (*cf.* Chapter VIII, § 8) "grammatical rhythm," as in the parallel verbs "crushed," "hammered," and "burnt"; then "rolled," "picked," and "rooted"; and the parallel nouns "blood," "hearts," and "trees." Notice also the internal rimes "made," "paid," and "shade." Example (5) is greatly similar in parallelism, reiteration, and rhythms to many passages in *Leaves of Grass*, yet in general there is an important difference: Lanier's reiteration and parallelisms function chiefly as tone-colors in passages which have a conventional rhythmical pattern, whereas in Whitman's verse they are more important for the rhythm which they establish for the passage.

Lanier frequently repeats a word or a phrase chiefly for its sound. For example, the weary monotony in *From the Flats*:

No humors, frolic forms — this mile, that mile; . . .
Her fancy fails, her wild is all run tame:
Ever the same, the same.

Sometimes a single vowel-tone is repeated for its lyric effect, as in the refrain of *Song for "The Jacquerie"*:

Over thee, Marie, and me,
Over me and thee.

It seems quite obvious that many of the phrases in *Sunrise* are repeated almost entirely for the sound, *e.g.*:

In my sleep I was fain of their fellowship, fain . . .
Came through the lapped leaves sifting, sifting,
Came to the gates of sleep.
(But would I could know, but would I could know,) . . .
So,
That haply we know somewhat more than we know.
. . . .
And lo, in the East! Will the East unveil?
The East is unveiled, the East hath confessed
A flush: 'tis dead; 'tis alive: 'tis dead, ere the West
Was aware of it: nay, 'tis abiding, 'tis unwithdrawn:
Have a care, sweet Heaven! 'Tis Dawn.

Alliteration is to be found here and there in most of Lanier's poetry, but it is used extensively in the later poems, especially in *Sunrise* (*cf.* passages quoted above). Some convenient examples are the following from *The Marshes of Glynn*:

And the *s*ea *l*ends *l*arge, as the marsh: *l*o, out of his plenty the
*s*ea
Pours *f*ast: *f*ull soon the *t*ime of the *f*lood-*t*ide must be:
Look how the *g*race of the sea doth *g*o . . .
And the *m*arsh is *m*eshed with a *m*illion veins, . . .
Passeth a hurrying sound of *w*ings that *w*estward *w*hirr; . . .

Syzygy is also used extensively in Lanier's versification, in conformance to his theory, yet it is impossible even to illustrate the device here, since it cannot be intelligently understood without a fair knowledge of the physiological principles of English phonetics. It is to be hoped that some competent phonetician will soon publish a study of the phonetics of Lanier's versification, for such a study would be of tremendous value not only to the student of Lanier but to all students of prosody. But in the meantime we may at least observe the ease with which most of Lanier's verse can be pronounced. In the following quotation the underscorings indicate where phonetic linking takes place:

And I would I could know what swimmeth below when the tide
    comes in
On the length and the breadth of the marvellous marshes of
    Glynn.

Poe and Lanier are probably the most careful American poets regarding syzygy, and Lowell the most careless.

4. VAGUE IMAGERY, THE RESULT OF LANIER'S THEORY

Since Lanier was a moralist and a would-be social reformer, *thought* in his poetry is highly important, as recent critics and biographers realize. The older attitude, that his theory and practice minimize thought and over-emphasize music, is, therefore, not entirely justifiable. Yet so far as prosody and versification are concerned, Lanier did place great emphasis on the music in his poetry; and to that extent, he sometimes neglected thought, though never intentionally. He did not hold Poe's theory of the necessity for "indefiniteness" in poetry, and he prided himself, to judge by one of his essays, on using the appropriate natural symbol; but in actuality, his later poems are often vague, a fault traceable directly, it would seem, to his attempt to produce the sound-patterns of music in the sounds of English verse. For instance, in the following passage from *Hymns of the Marshes*, the alliteration and vowel "colors" produce beautiful and poetic *sounds*, yet the resulting images are so nebulous that the imagination can scarcely comprehend them:

O cunning-green leaves, little masters! like as ye gloss
All the dull-tissued dark with your luminous darks that emboss
The vague blackness of night into pattern and plan,

Here, however, it may be argued that vagueness is part of the poet's scheme, suggestive of the indefiniteness of the leaves in the dark, and hence appropriate. This is undoubtedly true, but (and this is an interpretation, not an adverse criticism) the *sounds* in the lines seem to be much more important than the metaphors. Furthermore, many lines in this poem (and others) are equally vague as a result of Lanier's heavy concentration on sound. Consider, as a specimen, this description of a sunrise:

Now a dream of a flame through that dream of a flush is up
    rolled:

The remainder of the stanza is easier for the imagination to encompass, the rays of the sun on the clouds being compared to a bee-hive, and the sun to a bee:

The star-fed Bee, the build-fire Bee,
Of dazzling gold is the great Sun-Bee
That shall flash from the hive-hole over the sea.

Yet even these compound epithets, a favorite device with Lanier, are important for their sound and rhythmical function.

But perhaps the crowning example of word-music produced at the expense of a clear imagery is this stanza from the three-page sentence of *To Bayard Taylor:*

The cross of love, the wrench of faith, the shame
    Of science that cannot prove proof is, the twist
Of blame for praise and bitter praise for blame,
    The silly stake and tether round the wrist
By fashion fixed, the virtue that doth claim
    The giant of vice, the lofty mark that's mixed

This is not the place to judge whether music is more important in poetry than thought; yet there can be little doubt that in his later poems Lanier was trying desperately hard to realize his theory in his poetic practice, though he could not have gone much farther in the same direction without reaching unintelligibility, if indeed he did not sometimes do so.

It is difficult to determine how much influence Lanier's technique has had on the history of American versification, but certainly his prosody is important as a forceful statement of the "quantitative argument," and his own verse has undoubtedly stimulated some of the later poets in their experiments with word-music. His versification is perhaps most interesting, however, as an American culmination of melody in conventional meters. Swinburne of course went much farther, but the two poets have much in common. Certainly of all American versification, Lanier's seems most nearly akin to Swinburne's, notwithstanding its greater limitations.

In calling Lanier's technique a "culmination," we do not mean that he was chronologically the last American to give his main attention to melody, but he is the best representative of his particular manner. He started no new school or vogue. In fact, soon after his death (1881) American versification began travelling once more in the direction of another prosodic fashion. Emily Dickinson's first edition appeared in 1890, establishing a tradition for the subsequent theory of "Imagism," to which Lanier's later versification is almost antithetic, despite his freedom in varying the length of his lines and mixing meters (practices that are related to the technique of "free verse").

5. MINOR SOUTHERN POETS

The minor Southern poets of the later nineteenth century were in many respects less sectional than those of New England, New York, or California; and the influences which shaped their art were the same as those of their Northern brethren. Yet it is appropriate to consider them separately because their versification shares certain traits in common, they did influence each other to a considerable extent, and they did not greatly influence the poets of other sections.

Some of the traits of Poe's versification are found in the verse practices of William Gilmore Simms (1806–1870), Henry Timrod (1829–1867), and Paul Hamilton Hayne (1830–1886). All attempted blank verse without marked success, all wrote sonnets with erratic rime-schemes, and all were most successful with lyric forms.

Simms's *Norman Maurice* is hardly in the great English blank verse tradition. The short phrases, free use of feminine endings and final redundant syllables, and stychomythia prevent the long breath-sweeps, the flow and ebb, of the best blank verse. In this poem and in *Atlantic* the verse is nervous, jerky, and forced. *Albert and Rosalie* is smoother. His sonnets have usually a semblance of the Italian rime-scheme, but like many of his contemporaries he frequently used one English quatrain (*abab*) followed by an Italian quatrain (*abba*), or *vice versa*. An example of the English rimes arranged somewhat in the Italian manner is *Sympathy between the Past and Future, abba cddc effe gg*. By the Swanannoa rimes *abb acdc dede ff* — the final line being an alexandrine. Other characteristic examples of Simms's versification are the tail-rime arrangements of *The Cassique of Accabee, To Time,* and *The Land of the Pine*. In the latter trisyllabic substitution is used freely. A fairly typical stanza of *To Time* rimes *aaabcccbdddb. The Mock-Bird* has an unusual stanza of thirteen four-stress trochaic lines with a final alexandrine. *To the Breeze* has an arrangement which is characteristic of this group of poets, pentameters rimed alternately with intermittent three-stress lines. *Francesca da Rimini* is a translation of the fifth canto of Dante's *Inferno* in the original *terza rima*.

Timrod's blank verse is even more like Poe's than Simms's. In *A Mother's Wail* repetition and exclamations are used very much in the Poe manner. *Dramatic Fragment* shows great freedom in the placing of accents, use of extra syllables, feminine endings, etc. *Retirement,* however, is fairly regular. He did not write many sonnets, only one in the Italian form, two in an English-Italian combination, and twelve in unclassifiable forms. Pentameter in general is not characteristic of Timrod's versification. He was more successful with the ode, as in *The Cotton Boll,* a forerunner of Lanier's *Corn,* and *Ethnogenesis,* perhaps his best ode. In general Timrod's odes are nearer the Cowleyan form than those of Emerson and the transcendental poets, in which the short lines predominate. *Præceptor Amat, Vox et Prœterea Nihil,* and *An Exotic* illustrate Timrod's use of the anapest for lyrical purposes, and indicate that both Shelley and Lowell were significant influences in the formation of his poetic style.

The Problem is in the same meter as Poe's *Raven,* but Timrod's eight-stress trochees do not syncopate like Poe's. The verse is arranged as eight-stress couplets, but the meter might more accurately be described as four-stress, riming *abcb,* for the line is regularly broken into two equal portions by a very emphatic cæsura. One of Timrod's most skilful poems is *The Lily Confidante,* in trochees riming abc_4b_3. *Katie, Two Portraits,* and *Storm and Calm* are in octosyllabic couplets; *La Belle Juive* and *The Rosebuds* in octosyllabic triplets. Four-stress trochees and "clipped" octosyllabics, two of the most regular lyric measures, are particularly characteristic of Timrod's prosodic ideals and verse technique.

Paul Hamilton Hayne was the most voluminous of the minor Southern poets, and perhaps the most important after Lanier. In an article on Hayne, Lanier pointed out that "Hayne was at his best when he escaped entirely from the enervating influence of Morris and followed the example of Chaucer, who wrote of the vibrant life about him." [37] This criticism would seem to apply to subject-matter more than versification, but "Legends and Lyrics" (1865–1872) does contain many pentameter and octo-syllabic couplets which may have suggested the Chau-cerian manner to Lanier.

No other Southern poet handled blank verse with Hayne's ease, though his best is less skilful than Bryant's. *The Island in the South* suggests both Byron and Words-worth, and all of Hayne's blank verse is probably indebted to the recent English "closet dramas." He wrote a large number of sonnets, most of them in the Italian form, three in the English, and a few in the usual combination of the times. Most of them are competent, but few are comparable to the best of Longfellow and Boker. One of the irregular sonnets is *October*, riming *abab bccd dede ff*.

In his straining for melodious effects Hayne followed in the footsteps of Poe, and in his metrical freedoms he obviously followed Shelley. *Fire-Pictures* has an ode arrangement, but in it Hayne makes use of practically all of Poe's favorite devices of reiteration, parallelism, tone color, etc.; whereas *A Dream of the South Winds* and *The Breezes of June* are somewhat Shelleyesque, even in subject-matter. Hayne, like the other lyric poets of the South, was also fond of clipped octosyllabics, as in *The Lotus and the Lily;* three-stress trochees, as in *The Lily* and *The Meadow Brook*. The latter poem is particu-larly onomatopoetic. Some of the "Poems for Children" are almost Skeltonic, *e.g.*, *The Ground Squirrel*, which might be compared with Skelton's *Philip Sparrow*.

John Banister Tabb (1845–1909) extends beyond the limits of this survey of American versification, but it would be an oversight not to give him at least a note in a discussion of the minor Southern poets. Father Tabb was a disciple of Poe — and a staunch defender, as he

[37] Aubrey Harrison Starke, *Sidney Lanier* (University of Carolina Press, 1933), p. 202.

shows in several poems to the master —, but Poe's chief influence appears to have been to convince Tabb that a long poem does not exist. Tabb's poems, in fact, are far shorter than Poe's own. Most of them are about the length of Emily Dickinson's, with whom Tabb would inevitably be compared. But he used a greater variety of meters than Emily Dickinson, his rhythms are more regular, and his rimes correct. In fact, his craftsmanship is in every respect more finished. In addition to his short lyrics in the seventeenth-century English tradition, Tabb also wrote a number of sonnets in the Italian form, comparable in finish, ease, and grace to George Henry Boker's.

Father Tabb's versification is part of a tradition which has come down to the twentieth century in the work of those poets who excel in the brief lyric. But his influence may easily be over-emphasized, for on the one hand his work was part of a general movement which was already on foot, and on the other hand it was the so-called "discovery" of Emily Dickinson that turned most modern poets to the short lyric measures. Father Tabb, Helen Hunt Jackson, Lizette Woodworth Reese, and others were doing in the nineties what Sara Teasdale and certain contemporaries were to attempt later.

SELECTED BIBLIOGRAPHY

Sidney Lanier

Text

Lanier, Sidney, *Poems*, ed. by his wife. New York: Charles Scribner's Sons, 1923.

——, *The Science of English Verse*. New York: Charles Scribner's Sons, 1880.

——, *Music and Poetry*. New York: Charles Scribner's Sons, 1898.

Criticism

Beutzon, T. L. (Mme Blanc), "Un musicien poète," *Revue des deux mondes* (January 15, 1928), CXLV, 307-341.

Cady, Frank W., "Sidney Lanier," *South Atlantic Quarterly* (1914), XIII, 156–173.

Kent, Charles W., "A Study of Lanier's Poems," *Publications of the Modern Language Association* (1892), VII, No. 2, 33–63.

Miles, Dudley, "The New South: Lanier," *Cambridge History of American Literature*. New York: G. P. Putnam's Sons, 1918. II, Chap. IV, 331–346.

Starke, Aubrey Harrison, *Sidney Lanier, A Biographical and Critical Study*. The University of North Carolina Press, 1933. Esp. pp. 177–198, 346–361.

Williams, Stanley, "Sidney Lanier," *American Writers on American Literature*, ed. by John Macy. New York: Horace Liveright, 1931. Pp. 327–342.

MINOR POETS OF THE SOUTH

Baskervill, W. M., *Southern Writers*. Nashville, Tenn.: Publishing House of the M. E. Church South, 1898–1903. 2 vols.

Holliday, Carl, *A History of Southern Literature*. New York and Washington: Neale Publishing Company, 1906.

Huber, C. W., *Representative Southern Poets*. New York and Washington: Neale Publishing Company, 1906.

Link, S. A., *Pioneers of Southern Literature*. Nashville, Tenn.: Publishing House of the M. E. Church South, 1899–1900. 2 vols.

Manly, Louise, *Southern Literature from 1579–1895*. Richmond, Va.: B. F. Johnson Publishing Co., 1895.

Trent, William Peterfield, *Southern Writers*. New York: The Macmillan Company, 1905.
[Selections.]

CHAPTER XI

Emily Dickinson

I. INTRODUCTION

CONTRARY to popular belief, Miss Dickinson's poetry had many devotees before the twentieth century,[1] but the present generation of critics and poetry lovers likes to feel that it really "discovered" her, and recently the adoration of her technique has become almost a cult. As a consequence, many bitter literary battles have been fought in her name, for there are still some "die-hards," like Professor Pattee,[2] who refuse to accept her as a star leading to a new Jerusalem.

Thus our first problem in the study of Emily Dickinson's versification is whether her poetry is sufficiently important to deserve analysis. The judging of her work as poetry necessarily involves literary standards, æsthetics, and philosophical or thought content, none of which belong to the special subject of poetic technique. Whether or not her poetry is *great*, therefore, is not our problem, at least at present. Yet it does not seem that any one who is familiar with her influence on recent American poets could doubt the importance of her versification. Though she never wrote a word specifically on prosody, so far as we know (one never knows what new manuscripts her relatives may turn up!), her own technique has been accepted by the later poets (especially the *vers librists*) as

---

[1] *Cf.* Anna Mary Wells, "Early Criticism of Emily Dickinson," *American Literature* (November, 1929), I, No. 3, 243–259.

[2] Fred Lewis Pattee, *A History of American Literature since 1870* (New York, 1915), p. 341.

a challenge to the established conventions of English versification.[3]　And her versification is also important as a link between Emerson and the "New Poetry."

There is a great stumbling block for the student of Miss Dickinson's technique, namely, that we have no adequate text for a study of her method. The first edition of her poetry made its appearance posthumously in 1890, followed by the "Second" and "Third Series" in 1893 and 1896. These were edited by Miss Dickinson's friends, Mrs. Mabel Loomis Todd and Col. T. W. Higginson. In 1924 the poet's niece, Martha Dickinson Bianchi, edited *The Complete Poems of Emily Dickinson;* but in 1929 this edition was supplemented by *Further Poems of Emily Dickinson,* which had been "Withheld from publication by her sister Lavinia."

Mrs. Todd has explained the chief difficulties of the editors.[4] Emily did not write her poems for publication, and left her manuscripts in no condition for the printer. She wrote on scraps of paper, backs of old envelopes, bits of wrapping paper, and whatever was convenient. Some of her improvisations appear to have been revised, but these revisions often consist of several substitute words and phrases, no preference being indicated. Naturally the line divisions were erratic, sometimes the shape and size of the scrap of paper making it impossible for the poet to indicate clearly her divisions (if, indeed, she would have bothered with them anyway); and the editors tell us that her main punctuation mark was the dash. The handwriting itself offered the editors many difficulties,

---

[3] Miss Amy Lowell, for instance, says that, "thirty years after her death the flag under which she fought had become a great banner, the symbol of a militant revolt." *Poetry and Poets* (Boston, 1930), p. 89.

[4] *Harper's Magazine* (March, 1930), CLX, 463–471.

but also some aid, since we are told that the chronology of the poems can be fairly accurately judged from the handwriting — though unfortunately for the student of versification, no attempt has been made in the various editions to indicate chronology in any way.

The most serious of all textual problems, however, is the skepticism of some scholars regarding the editors' readings of the manuscripts, which, it is to be regretted, have not been made generally accessible to scholars. Professor Prescott has questioned especially the editing of *Further Poems*. He quotes the following poem:

> Too much of proof affronts
> Belief.
> The Turtle will not try
> Unless you leave him;
> Then return —
> And he has hauled away,

Adding: "The line division is so inexpressive of the obvious rhythm — the 'common measure' in which nine-tenths of all Emily's poems are written — that one suspects the editors of having made six lines out of four (ending respectively *belief, try, return,* and *away*). This suspicion is strengthened by other considerations: 1. This same poem when quoted in the Introduction is divided not into six, but into five lines. 2. Where other poems appear (in part) in both Introduction and text the two in almost every case disagree, in line division, punctuation, or wording. Sometimes these changes alter at least the suggestion of the poems. 3. Many pages in the manuscripts, the editors tell us, are 'difficult to read' — the writing often 'so bold that there are but two words on a line.' Have the editors read correctly?"[5]

There can be no justification of these inconsistencies which Professor Prescott points out, but there are many

---

[5] F. C. Prescott, "Emily Dickinson's *Further Poems,*" *American Literature* (November, 1929), I, No. 3, 306–307.

people who believe that Emily Dickinson's irregular line divisions were intentional and that they are more expressive than a regular arrangement could be. This latter class, including many of the *vers librists*, is not disturbed by the textual arrangement which we have at present. But until we have at least further proof that the editors have "read correctly," or a more general agreement regarding the arrangements of Emily Dickinson's poems, no definitive exposition of her versification can be given; for the irregular line division is one of the two most important innovations in her verse technique (the other regards rime, see § 4). What we really need is a complete edition edited by several competent, and preferably well-known, scholars, a sort of jury to decide upon the Emily Dickinson canon. Until something like that is done, our analyses and conclusions regarding her versification must be tentative, given with the understanding that further manuscript studies of her poems may modify our interpretations, inasmuch as changes in line divisions, in punctuation, and in wording affect rhythm very fundamentally.

3. THE QUESTION OF IRREGULAR METER

In the Preface to the first volume of Emily Dickinson's *Poems*, Colonel Higginson says, "Though curiously indifferent to all conventional rules, [she] had yet a rigorous literary standard of her own, and often altered a word many times to suit an ear which had its own tenacious fastidiousness." [6] Indifference to *all* conventional rules is pretty sweeping, as well as ambiguous, though the Colonel apparently meant indifference to the "classical" rules of versification. The last clause of the quotation, however, indicates that he did not understand her technique, for the vague assertion that she was careful in her choice of words is exactly the kind of statement that Whitman's loyal but puzzled admirers made about his

[6] *Poems by Emily Dickinson* (Boston, 1890).

craftsmanship. But when the Colonel adds that Emily's
"words and phrases" were "often set in a seemingly
whimsical or even rugged frame," he errs absurdly, since
rugged is the last word that ought to be applied to Emily
Dickinson's versification. "Fragile," "lace-like," "deli-
cately-carved" are far more accurate; certainly never
"rugged."

Mrs. Todd's Preface is better: "Like impressionist pictures, or Wagner's rugged music, the very absence of
conventional form challenges attention . . . her verses
all show a strange cadence of inner rhythmical music.
Lines are always daringly constructed, and the 'thought-
rhyme' appears frequently, — appealing, indeed, to an un-
recognized sense more elusive than hearing." [7]

Here we have the word "rugged" again, and "thought-
rhyme" is also puzzling, as Amy Lowell admitted.[8] But
this last phrase may mean that parallel words are substituted for rime; and the influence of biblical rhythms upon
Emily Dickinson's work is obvious, though as her niece
says, not "obtrusive." [9]

Nevertheless, it is to be regretted that both of these
early editions so greatly emphasized the metrical irregularities; for it must have been, however they attempted
to define it, their failure to recognize conventional meters
(and rimes) in her verse that made them regard the technique as "rugged." We say this emphasis was regrettable because the truth is that, aside from rimes, Emily
Dickinson's versification is not a great deal more irregular
than Emerson's. Her poetry was startlingly original for
her age, but its originality lies more in the thought than
in the metrical technique.

Some of her rhythms are irregular, yet the majority of
them are surprisingly regular for the epigrammatic dic-

[7] *Poems by Emily Dickinson*, Second Series (Boston, 1893).
[8] Amy Lowell, *Poetry and Poets* (Boston, 1930), p. 95.
[9] *The Poems of Emily Dickinson*, ed. by Martha Dickinson Bianchi
and Alfred Leete Hampson (Boston, 1930), p. viii.

tion and thought. We have already cited "Too much of proof affronts belief" in Professor Prescott's criticism of the editors. Arranged as "common meter," the poem scans as follows:

> Too much of proof affronts belief.
> The Turtle will not try
> Unless you leave him; then return
> And he has hauled away.

Another representative example is "I fit for them," which is printed as a nine-line poem, in irregular verses and exceedingly puzzling rimes. But this poem is also nothing but common meter, and if arranged as four regular 4 + 3 quatrains even the rimes are less irregular: "fit" in the second line riming with "sweet" in the fourth, and "them" in the second line of the second quatrain riming with "aim" in the fourth line. These consonant-rimes are a usual practice with Emily Dickinson (see § 4). The first two lines of the poem show how the irregular verses straighten out when arranged to indicate the natural rhythms in which the poem was written:

> (1) I fit for them,
>   I seek the dark till I am thorough fit.

> (2) I fit for them, I seek the dark
>   Till I am thorough fit.

It is interesting that some very fine specimens of "common meter," arranged as irregular-length lines, are quoted by Miss Lowell in an essay in which she cites Emily Dickinson as a forerunner of Miss Lowell's own "school." "They bothered the critics dreadfully," says Miss Lowell, "these original, impossible poems where form (conventional form) was utterly disregarded . . ." [10] From *The Single Hound*, the following poems are quoted, all of which, supposedly, "utterly disregard conventional form." No. LXVI is printed in nine lines, but if lines seven and eight (each two-stress) are combined, we have two 4 + 3 quatrains. No. XLII is in ten lines, but if the two final lines (each composed of two phrases) are broken up, we have three trimeter quatrains, each ending with a period, and riming *abcb*. No. XXX is simply a seven-stress couplet, which of course is metrically the same as a quatrain of "common meter." No. LXVII is printed as eleven lines, but is simply two 4 + 3 quatrains, with *abcb* rimes, the first quatrain rimes being conventional, "street" and "beat," and the second quatrain having final consonant rimes, "steed" and "played." As the poem is printed, the rimes are without order, but in ballad quatrains, they come at the right places.

Despite her own statements that the poems utterly disregarded conventional form, Miss Lowell acknowledges the fact that "Emily Dickinson had no conscious idea of any form of verse other than the metrical . . . she did her best to cram her subtle rhythmic sense into a figure of even feet and lines." [11] But she thought that Emily's "genius revolted," carrying her "over into cadence in spite of herself." Miss Lowell also believed that her own doctrine [12] of "verse based upon a unit of time instead of a unit of accent . . . would have liberated Emily Dickinson from the bonds against which she chafed." [13]

There was undoubtedly a conflict of some sort in Emily Dickinson's technique, for some of her poems do seem to hang between regular meters and "free verse"; yet her few irregular poems appear to have blinded many people to the fact that the majority are in regular meters. Professor Prescott's estimate of nine-tenths "common meter" seems a little bit high, though it is safe to say that two-

[10] Amy Lowell, *op. cit.*, p. 93.
[11] *Ibid.*, pp. 105–106.
[12] *Ibid.*, p. 106.
[13] *Ibid.*, p. 106.

thirds of her poems are in this measure. Conrad Aiken was mistaken when he said that of six hundred poems practically all were in octosyllabic quatrains or couplets; [14] however, a large number are, and the regular trimeter quatrain is also used a good deal. Emily Dickinson hardly ever used pentameter, but we do find it occasionally (*cf.* III in *The Single Hound*, a regular five-stress quatrain). Even the irregular poems are mainly four- and three-stress, and in many cases "common meter" is obviously the underlying pattern.

We must conclude, therefore, that Emily Dickinson's metrical irregularities have been grossly exaggerated, the mistaken conception being based mainly on the irregular line divisions. And in view of the reported condition of her manuscripts, it is impossible to decide whether she had any intention of substituting "cadence" for meter in her versification. But no matter how the lines are printed on the page, when the poems are read aloud the conventional iambic rhythmical patterns are plainly discernible.

4. EMILY DICKINSON'S RIME

Some of the early critics assumed that Emily Dickinson's erratic rimes were the result of a faulty ear for sounds, yet it seems very unlikely that a person with her sense of rhythm would be unable to distinguish a good rime from a bad one, though a recent critic in *Poetry* still refers to her "almost comic gaucherie in the finding of rhyme." [15]

It does seem certain, however, that while Emily at no time completely and intentionally abandoned rime, she did not hesitate to sacrifice accurate rimes whenever they stood in the way of the expression of her thought, as was

---

[14] Conrad Aiken, "Emily Dickinson," *Dial* (April, 1924), LXXVI, 308.
[15] Edward Sapir, in a review of the *Complete Poems* and the *Life and Letters*, *Poetry* (1925), XXVI, 99.

so often the case. Her practice, then, stands somewhere between the unrimed verses of Emerson's notebooks and the approximate rimes of Emerson's revised poems. And this comparison is more than an analogy, for her manuscripts are probably little more than mere notes; and whereas Emerson suppressed the spontaneity of his notebooks in favor of revisions in more conventional forms, she appears to have found increasingly greater satisfaction in her most natural and uncurbed manner.

Miss Susan Miles has an interesting theory that Emily Dickinson's irregular rimes have an artistic and psychological significance, and in nine cases out of ten express or imply defeat, struggle, frustration, suspense, failure, disillusion, etc. This theory leads Miss Miles to work out a classification of Emily's rimes:

(1) "Sometimes the expression demanded a three-quarters rhyme, that is an echo of the final consonant (if any) and the substitution of a long for a corresponding short vowel, or of a short for a corresponding long;

(2) "sometimes the expression demanded a half-rhyme, that is, an echoing vowel and a contrasting consonant, or an echoing consonant and a contrasting vowel;

(3) "sometimes a non-rhyme, that is, a sound which echoes neither final consonant nor vowel, but which clangs out its contrast to both." [16] [And probably this was what Mrs. Todd meant by "thought rhyme."]

There appears to be some justification for this theory, and it is in no way invalidated by the suspicion that Emily Dickinson was probably unconscious of the artistic significance of the three-fourths, half-, and non-rimes which Miss Miles points out. But the theory must be

[16] Susan Miles, "The Irregularities of Emily Dickinson," *London Mercury* (1925–1926), XIII, 145–158.

accepted, if at all, only as a working principle. Miss
Miles herself inadvertently demonstrates that it cannot
be applied with reliable accuracy. For instance, she
cites the poem "I felt a clearing in my mind," the rimes
in the first quatrain being "split" and "fit," and those
in the second quatrain being "before" and "floor."
Then she points out the appropriateness of the first
accurate rime and the second "three-quarters rhyme."
But why are "before" and "floor" not "full" rimes?
The final consonant is repeated, and in both words the *o*
is long. Or at least it is in American speech, if not in
Miss Miles's English pronunciation (thus illustrating one
of the dangers in theories and critiques on the subject of
rime).

And yet whatever we may think of the æsthetic and
psychological aspects of this theory of Emily Dickinson's
rimes, Miss Miles's classification is a convenient one.
Without it, we would have difficulty in labeling the rimes
in "Some have resigned the Loom":

. . . Loom,	a
. . . tomb	a
. . . employ	b
. . . feet	c
. . . gate,	c
. . . [at you and] I.	b

The rimes marked "a" are "full" or accurate rimes,
those marked "c" are half-rimes ("an echoing consonant
and a contrasting vowel"), and there is a suggestion of
assonance in "employ" and "I" (though we might add a
fourth classification and call it a one-fourth rime). This
poem, however, is uncharacteristic in the rime-scheme
indicated above, for Emily Dickinson's usual scheme is,
as we have noticed, *abcb*. This is significant because the
scheme itself reduces rime to a minimum.

Of course the final rime in this poem would be less
far-fetched if the line were grammatical, "at you and me."

Just how the defenders of Emily Dickinson's every practice would justify this phrase is difficult to see, for it
does not seem that the bad grammar serves any artistic
or poetic purpose. The truth probably is that here, as
in many other places, she was simply careless in composing the verse and too indifferent to revise it carefully
afterward.

Further illustrations of her half-rimes (the most numerous variety of her inaccurate ones) have already been
referred to as "final consonant rimes" in the preceding
section on meter. For example, in "I fit for them" the
rimes are "fit" and "sweet," "them" and "Aim"; in
"Like Brooms of Steel," "Street" and "heat" is a full
rime, but "Steed" and "played" is only a half-rime. In
"I bet with every Wind that blew," there is another
half-rime, "chagrin" and "Balloon."

In "Of tribulation these are they," the rimes of all four
quatrains repeat only the final consonant (or two consonants, as once in the second quatrain): "white" and
"designate," "times" and "palms," "soil" and "mile,"
"road" and "Saved."

Among the "full" rimes, the light-ending (*i.e.*, rime on
a final unaccented syllable) is found frequently, as, for
instance, "bee" and "revery" in "To make a prairie."
Wherever a poem contains triplet rimes (rare but used
occasionally), some of them are almost certain to be
"light." "A Spider sewed at night" is a good illustration.
The first three lines end with "night," "light," and
"white"; then follow the half-rimes "dame," "gnome,"
and "inform"; and finally these lines:

> Of immortality
> His strategy
> Was physiognomy.

Sometimes the repetition of a word and not rime gives
form and symmetry to the poem. The reiteration may
take place anywhere in the line, but the initial position is

frequently used. In "Glowing is her Bonnet," No. LXI
in *The Single Hound,* the phrase "glowing is her" is
repeated three times in the first quatrain, and the second
quatrain has similar repetitions.

The parallelism, however, in most of Emily Dickinson's
poems is more subtle and irregular than in this poem, and
the reiteration (a natural concomitant of parallelism)
does not usually extend over so many lines, though in
"Bring me the sunset in a cup," all four of the six-line
stanzas are marked out by the repetition of phrases,

> Tell me how far the morning leaps,
> Tell me what time the weaver sleeps, etc.

In fact, this sort of parallelism of both thought and words
is used extensively in the sections of poems which the
editors call "Life" and "Nature," the latter containing
more parallelism than the former (*cf.* "The Wind began
to rock the grass").

But parallelism and reiteration in Emily Dickinson's
versification do not crowd out meter and rime. They
help to form patterns and to reinforce the metrical
rhythms, yet they are not, as with Whitman's verse,
rhythmical principles in themselves.

5. THE LINK BETWEEN EMERSON AND "IMAGISM"

The resemblance of Emily Dickinson's rhythms and
imperfect rimes to Emerson's is important, but is superficial in comparison to the deeper and more significant
relationships of style and epigrammatic manner. Of
course Emily's fractures of grammatical rules and dictionary pronunciations are hardly ever paralleled in Emerson's
verse, but even these faults are not difficult to reconcile
with Emerson's doctrines of spontaneity and individualism
of poetic technique. Conrad Aiken has made a still more
important comparison: "The thought is there" in Emily
Dickinson's poems, he says, "hard, bright, and clear;

and her symbols, her metaphors, of which she could be
prodigal, have all analogous clarity and translucency . . .
Emerson's gnomic style she tunes up to the epigrammatic
— the epigrammatic she often carries to the point of the
cryptic, she becomes what one might call an epigrammatic symbolist." [17]

The epigram is so packed with meaning that the thought
becomes of far more importance than rhythm, rime, and
word-music.   There is some beautiful music in Emily
Dickinson's poems, yet in reading them we are usually
far more conscious of the thought than the music.   This
fact probably explains why her versification has been so
puzzling to some critics.   She often had to sacrifice versification for a closely-packed metaphor or a barbed epigram, not because she had any intention of breaking the
conventional rules but because what she had to say did
not precisely fit the accentuation and form which the
conventional scheme demanded.   This is especially true
in those poems which Professor Elliott calls too "Emer-
sonianly enlightened, to arrive." [18]

As we have seen, her irregularities of meters are more
likely to consist of uneven-length lines rather than erratic
accentuation; but the line-divisions have been taken up
by the "free versifiers" as a valuable precedent for them.
And Mr. Aiken's characterization of her thought as "hard,
bright, and clear" is the central ideal of the "Imagists."
Finally, Emily Dickinson's poetic style is ejaculatory,
suggestive rather than completely formed, and it is perhaps in this respect most of all that she is a link between
Emerson and the "Imagists." [19]

[17] Conrad Aiken, *op. cit.*, p. 306.
[18] G. R. Elliott, in a book review of *Further Poems, American Literature* (January, 1930), I, No. 4, 442.
[19] "Imagism" is the self-styled name given to a group of English
and American poets who in 1914 decided to "reform" their native
prosody.   The Americans were Miss Amy Lowell (the chief organizer
and spokesman), Mr. John Gould Fletcher, and "H. D." (Hilda Doolittle).   In 1915 they published an anthology called *Some Imagist*

SELECTED BIBLIOGRAPHY

TEXT

Dickinson, Emily, *Poems*, ed. with an introduction by Martha Dickinson Bianchi and Alfred Leete Hampson. Boston: Little, Brown and Company, 1930.
[This is the only complete edition, in that it includes the *Further Poems* not in the earlier so-called "complete" edition.]

CRITICISM

Aiken, Conrad, "Emily Dickinson," *Dial* (April, 1924), LXXVI, 301–308.

Lowell, Amy, *Poetry and Poets*. Boston: Houghton Mifflin Company, 1930. Pp. 88–108.

Miles, Susan, "The Irregularities of Emily Dickinson," *London Mercury* (1925–1926), XIII, 145–158.

Prescott, F. C., "Emily Dickinson's Further Poems," *American Literature* (November, 1929), I, No. 3, 306–307.

Wells, Anna Mary, "Early Criticism of Emily Dickinson," *American Literature* (November, 1929), I, No. 3, 243–259.

Poets, with a preface setting forth the "creed" of the "movement." The following is a condensed version of the creed: (1) "To use the language of common speech, but to employ always the exact word," (2) "To create new rhythms as the expression of new moods — and not to copy old rhythms, which merely echo old moods," (3) "absolute freedom in the choice of the subject, (4) "To present an image . . . and not deal in vague generalities, however magnificent and sonorous," (5) "To produce poetry that is hard and clear, never blurred nor indefinite," (6) "concentration is of the very essence of poetry." The Imagists insisted upon the freedom to use "free verse" if they chose to do so, but their movement only partly coincides with the free verse tendencies of the times. References: Amy Lowell, *Tendencies in Modern American Poetry*. Boston: Houghton Mifflin Company, 1917. Glenn Hughes, *Imagism and the Imagists*. Stanford University Press, 1931.

INDICES

GLOSSARIAL INDEX OF TECHNICAL TERMS

(Note: All numbers refer to pages. Italicized numbers refer to definitions.)

Accent, the relatively greater expiratory force or stress placed upon one syllable over another: xx, *xxiv–xxvi*, xxvii, xxviii, xxxii, xlii, xliv, 58, 59, 84, 91, 97, 103, 113, 140, 141, 143, 144, 160, 166, 178, 198, 200, 207, 208, 249, 251, 252, 253, 269, 274, 279–283, 292, 293, 303, 313.

—, metrical accent (or stress), xxvii–xxviii, *passim*.

—, primary, *xxiv–xxvi*, *passim*.

—, secondary, *xxiv–xxvi*, *passim*.

—, weak secondary, *xxiv*, xxviii, 97, *passim*.

Alexandrine, an iambic verse of six feet, xxxix, 45, 46, *47–51*, 52, 65, 103, 183, 207, 267, 272, 291, 302.

—, unrimed, 151.

Alliteration, recurrence of the same initial consonant or vowel sounds, *xxii*, xxxiv, xlv, 34, 39–40, 60, 67, 69, 70, 75, 78, 83, 85, 135, 159, 165, 169, 182, 200, 208, 263, 283, 294, 298, 299.

Amphibrach, a classical foot composed of three syllables, unstressed, stressed, unstressed (× / ×), *xxvii*, 11, 291.

Amphimacer (or cretic), a classical foot composed of three syllables, stressed, unstressed, stressed (/ × /), *xxvii*, 18, 106.

Anacrusis, a prefix of one or two unaccented syllables to a verse properly beginning with an accented syllable, 48.

Anapest, a metrical foot composed of two unstressed and a stressed syllable (× × /), xx, *xxvi*, xxvii, xxxviii, 2, 11, 14–18, 19, 21, 28, 41, 42, 60, 76–78, 86, 106, 136, 137, 145–146, 152, 161, 166, 167, 169–171, 198, 202–204, 213, 229, 255, 257, 259, 262, 265–266, 286, 287, 289, 290, 291, 292, 293, 303.

Arsis, unaccented part of a metrical unit (in classical pros.), 36.

Assonance, resemblance of sounds between the last accented vowel and vowels which follow it in one word and similarly situated vowels of another word; a kind of vowel rime, the consonants being unlike, xlv, 70, 263.

Bacchic, a classical foot composed of an unstressed and two stressed syllables (× / /), *xxvii*, 167.

Ballad stanza, an iambic quatrain arranged $a_4b_3c_4b_3$, xl, 19, 22, 51, 71, 128, 129, 138–140, 147, 148, 151, 152, 164–168, 169, 190, 194, 197–199, 212, 213, 291.

Ballade, a French form of verse, imitated by some English and American poets, in which three or four rimes are used in three stanzas of eight or ten lines each, the stanzas ending with a refrain and the whole poem with an envoi, 214.

"Bastard feet," *60n*.

Blank verse, unrimed five-stress iambic verse, xxvii, xxix, xxxiii, *xxxvi–xxxvii*, xxxix, 2–8, 11, 24, 25, 30, 31–37, 54, 72–74, 88, 96–102, 143–144, 159, 185–187, 195, 206–207, 210, 250, 268, 271, 287, 288, 302, 303, 304.

"Blending," *see* Substitution.

Breath-sweep, a phrase or clause read with one exhalation, *xxxii–xxxiii*, 8, 72, 73, 88, 106, 107, 144, 176, 186, 195, 206, 268, 287, 302.

Cadence, rhythmical and musical modulation of sound, xxxi, xxxiii, xxxv, xlii, xlvi, 36, 37, 38–39, 43, 45, 46, 97, 111, 119, 134, 137, 142, 144, 148, 149, 160, 161, 180, 186, 205, 206, 230, 231, 232, 255, 256, 257, 262, 269, 287, 290, 292, 313, 314.

Cæsura, a pause in the reading of the verse (usually indicated by the punctuation), occurs rarely after the first syllable or before the last; the most frequent pauses are near the middle and at the end of the line, but the middle pause is usually referred to as the cæsura, xxix, *xxxii*, xxxvii, xl, 11, 33, 48, 50, 75, 106, 134, 144, 164, 170, 172, 182, 183, 195, 254, 303.

—, feminine, a cæsura which occurs within a foot, *xxxii*, 203, 257, 258, 259.

—, masculine, a cæsura which coincides with a foot-division, *xxxii*, 106.

—, Poe's "cæsura," 59*n*.

Catalexis, omission of a syllable at the end of a verse, 164.

Changing figures, a series of figures of speech used in a schematic order — *cf.* "parallelism" —, 36, 188, *236–238*.

Chant royal, a medieval French form of verse composed of five stanzas of eleven lines each and an envoi of five lines, the entire poem being written on the five rimes of the first stanza; probably an extended form of the ballade, 214.

Choriamb, a classical foot composed of four syllables, the first stressed, the second and third unstressed, and the last stressed ($/ \times \times /$), 161.

Clipped, *see* Headless line.

Closed couplet, *see* Couplet, closed.

Common measure, either seven-stress couplets or $4 + 3$ measure riming *abcb*, xxxviii, xl, 309, 312, 313, 314.

Concealed rime, *see* Rime.

Consonance, similarity of consonant sounds, 68, 315.

Contraction, reduction of the number of syllables by omission of a letter (or letters), 61, 65, 251.

Couplet, closed, heroic couplet ending with a full stop, xxxviii, xli, 21.

Couplet-mould, closed heroic couplet, xxv, 2, 7, 14, 144, 205, 267.

Cretic, *see* Amphimacer.

Dactyl, a metrical foot composed of a stressed and two unstressed syllables ($/ \times \times$), *xxvi*, xxvii, 53, 60, 179, 180, 181, 182, 229.

—, unrimed, 272.

Diiamb, a metrical foot composed of two iambs ($\times / \times /$), 106.

Dimeter, two-stress verse, *xxvi*, 117, 118, 179–180, 191, 253, 254, 260, 274, 275, 287, 290.

—, unrimed, 80, 263.

Doggerel, irregular, awkward, and unrhythmical versification, usually with low style and coarse subject matter, xxxviii, 17, 23, 87, 201.

Eight-stress verse, xxxi, 74–76, 163–164, 258, 264–265, 272, 303.

Elegiac stanza, a four-line stanza riming *abab*, 19, 23.

Elision, two syllables which are pronounced so lightly and quickly that they are equivalent in weight and time to only one syllable are scanned as one syllable, *xxix–xxx*, xl, 6, 9, 28–29, 34, 60, 64, 65, 97–98, 109*n*., 205, 251.

INDEX OF PERSONS AND WRITINGS
CITED

329